Anti-Discriminatory Practice
A Guide for Those Working with Children and Young People

Third edition
Rosalind Millam

continuum

Continuum International Publishing Group
The Tower Building   80 Maiden Lane
11 York Road   Suite 704
London SE1 7NX   New York, NY 10038

www.continuumbooks.com

British Library Cataloguing-in-Publication Data
A catalogue record for this book is available from the British Library.

ISBN: 978-1-4411-7741-4 (paperback)

Library of Congress Cataloging-in-Publication Data
Millam, Rosalind.
Anti-discriminatory practice : a guide for those working with children and
young people / Rosalind Millam.– 3rd ed.
     p. cm.
Includes bibliographical references and index.
ISBN 978–1-4411–7741-4 (pbk.)

1. Child care services--Standards--Great Britain. 2. Multiculturalism–
Great Britain. 3. Discrimination--Great Britain. 4. Equality–Great Britain.
5. Multicultural education--Great Britain. 6. Discrimination in education–
Great Britain. I. Title.

HQ778.7.G7M55 2011
362.7'120941–dc22
                                                    2010021287

Typeset by Newgen Imaging Systems Pvt Ltd, Chennai, India
Printed and bound in India by Replika Press Pvt Ltd

Contents

4 The Role of Play

Preface

This is the revised third edition of this book and anti-discriminatory practice continues, rightly, to be an issue that everyone working with children, families, colleagues and individuals, need to be aware of, aspire to and be working towards. Anti-discriminatory practice acknowledges, values and addresses the needs of the various groups and individuals who go to make up the society in which we live. There are many reasons to work within an anti-discriminatory framework, including the fact that practitioners have a moral obligation, to ensure that all individuals feel valued, respected and have a positive sense of self, as well as the legal obligation to do so. The first edition of this book was published back in 1996 with the second edition following in 2002. Much has changed in the early years and childcare field during this time. When the Children Act 1989 arrived, it was a landmark piece of legislation that brought many principles including the requirement for practitioners to ensure that the welfare of the child is paramount, and to take into account a child's race, religion, culture and language. This Act, and many subsequent pieces of legislation, caused practitioners to evaluate, reflect on and update their practice. Like all things, legislation needs to be refined and updated. We now have another Children Act. The Children Act 2004 embedded the Every Child Matters agenda into legislation ensuring that all practitioners working with, and for, children from birth to their 19th birthday actively promote and ensure that the five Outcomes for Children; Stay Safe; Be Healthy; Enjoy and Achieve; Make a Positive Contribution and Achieve Economic Well-Being, are embedded into their practice. The Children Act 2004 was followed by the Childcare Act 2006, bringing with it the Early Years Foundation Stage and other duties. There have been many more changes in legislation recently, and this can be confusing and challenging for practitioners as it impacts on all areas of practice from recruitment and selection of staff, to planning, the physical environment and how practitioners work with individuals on a day-to-day basis. This new edition updates previous editions and explores legislation that has come into force since 2002. The only constant in life is change. Legislation changes, qualifications are updated, what is deemed 'good practice' at work changes, communities and environments alter and, importantly, practitioners change. Change happens even when we are not aware of it. The person you were in 2002 when the second edition of this book was published is still there, but you have had new experiences, attended training sessions, maybe added a new qualification to your CV or changed employment or job roles. Hopefully you have evaluated and reflected on your practice. All this influences your growth and development both as an individual and a practitioner.

The new edition of this book examines and explores some of the changes that have taken place since 2002 and what they mean to practitioners. This edition has been updated and reorganized into, what is hopefully a useful and comprehensive book for practitioners. It contains new and updated material as well as the original concept of 'a chance to think' boxes that enable practitioners to reflect on what has been said in the book and how it may impact upon practice. The five chapters in this book address different issues, starting with the importance of working within an anti-discriminatory framework. Each chapter examines the theoretical issues being discussed, so that practitioners have an outline of background information. Chapter 1 examines the reasons for working within an anti-discriminatory framework as well as exploring attitude development. It also looks at some of the research relating to anti-discriminatory practice and presents an overview of the legislation. It then moves on to look at some of the issues relating to working with parents, families and colleagues. Chapter 2 examines race, religion and culture; what they are and the influence they have on individuals and their development. Chapter 3 provides an overview of many religions; their history, beliefs, major festivals celebrated, symbols that have meaning or are important to each religion, and dress and dietary requirements of each religion. Chapter 4 explores the crucial role of play in working with children in an anti-discriminatory framework. It gives the legal overview in relation to play and it looks at how and why children play, and what they learn from it. It examines the role of the adult in children's play, including how to observe, plan, provide and evaluate children's play within an anti-discriminatory framework. It also provides some practical ideas and examples of how to incorporate anti-discriminatory practice in all areas of play. Chapter 5 examines child development, identity and self-esteem. It discusses the importance of understanding child development and the many influences on it. The chapter moves on to identify the crucial role of practitioners and how they support development. It ends by highlighting the development of identity and self-esteem; including what it means, why it is important, what affects and influences it, and how to support it. Each chapter has the 'chance to think' boxes in them. These are based on real examples from practice. Some suggest practitioners write down answers and these can be used to reflect on practice, as well as evidence for qualifications, for use in continuing professional development files, or as a starting point for discussions with colleagues or as an reflective practice exercise in staff meetings. Some suggested answers are given in the appendices at the end of the book for people wishing to compare their answers with some already provided by other practitioners.

A list of useful publications, resources and websites is given at the end of each chapter so that practitioners can undertake further reading or gather additional information There is also a list of useful organizations, resources and websites given at the end of the book.

Practitioners who have worked with children, families and colleagues have acknowledged for many years the need to respect and value all people and treat them as individuals. When we work with children, families and colleagues it is important to recognize and take into account the overlapping and important roles that everybody has in each other's lives. People are not isolated individuals. They have a birth family that they may or may not live with; they have friends and a peer group; there are significant adults with whom they come into contact; such as a key person, as well as the people they meet on a daily basis, for example, the bus driver, or the people they meet when they go for walks and characters they see when they watch television. All of these people and the things individuals do or do not do, along with the environment they live in, have a huge effect on them and their development.

Addressing the issues of anti-discriminatory practice can still sometimes feel threatening or worrying to practitioners, particularly given the changes in legislation and day-to-day practice. Some people are not sure what this entails; some feel that it does not really apply to their settings; others feel that they are already working in a way that encompasses these changes; some practitioners are worried about getting it wrong and upsetting people; while others do not know where to start.

We saw earlier that anti-discriminatory practice acknowledges, values and addresses the needs of the various groups and individuals that go to make up the society in which we live. These include gender, age, disability, sexual orientation, economic background, race, religion, culture, language, ability, faith, legal status, family structure and ethnicity among other factors. Of course it is important to recognize that one individual will be made up of many parts, and that we are all individuals. We may be seen by others as belonging to, or being part of, a specific group; and we may be labelled accordingly, for example, in terms of our age. Anti-discriminatory practice actively takes account of the many different facets of individuals and groups and acknowledges them in all aspects of work. Sometimes this can feel threatening and sometimes it can feel comfortable, as all individuals have some things in common and some things about them that may be different from you as a practitioner. All practitioners need to think about how they recognize this and support people in becoming comfortable with difference.

This book addresses the need to be aware of and promote an anti-discriminatory framework in all areas of work. It looks at what legislation requires of practitioners; it examines research to show why this is good practice, and it provides practical suggestions on how this can be achieved. The most important aspect of working in this way is for practitioners to examine and reflect on their own attitudes towards anti-discriminatory practice. This is the one issue that this book addresses throughout. Reading a book will not change anyone's attitude, but it will, I hope, address issues that will cause practitioners to examine the opinions and attitudes they hold and how these affect and influence their work with children, families and colleagues.

This book is designed to give practitioners an understanding of anti-discriminatory practice and a starting point for addressing the issues involved. I hope it will give practitioners the urge to explore issues of good practice and to work in a way that reflects this. Some practitioners may feel that they need to follow up some of the issues raised in this book with further reading or training.

Whom the book is for and how to use it

This book will be useful for practitioners working towards a qualification related to early years and childcare. It will also be useful for practitioners working with children and young people, as well as practitioners undertaking related training and courses, or practitioners who need to up date information. It can be used as a point of reference for anyone who may need it, including early years practitioners, foster carers, residential workers, teachers, social workers and trainers. Practitioners can use this book in many ways; as a reference guide, to help develop and reflect on practice, as a starting point for discussion with colleagues, to help gather evidence for courses, to gain new ideas for activities, or as a signpost to further reading or helpful organizations.

The same terminology has been used throughout the book. Frequently used words included *practitioner* (any individual who is working with children, young people, parents and colleagues on a paid or voluntary basis or as a trainee). *Setting* (the place where practitioners work) and *parents* (people who may be natural parents, foster parents, adopted parents or people with parental responsibility).

Acknowledgements

Thank you to all the individuals who read and commented on this book and to all who gave permission for the photographs used. Thank you also to all the children, settings and practitioners who contributed to this book, and a big thank you to Teum and Mattewos for their love and support.

What Do We Mean?

In Britain today there are many different types of childcare services. These include day nurseries, nursery schools, playgroups, nurseries, childminders, children's centres, nannies, foster care, residential settings schools, breakfast clubs, after school clubs and play schemes to name but a few. Each type of provision will offer a different type of service. Families will sometime choose which provision best suits their needs, and sometimes make a decision on which service to use based on other factors such as cost or proximity to home or work. Other families will be using settings as they may have been required too, for example, due to legal issues. Services may be run by a variety of organizations, including private and voluntary organizations, registered charities, education departments, primary care trusts and local authorities. Some settings will be run in partnership with many organizations working together either on the same site or across several sites. Settings may be based in rural locations, villages, towns or in cities. Some settings may be large, others small. Some may be located on more than one site. Some settings may be home based, others purpose built and others may have to set up and tidy up every day in a shared building. Some settings may be multi-agency settings with professionals from many different disciplines working together, others may have only one person working there. All settings are equally important and all practitioners have a responsibility to the children, families, colleagues and other professionals they come into contact with to work within an anti-discriminatory framework. Children may attend settings for a variety of reasons. Their parents may work or study, and so need childcare. Some parents may not work but want their children to experience playing with other children. Once children reach school age, by law they must have educational provision. For some children this means going to school, and for other children being educated at home. Some children may be defined as 'children in need', a definition used in the Children Act 1989, meaning that children may require some form of childcare provision or support. Some children may be 'at risk'; or they may have a special need such as the need for speech therapy; or their parents may need a respite break. Other children may be defined as being 'looked after' by the local authority, which means that the local authority has responsibility for those children as set out in the Children Act 1989. Some children and families may make use of more than one type of provision, for example, a child may live with foster parents and also attend a nursery school. Another child may go to a childminder in the morning, then go to school and subsequently attend an after school club. Yet another may have a nanny and another be at home with parents and attend a playgroup or parent and child groups. Whatever the type of provision or the reason for a child's attending, all provisions have at least three things in common; children, parents and staff.

In this chapter we will be examining the necessity to work with children, families and colleagues within an anti-discriminatory framework. This is important for both legal and good practice reasons, in whatever setting we work. It does not just apply to particular settings, or only in particular places such as large towns, but to all practitioners and all settings. We will look at why this is important and examine research into how children see colour and gender in particular. We will see that both adults and very young children can have discriminatory attitudes; for example, they can be racist. We examine how practitioners can begin to try and challenge such attitudes and help form more positive attitudes by working within an anti-discriminatory framework, and the benefits this will bring to children, parents and staff. We try to understand what is meant by anti-discriminatory practice and how this may differ from other approaches. An anti-discriminatory framework is required by law, and this chapter will examine some of the legislation within which practitioners operate.

It is important that issues of anti-discriminatory practice are addressed and resolved for all children and adults in all settings. Inequality is a very real issue and must be addressed at all levels and in all areas in settings, including: accessibility of the setting, both physically, and for the individuals attending (and for those not attending – examine why?); the management of the setting; recruitment, selection and retention of staff; policies, procedures and practices; play and its planning and evaluation; how the physical space is used; purchasing and using equipment and resources; record keeping; communication; working with parents; working with others; team work and working with colleagues and all other aspects of work.

Working in an anti-discriminatory framework can affect and influence the lives of everyone. This is important as inequality is deep-seated in society and practitioners have a duty to work to make the world a fairer place for everyone, so that the children we work with today have the chance to be the very best people they can actually become.

The report of the National Equality Panel titled 'An Anatomy of Economic Inequality in the UK' published in 2010, shows how deep rooted inequality is. It found that:

> Girls have better educational outcomes than boys at 16 . . . and more women than men now have higher education qualifications than men in every group up to the age of 44 . . . However, women are paid less than men – 21 per cent less in terms of median hourly pay.

Looking at test scores in education it found that,

> at 16, however, Pakistani, Black African and Black Caribbean boys in England have median scores well below the national figure for all pupils. Children recorded as having Traveller or gypsy backgrounds have assessments that fall further behind during the school years, resulting in much worse results at 16 than others. This gap appears to have widened in recent years.

The impact of social background is seen very early on in life. The report found that

> Children entering primary school in 2005–2006 whose mothers had degrees were assessed 6 months ahead of those who had no qualifications above Grade d at GCSE. In addition, every £100 per month in income when children were small was associated with a difference equivalent to a month's development.

Children with a higher social class background who start with a low assessment of relative cognitive ability when young eventually overtake those with a lower social background who were initially assessed as having highability.

> Looking from age 3 to age 14, differences in assessment related to family income, father's occupation and mother's education widen at each stage (although they then narrow slightly between 14 and 16), in contrast to differences related to ethnicity, which narrow or even reverse during childhood.

Looking at these results reinforces the important and necessity of working within an anti-discriminatory framework.

Sometimes when we start to talk about things such as, culture, race, religion, gender, disability, age, discrimination, stereotyping and the need to work within an anti-discriminatory framework, people may begin to feel uncomfortable. This may be for a variety of reasons. Some adults do not really understand the concept of anti-discriminatory practice or know the difference between, for example, discrimination and stereotyping. Later on in chapter this we will try and define some of the terms commonly used so that people can feel less uncomfortable with them. It might be that people feel uncomfortable because they do not think it is an issue that needs addressing with young children; they believe that young children are not capable of having discriminatory attitudes, and they do not want to shatter this illusion. Other people may want to start addressing these issues but are worried that it is too big a task, or they do not know where to start; other individuals are aware of the need to work within an anti-discriminatory framework, but are so worried about getting it wrong or upsetting people that they are frightened to do anything about it. It is important to recognize that, no matter how hard we try, no one can get it right all the time, but that should not stop people from trying. Some people will be worried about beginning to address these issues because they will have to examine their own attitudes towards the various groups that go to make up the society in which we live. Some people feel uncomfortable about doing this because it can focus on things they would rather not admit to, or cause them to question the attitudes they hold. Everyone will have some sort of attitude or opinion about most things, including the different groups that make up the society in which we live. The Concise Oxford Dictionary defines 'attitude' as 'a settled way of thinking and behaviour reflecting this' and 'opinion' as ' belief or assessment based on grounds short of proof – a view that is held as probable'.

A Chance to Think 1.1

Attitudes

The society in which we live is made up of many different individuals, who are sometimes classified into groups, for example, according to the religion to which they belong, or as being a particular age, sex or sexual orientation, or because of their racial or cultural background. One individual may belong to many different groups. Think about two different groups in society and the way you view them. One group should be people you have daily contact with and the second group, people you have little contact with. Write down your thoughts on these two groups.

What is your attitude to the group of people you have daily contact with?

What is your attitude to the group of people you have little contact with?

What has influenced your thinking about these two different groups of people?

Having various attitudes and opinions is a natural part of life. Triandis (1971) says that people have attitudes for a variety of reasons because they: (a) help them to understand the world around them by organizing and simplifying a very complex input from their environment; (b) protect their self-esteem by making it possible for them to avoid unpleasant truths about themselves; (c) help them adjust to a complex world by making it more likely that they will react so as to maximize their rewards from the environment; and (d) allow them to express their fundamental values. The Early Years Foundation Stage (EYFS) (see Childcare Act 2006 in this chapter for more information) recognizes the impact attitudes have on young children. The statutory booklet says:

> providers have a responsibility to ensure positive attitudes to diversity and difference – not only so that every child is included and not disadvantaged, but also so that they learn from the earliest age to value diversity in others and grow up making a positive contribution to society.

As well as attitudes, everybody also has values that are important to them. Values originate from one's own principles or standards, one's judgment of what is valuable or important in life. A person's attitudes, opinions and values are influenced and formed by many things including: the attitudes and values of parents and other significant adults; religious and cultural background; images in the media; the influence of friends; that person's own experiences and day-to-day things that happen in the world around them. People may have to juggle several different sets of values. For adults this will include personal values that is, those values that are important to them as individuals. They may then have professional values that have been influenced or formed by the profession or employment they work in. A third set of values may derive from the organization in which they work. Children may also have to juggle different sets of values, including the values of the family in which they are brought up, values of the setting they attend and the values of their friends or peer group. These value systems may lead to a conflict within individuals when they have to balance these different sets of values on a day-to-day basis. Here it is important to realize that some of the attitudes people hold towards some individuals and groups may be stereotypes or prejudices. The Concise Oxford Dictionary defines 'stereotype' as 'a person or thing that conforms to an unjustifiably fixed, usually standardised, mental picture'. Its definition of 'prejudice' is ' a pre-conceived opinion or(followed by against , in favour of) bias or partiality'. Therefore stereotypes and prejudices are not based on what actually is, but are views that people have gained from the experiences they have had or the images and attitudes around them, which may be inaccurate. Stereotypes and prejudices can lead to discrimination. This is defined as 'unfavourable treatment based on prejudice'. Discrimination may in turn lead to oppression, which is defined as 'the act or instance of oppressing, the state of being oppressed, prolonged harsh or cruel treatment or control'. It is important to recognize the impact of attitudes, stereotypes, discrimination and oppression can have on individuals, organizations and society for practitioners to be able to work within an anti-discriminatory framework in all aspects of their behaviour and practice. Neil Thompson said in 2001, ' practice that does not take account of oppression and discrimination cannot be seen as good practice, no matter how high its standards may be in other respects'.

It is important to recognize that everybody forms stereotypes and has prejudices and attitudes. It is what is done with them and how they are expressed through a person's behaviour, actions and language that is important, as this will play a part in influencing how young children develop their own attitudes. It is important for people working with children to have a positive attitude about themselves and an understanding of who they are. Practitioners are seen as role models by children, parents and colleagues. They will have to answer what may be potentially difficult questions or challenge unacceptable behaviour. It is important that practitioners are willing and able to deal with this and, if necessary, say that they do not have all the answers but are prepared to try to find out. This chapter will not change people's attitudes, but it will, I hope, get people thinking about and questioning: the attitudes they hold about themselves, individuals and the groups that make up society; why they hold them; how they are expressing them and the effects that this may be having on children, parents and colleagues in the setting.

A Chance to Think 1.2

Myself

Think about yourself. Martians have landed from outer space and you have to describe yourself to them. Some of the things they want to know are: how you look, where you come from, what your background is, what you believe in, where you fit in your family, what you like and dislike about yourself. Write down what you would say to them.

How do you feel about what you have said?

Now describe one of your colleagues to them.

Are there any similarities or differences between the two of you?

How do you feel about this?

The way that we feel, about ourselves and other people, develops very early in life. Sometimes workers like to think that young children are unable to be unkind or have negative attitudes towards themselves and other people. It is often easier to believe that young children cannot notice, for example, disabilities, gender or the colour of a person's skin and have an attitude towards them. Practitioners making colour tables or playing colour matching games know that children recognize the difference between red and green, but still find it hard to believe that children notice the difference in skin colour. This may be because it can be uncomfortable to acknowledge the fact. When we acknowledge it, something has to be done about it and the way people work, and, as we have said, this can be threatening to some people. We shall now look at some of the research that has been undertaken on how children develop attitudes in particular to colour and gender.

Research

It is not possible to examine all the research that has taken place in the childcare field, but some of the main areas of research will be examined here to provide an insight into how children develop attitudes towards colour and gender. We will show that children do develop attitudes very early in life and, if they have attitudes towards colour and gender, then it follows that they will be developing attitudes towards other groups, such as people with disabilities, language, and people from perceived minority groups.

One very early piece of research conducted in the USA by Vaughan in 1964 showed that white American children as young as three were showing signs of racial prejudice. It might be easy to say that as this is such an early piece of research, it is out of date, or that more up to date research will have different findings. Unfortunately that is not the case. David Milner in 1983 found that by 2 years of age children are noticing differences in skin colour, and that between 3 and 5 years of age they are beginning to attach values to it, meaning that they perceive that people with white skin are generally seen as having the most powerful place in society. Between 3 and 5 years of age children begin to discriminate on ground of racial origin. Even before that, babies as young as 6 months old find skin colour differences interesting and look longer at a picture of a face with a new skin colour. This has implications for everyone. Jocelyn Maximé has found that children develop negative messages about racial groups. In her book on how and why children hate, Jocelyn Maximé (1993), found that the negative development of black children's view of their sense of racial identity can have serious and harmful consequences for some children, including self harm. The development of identity and self-esteem will be discussed in more depth in Chapter 5.

The media, TV, the internet, newspapers and so on, can both reflect and influence the attitudes individuals hold. A newspaper headline in 2010 said in large letters, 'Tory: Town has too many P***S'. It went on to say 'there are too many takeaways and too many P***s. It's why people do not come here'. This is paper is read by many people and this article is harmful to everyone as the views it contains are racist and discriminatory. We saw earlier that Maximé found that black children can have negative views about their identity. Articles like this one only serve to reinforce this.

A Chance to Think 1.3

Skin Colour

Research tells us that children as young as 3 years old notice differences in skin colours and that they have clearly defined attitudes about them. What do you think some of these attitudes may be?

Where do you think children learn these attitudes from? How do you think that awareness of skin colours may influence children's behaviour?

Compare your answers with the sample answers in Appendix 1.

How do children develop these attitudes? The people who generally have the most influence in the development of young children's attitudes are their parents. Parents are role models to children and children will copy what their parents do and say. This is known as 'modelling'. Children also develop attitudes from the images they see, or do not see, around them: on television; in computer games; in comics and from books; in the toys they play with; in the environment and in everything they come into contact with. Television plays a particularly powerful role, as many families have access to a television. The BBC television programme 'Child of Our Time' found that by the age of 3 a child watches around 3 hours of television a day and that many 3-year-olds have a television in their bedroom. When added together, this is a great many hours over the period of a year. While there are many good children's programmes on television there are also some that do not give positive messages about skin colour and reinforce stereotypes and prejudices. Many children watch programmes on their own without an adult present, so that if they have questions or something comes on the screen that needs clarification that opportunity is missed. Some children are also watching programmes that are not designed for children or are not appropriate for their age and that they may not be able to understand. The things children do not see or hear also play a part in how they perceive the world to be. For example, if children so not see images of people with disabilities or of black people in positions of power, they may assume that people with disabilities do not have an important place in society or that it is not possible for black people to have positions of power. The word 'black' is being used here to encompass all the perceived minority groups who may experience discrimination owing to race or ethnic origin. It is to acknowledge that this is a simplified way of classifying people not perceived to be white, and that some individuals would not wish to use this classification.

A Chance to Think 1.4

Television

Conduct a survey with the children you work with to find out their favourite television programmes. Try and watch them. Look carefully to see what sort of visual images they are portraying and what language they are using. See which children are featured in the leading roles or of any of the characters are in what could be considered to be stereotypical roles.

What sort of images do you see?

What sort of language is being used?

What messages do you think children are getting from this?

If you cannot watch the programmes, ask the children about them, who are in them, what happens and why they like them.

We have seen that very young children can have racist attitudes. This has negative effects on the development of both black and white children. If people feel discriminated against, their self-esteem and sense of identity can be damaged. The development of self esteem will be discussed in more detail in Chapter 5. All children need to feel valued and respected and to have the chance to fulfil their full potential. Often this is not the case. We have seen how parents' attitudes are passed on to their children. The same can happen with the attitudes of people who work with children. There has been a great deal of research into the attitudes of teachers towards pupils and how this can affect children and their learning. A 2009 study in the United States into the impact of teachers' expectations on diverse learners' academic outcomes found that 'research indicates that both black and white teachers perceive white students more positively than they do minority students, including those who speak English as their second language', and that 'children's academic outcomes are strongly influenced by teachers' perceptions, with teachers holding students to different academic standards depending on their race and social class'. This has a profound impact for practitioners who have long understood that they are role models for children. The way practitioners work with children and the expectations they have of both their achievements and behaviour can have an effect on how children achieve and behave. If practitioners have high expectations of children they will live up to them, but if they have low expectations, children may not achieve much because practitioners do not expect much of them. This is known as the 'self-fulfilling prophecy'. It may be easy to dismiss this research as it is from the United States and therefore not relevant to the United Kingdom, but similar research in the United Kingdom is reaching the same results. A Department for Education and Skills publication in 2004 titled 'Understanding the Educational Needs of Mixed Heritage Pupils' found that

> White/Black Caribbean pupils also face specific barriers to achievement. Low expectations of pupils by teachers often seem based on a stereotypical view of the fragmented home backgrounds and 'confused' identities of White/Black Caribbean pupils. These pupils often experience racism from teachers and from their White and Black peers targeted at their mixed heritage.

Another Dfes publication, the in 2006 found that 'discrimination against the grandchildren and great grandchildren of the early Black migrants persists in the form of culturally unrepresentative curricula and low expectations for attainment and behaviour on the part of staff'. It also said that

> that Black pupils are disciplined more frequently, more harshly and for less serious misbehaviour than other pupils; that they are less likely to be praised than other pupils; that this differential treatment by school staff can be observed very early on in a child's education; and that such a differential approach is likely to be unwitting on the part of teachers.

While the report found that teachers may be doing this 'unwittingly' this can still have major consequences for children on all aspects of their development and in particular on self-esteem, sense of identity and academic achievements. Research shows that if people feel that they are not going to succeed they will not try. If they do not try, they cannot fail. This report also looked at exclusion from school and it found that,

> Rates of exclusion are much higher for Black young people than for any other groups apart from Traveller groups. Between 1995 and 2000 there was a decline in exclusions, and the gap between exclusion rates for Black pupils and others closed significantly. However, the gap persists and shows no sign of disappearing. In fact, since 2000, the proportion of Black pupils excluded has increased, and more rapidly than for any other group.

Other research has also found that even very young children attending nursery are being excluded. This is very worrying, as many children who have been out of school for long periods of time, never return to school, and thereby miss out on vital parts of their education. This then affects and influences their life chances. What can be done to ensure that exclusion does not continue to occur? One suggestion put forward is that of segregated schools where children are taught separately in a community or faith based school. Another group of children who may experience difficulties with their education because of people's attitudes towards them are those children who are 'looked after'. The 'Care Matters Time for Change 2007' White Paper found:

> As a result of their experiences they (i.e. children who are looked after) have often had a disrupted education; they may have difficulties with their social and emotional wellbeing, and they often lack stable relationships in their lives, resulting in attachment problems and a lack of resilience. In 2006, only 12% of children in care achieved 5 A*–C grades at GCSE (or equivalent) compared to 59% of all children; Their health is poorer than that of other children. 45% of children in care are assessed as having a mental health disorder compared with around 10% of the general population; Over 50% of children in care responding to *Care Matters* said that they had difficulties accessing positive activities; 9.6% of children in care

aged 10 or over, were cautioned or convicted for an offence during the year – almost 3 times the rate for all children of this age; 30% of care leavers aged 19 were not in education, employment or training (NEET). Some groups of children are over-represented in the care population, for example, disabled children, and some ethnic minority groups.

The 2009 Ofsted report 'Care and Prejudice' reported on children and young peoples' views on being in care. It said that in relation to education, being in care can make a difference to how teachers react to children. One child said, 'Teachers treat me differently to when I wasn't in care'. They also found that 'being in care could make you more likely to get in trouble with some teachers, but more likely to get away with other things with other teachers'. Research and its outcomes have important implications for practitioners, for as has been demonstrated, they hold powerful positions in children's lives. Practitioners need to recognize and examine their own attitudes and to evaluate constantly how these attitudes may be transmitted to children. It is possible that people do not realize that they hold discriminatory attitudes, or that they may be treating some children less favourably than others. It is often useful to spend some time trying to assess the expectations they have of children in their particular setting, to examine why they hold those expectations, and, if necessary, to re-evaluate them. As we have seen, much research has taken place in this area. Much research has also been undertaken into studying gender and how people expect boys and girls to behave. Some people expect males and females to behave in what they consider to be appropriate sex role ways in light of what society considers to be masculine and feminine behaviour. What is considered to be masculine and feminine behaviour varies between societies. Margaret Mead, an anthropologist, studied three tribes in New Guinea, where she found that among the Araspesh, men and women exhibited the same sort of gentle and nurturing behaviour. The Mundugumor adults both behaved in the same way, but this time they both exhibited assertive and independent behaviour, whereas the Tchambuli men behaved in what Western society would consider to be a feminine way, and that the women behaved in a way that Western society would consider to be masculine. The way children learn to be male or female is due to both the sex they were born to and the gender role in which they are brought up. Sex typing and gender identity are different. Sex typing is when a person takes on the characteristics and behaviour that are caused by the environment and are considered to be acceptable and appropriate for males and females. Gender identity is the degree to which people consider themselves to be male or female. There continues to be a debate about heredity and environment, including sex and gender; in particular as to how much children inherit in their genes and how much they learn from the moment of birth. This is known as the nature / nurture debate. There are a number of fascinating experiments that look at gender differences and the nature / nurture debate. On 'Child of Our Time', a BBC programme following a number of children born in 2000, they tested children's musical preferences at 1 year of age, and found that the majority of boys went for loud rock, while most of the girls preferred softer music. The reason given for this is that baby girls tend to have more acute senses, can perceive quieter sounds, subtler scents and a softer touch than boys. They also conducted an experiment into how quickly and effectively parents transferred their views about gender onto their children. They took several young babies and dressed them up as the opposite sex that is, girls in boys' clothes and boys in girls' clothes. When the child's parent was asked to leave the room the child, dressed in clothes of the opposite sex, was entertained by another parent, who did not know the child. In the room were some toys; a car, a plane, a rattle and a couple of dolls. The adult had to choose a toy for the child. Every parent chose a car or a plane for the baby they thought was a boy, but for the babies that were dressed as a girl they usually chose a doll. The 'girls' (i.e. the boys dressed as girls) were offered the car and plane, especially if they rejected the doll, but the 'boys' (i.e. the girls dressed as boys) were never offered the doll, even if they cried and tried to reach for it. From nature we know that males and females are genetically different. Males have an X and Y chromosome and females have two X chromosomes. Their genetic make-up affects their reproductive physiology and genitalia, but does it affect anything else? Another difference between male and female bodies is in the hormones that they produce. Both males and females have oestrogen and testosterone in their bodies. Oestrogen is the female sex hormone. Females have more oestrogen in their bodies than males do and it helps develop some of the female characteristics. Testosterone is the male sex hormone. Males have more testosterone in their bodies than females do and it helps develop some of the male characteristics. The levels of oestrogen and testosterone present in the body have an effect on it. This can be seen in the development of a person's body and also in a child's behaviour. Boys experience surges of testosterone at various points in their lives including at around age 4, just before they start school and as a teenager around the age of 13. There is now a great deal of research into brain development and how the male and female brains are different. Girls' brains develop more quickly than boys' do. Also the way the brains develop are different. The brain is made up of many areas but has two halves to it; the left and right hemispheres. The left hemisphere is responsible for, among other things, language and conscious self-image. This is generally better developed in females, leading to girls being better at language, communication and listening. The right hemisphere is responsible for emotions, spatial awareness and unconscious self-image. Girls use both sides of the brain for working out some things, whereas boys use just one side. For working out some things requiring spatial awareness boys use the left side, leading to boys being better at working out spatial problems. The two hemispheres are joined together by the corpus callosum and this is generally larger in girls which means the brain is able to send more messages between the two hemispheres. Both nature and nurture play a large part in how an individual develops. We have seen some of the effects and influences of nature. As well as influencing gender, genes also affect eye colour, skin colour, hair colour, and many other aspects that go to make a person an individual. Nurture and the environment a child grows up in also have a huge effect on how they develop in relation to gender issues. This can include the names that children are given and how people respond to them. Also the colours and styles of the clothes that children wear which then influence how adults respond to them. Girls tend to wear more pink and multi-coloured clothing; boys tend to wear more blue and brown clothing. Both children's names and clothing are seen by people as signposts to the sex of a child. Children also receive messages about being male or female from the role models in the community they live in, as well as from other significant adults and their peer group, the media, religions, cultures, the home and wider environment.

Boys taking time out to relax

By the time they are 3 years old most children are able to say whether they are boys or girls and have noticed that males and females are anatomically different. They know that men have penises and stand up to urinate and that women sit down to urinate. By the age of 5 boys know it is better to be a boy than a girl.

A Chance to Think 1.5

Gender

We have seen that young children have opinions about gender. These attitudes have to come from somewhere, and like opinions about skin colour, they are influenced by the adults around them. Everyone has opinions about some of the toys they think children should play with, or not play with. Think about the toys you have in your setting or toys you have seen children play with. Write down three lists:

- One containing toys that you think appropriate for boys to play with;
- One containing toys you think appropriate for girls to play with;
- One containing toys you think appropriate for both boys and girls to play with.

These lists may give you some indication as to your attitude towards children's toys. Everyone has an attitude to children's toys, but the most important thing is how this translates into a person's behaviour. Now think about your behaviour and how you use toys in your setting.

What messages do you think are being given to the children in the way you encourage them to play with toys?

Miller (1987) conducted research into children's toys. She began by trying to find out whether adults did classify children's toys according to gender-appropriate lines by asking psychology students to classify 50 toys according to whether they considered them to be appropriate for girls or boys. Of the 50 toys, they considered 24 significant as appropriate for boys, including guns, doctor sets, tricycles, remote control card, microscopes and blocks. Only 17 of the toys were considered to be significantly appropriate for girls, including teddy bears, telephones, dolls and dolls' houses. The toys considered as being appropriate for both boys and girls included paints and a chalk board. We can see that these have been rated according to very traditional gender stereotypes. Miller then asked the students to say what kind of development they felt the toys promoted. She found that boys' toys were thought to promote sociability, symbolic play, constructiveness, competition, aggressiveness and handling, whereas the girls' toys were thought to promote creativity, nurturance, attractiveness and manipulative skills. It may be easy to say that as this research was conducted in the 1980s it is no longer valid, or that it no longer holds true. This is not the case. More recent research into gender stereotyping of children's toys in 1999 by Campenni is still finding that toys are stereotyped according to gender, with feminine toys being more gender stereotyped than boys' toys. Interestingly the research found that parents were more gender neutral in rating the toys than non-parents. Parents buy toys for their children; they play with the toys with their children and as we saw earlier, pass on their attitudes to children, including attitudes around gender expectations. Research into the environment which parents provided for their children under 2 found that boys are provided with more sports equipment, tools and large and small vehicles. Girls had more dolls, fictional characters, children's furniture and toys for manipulation. Girls wore pink and had pink pacifies and jewellery. Boys wore more blue and had blue pacifiers. The research concluded that as the environments were so different this would have an impact on development and the type of activities children may prefer. We saw earlier in this chapter the BBC series 'Child of Our Time' experiment into parents' views on gender and toys. Do the toys that children play with influence them? Maccoby and Jacklin (1974) found that boys and girls do indeed have different intellectual and cognitive skills. On average, girls have better verbal skill and boys have better mathematical and spatial skills. We saw earlier on that this may be due to the differences between male and female brains. We also saw earlier in this chapter that children model the behaviour they see around them. So if adults classify toys along gender-appropriate lines then children may also do this. Research shows that this does happen. By the age of 2 boys are choosing gender-appropriate toys; girls on the other hand tend not to choose gender-appropriate toys until the age of 4, when they start to show a strong preference for feminine toys. By the time children are 6 they say which toys are for boys and which toys are for girls. For some children this happens earlier, even in homes that have tried not to stereotype toys. A 4-year-old boy was looking at a toy catalogue with his parent said, 'I don't want to look at those pages they are all girls' toys'. Even with toys that can be considered gender neutral, such as bikes, the colour of the toy can play an important role in who plays with it. As a play leader of an after school scheme commented, 'since our blue bike broke and we only have a pink one left the boys say they have no bikes to play with'. Indeed the boys would not ride the pink bike and found other toys to play with until the blue bike was repaired. Boys and girls, even when given the same toys to play with, will play with them in different ways, for example, the way girls play with blocks is different from the ways boys play with them. This has implications for practitioners. If children as young as two or three are choosing to play with gender-appropriate toys and developing different skills, than practitioners need to ensure that all children have the opportunity to, and are encouraged to play with, all toys. Practitioners often say that they set the toys out and all children have equal access to them. It can be useful for practitioners to observe their setting and the toys in it to see how children are playing, and with which toys. We have seen how children develop attitudes about colour from the things they see in the environment around them. The same things that influence how a child develops these attitudes also influence the attitudes a child develops towards gender roles. In the way that children are portrayed by the media, in advertising and even in the displays in shops, very strong messages are being given about gender roles. A childcare worker went into a store to buy a present for his niece. There were two displays, one labelled as 'toys for girls' and one labelled as 'toys for boys'. The computers were in the boys' display, so the worker asked the shop assistants if he could buy a computer for his niece, and was told that he could, that they were not intending to imply that only boys could use computers and that they had not realized that this was the message they were giving out. Many toy stores and toy catalogues are still laid out in this way. All the resources that are used with children give out important messages. How resources can be used and evaluated will be looked at in more detail in Chapter 4. There has been much research into how young children get messages about gender roles from books. A study by Crabb and Bielawski examined children's books published between 1937 and 1989 for gender representation. They found that many female characters were shown using household artefacts and a larger proportion of males were shown using non-domestic product artefacts. There was no change over the time between 1937 and 1989 in how female characters were portrayed. Research also shows that the roles children play in stories can be classed as stereotypical, with boys being portrayed as independent, brave and strong, and girls being portrayed as dependent, emotional and passive. This research has been replicated since with the same findings.

A Chance to Think 1.6

Children's Books

Find a selection of the children's books in your setting. Read them to yourself and look at the visual images they are showing of male and female roles. See who the central characters are and what role they are playing.

What sort of activities are females shown to be doing?

What sort of activities are males shown to be doing?

What sort of messages do you think this is giving to all the children in the setting?

See if you can find any books that you would recommend, that show females and males in positive non-stereotypical roles. Write a list of these and keep it in the setting, so that you can borrow them from the library to read to the children.

We saw earlier in this chapter that research into black children's education and that of 'looked after' children showed that workers can have a profound effect on a child's educational experience. The same can be said of children's experiences as defined by their gender. We can see from the research mentioned that children are getting some pretty powerful messages about the roles people are allocated in society, either because of their colour or because of their gender. This is also true of people with disabilities, homosexuals, elderly people, and anyone who is part of a perceived minority group. Such messages can lead people to develop prejudices and negative attitudes. People who work with young children need to be aware of this and to make a concerted effort to combat the effects of discrimination.

Legislation

In Britain today there are many laws that practitioners working with young children and families need to be aware of and work within. What is contained within these laws affects many of the different aspects of work with children, families, colleagues, adults and other professionals. Legislation is constantly being reviewed and new legislation is coming into force all the time. It is essential that practitioners are aware of the changes and developments in legislation and keep up to date with them. There is a great deal of legislation that practitioners need to know about and work within regarding anti-discriminatory practice. Although some of the legislation will relate to practitioners wherever they work and whatever role they are in, other legislation may relate to a particular area of work, work role or a specific organization. Some legislation may affect workers in the four nations of the United Kingdom differently, particularly as Scotland and Northern Ireland's legal frameworks are slightly different from that of England, and Wales now has a National Assembly legislating for the Principality. Practitioners also need be aware of European laws and other conventions, for example, the United Nations Convention on the Rights of the child, as these may have an effect on their work. While legislation is important because it protects people the one thing it cannot do is change people's attitudes. We have seen when examining research that people do have attitudes to issues, and it is important that those attitudes do not spill over into discrimination. Legislation is in place to ensure that people are clear about what is legally acceptable and what is not. For childcare practitioners, good practice should ensure that practitioners are constantly able to evaluate practice and to receive appropriate support and training particularly in the area of anti-discriminatory practice, to ensure that practice goes above and beyond what is required by law. The following is an overview of the major points with regard to anti-discriminatory practice contained in the legislation that affects child-care practitioners. For practitioners requiring more detailed information, a resource list is given at the end of the chapter. It is important to remember that while the United Kingdom as a whole has legislation that relates to everybody, since devolution each of the four nations that make up the United Kingdom has its own powers. This means that each has its own legal system, that is, The Houses of Parliament in Westminster, The Welsh Assembly, The Northern Ireland Assembly and Scottish Parliament. It is important that practitioners check their own nation's legislation as well as the legislation that comes out of Westminster.

Equal Pay Act 1975

This act says that men and women must be paid the same when doing equal work. Although issues around pay have improved since this piece of legislation was enacted there are still differences between men and women's pay. The report Framework for a Fairer Future the Equality Bill in 2009 found that women on average earn 22.6 per cent less than men.

Sex Discrimination Act 1975

We have seen how discrimination can have a negative effect on the development of both girls and boys, and this Act ensures that neither women nor men suffer discrimination on the grounds of their sex. It also prevents discrimination on grounds of marital status. Despite the Sex Discrimination Act, the status of women and men in society are still unequal. The Act also allows for positive action. This means allowing to advertise for a particular gender if it is a requirement of the job. This Act has been updated by several European directives. The Equality Act 2006 has inserted new duties into the Sex Discrimination Act 1975. The Equal Opportunities Commission that used to be responsible for administering the Act has been replaced with the Equality and Human Rights Commission that came into existence following the Equality Act 2006.

Race Relations Act 1976

The Race Relations Act came into being to ensure that people do not suffer discrimination on racial grounds. The Act defines discrimination in four ways: direct discrimination, indirect discrimination, segregation and victimization.

Racial grounds are defined as those of colour, race, nationality (including citizenship) or ethnic or national origins. It does not cover religion unless a group has established racial identity around religion for example, Sikhs. These words can unintentionally be misused. The following are all from the Concise Oxford Dictionary.

- race: each of the major divisions of humankind, having distinct physical characteristics; a tribe, nation, etc, regarded as of a distinct ethnic stock; nationality; the status of belonging to a particular nation; a nation; an ethnic group forming part of one or more political nations.
- citizen: a member of a state or commonwealth.
- ethnic: (of a social group) having a common national or cultural tradition; demoting origin by birth or descent rather than nationality; relation to race or culture (ethnic group, ethnic origins).

Direct discrimination occurs when a person is not treated in the same way as someone else on racial grounds and is illegal. Some people may not realize that they are being discriminatory, but this does not make their behaviour acceptable. It is unlawful whether people realize they are doing it or not. An example of direct discrimination in a childcare setting would be when a setting would not admit traveller children.

Indirect discrimination may also not be intentional, and again the person who is doing it may not realize it is happening, but it is still unlawful. It occurs when settings have rules and regulations or practices that some groups are unable to fulfil due to racial grounds. An example of indirect discrimination in childcare settings would be where cooking ingredients used always meant a child could not do cooking, for example, a Sikh child would not be able to take part in a cooking activity which involved beef products.

Segregation means 'to separate people or to keep them apart'. The Race Relations Act makes it unlawful to segregate people on racial grounds. An example of this would be when black children had to play outside at a different time from white children.

Victimization takes place when a person is in the process of taking action under the Act and receives different treatment from other people in the same situation. An example of victimization in a childcare setting would be where a setting refused to enrol a particular student because in the past, when the student had his/her own child in the setting, she had complained about racial discrimination in the setting.

The Race Relations Act does allow for positive discrimination, such as where there is s need in the setting to have a bilingual speaker, or where race is a genuine occupational qualification. Like the Sex Discrimination Act 1975, The Race relations Act has also been updated by several European directives . The Commission for Racial Equality that used to be responsible for administering the Act has been replaced with the Equality and Human Rights Commission that came into existence following the Equality Act 2006.

A Chance to Think 1.7

Race

You have just started in a setting that has a morning session and an afternoon session. You have noticed that the majority of the children in the morning session are white and the majority of the children in the afternoon session are black and younger than the children who attend the morning session. When you ask the manager why this is, she says, 'That is just the way it is'.

What do you think of this situation?

What do you think may be happening?

Compare your answers with the sample answers in Appendix 1.

Education Reform Act 1988

The Education Reform Act brought about major changes to the education system, with one of the most significant being the introduction of the National Curriculum. This is the framework used by all maintained schools. The Act stipulates that schools must offer a curriculum that is balanced and broadly based and that is should: (a) promote the spiritual, moral, cultural, mental and physical development of pupils at the school and in society; and (b) prepare pupils for the opportunities, responsibilities and experiences of adult life (see Table 1.1). The National Curriculum introduced the term 'Key Stage'. There are four key stages and also The Early Years Foundation Stage which will be discussed later in this chapter.

The Act also says that state schools must provide religious education that is of a broadly Christian nature. This has implications for all schools as society today is made up of many different religions. These are discussed in greater depth in Chapters 2 and 3.

Children Act 1989

The Children Act 1989 has had a huge impact in the field of childcare. It affects all areas and types of childcare including childminding, nurseries, foster care

Table 1.1 Key Stages and national tests.

Age	Stage	Year	Assessment
3–4	Early Years Foundation Stage		
4–5		Reception	
5–6	Key Stage 1	Year 1	
6–7		Year 2	Teacher assessments in English, maths and science
7–8	Key Stage 2	Year 3	
8–9		Year 4	
9–10		Year 5	
10–11		Year 6	National tests and teacher assessments in English, maths and science
11–12	Key Stage 3	Year 7	Ongoing teacher assessments
12–13		Year 8	Ongoing teacher assessments
3–14		Year 9	Teacher assessments in English, maths and science and the other foundation subjects
14–15	Early Year Stage 4	Year 10	Some children take GCSEs
15–16		Year 11	Most children take GCSEs or other national qualifications.

Source: DCSF parents website 2009.

and residential care. It introduced may new principles. These include the following:

- The welfare of the child must come first.
- Local Authorities and education departments are required to provide for children in need.
- Organizations must work together in the best interests of the child,.
- Childcare provision must take into account a child's race, religion, culture and language.
- People working with children must work in partnership with parents and those who have parental responsibility.

As mentioned at the beginning of this chapter the Children Act brought into use two phrases; 'children in need' and 'looked after children'. The Act says a child should be taken as being 'in need' if

(a) he is unlikely to achieve or maintain, or have the opportunity of achieving or maintaining, a reasonable standard of health or development without the provision for him of services by a local authority under this part; (b) his health or development is likely to be significantly impaired, or further impaired, without the provision for him of such services or (c) he is disabled.

A child is defined as being 'disabled' if 'he is blind, deaf, dumb or suffers from mental disorders of any kind, or is substantially and permanently handicapped by illness, injury or congenital deformity or such other disability as may be prescribed'. The term 'looked after' is defined as follows: 'A child is looked after by the local authority if he is in their care by reason of a court order or is being provided with accommodation for more than 24 hours by agreement with the parents or with the child if he is aged 16 or over.'

The Act is complex and comprehensive. It contains 12 parts as follows:

   I Introductory issues;
  II Orders with respect to children in family proceedings;
 III Local authority support for children and families;
 IV Care and supervision;
  V The protection of children;
 VI Community homes;
 VII Voluntary homes and voluntary organizations;
VIII Registered children's homes;
 IX Private arrangements for fostering children;
  X Childminding and day care for young children;
 XI The Secretary of State's supervisory functions and responsibilities;
XII Miscellaneous and general.

Practitioners need to be familiar with those parts of the Act that relate specifically to their area of work. The Act covers many areas involved in working with children and has many requirements including:

- Record-keeping;
- Court orders;
- Ratios of children to adults;
- The environment;
- Children's rights;
- Protection of children;
- Parental responsibility.

Practitioners need to ensure they have an overall knowledge of the Act and how it affects their day-to-day work. Following the Act came Regulations that are additions to the Act, which practitioners need to be aware of.

A Chance to Think 1.8

Race, Religion, Culture and Language
As part of reflecting on the work in your setting process of your setting you are holding a staff meeting to look at how the setting provides for the racial, religious, cultural and linguistic needs of the children.

You have been asked to prepare a list of what you are doing to take to the meeting to discuss with your colleagues.

Compare your list with the sample answers in Appendix 1.

Disability Discrimination Act 1995

The Disability Discrimination Act 1995 covers three areas where disabled people have been given new rights: (a) employment; (b) getting goods and services; and (c) buying or renting land or property. The Act defines a disabled person as someone who has 'a physical or mental impairment which has a substantial and long term adverse affect on (their) ability to carry out normal day-to-day activities'.

Part 2 of the Act relates to employment. In terms of employment, employers discriminate against a disabled person if (a) a disabled person is treated less favourably than a person who is not disabled and (b) the treatment cannot be shown to be justified. The Act states that in terms of disability and employment some discrimination may be 'justifiable'. Employers have a duty to make adjustments to enable disabled people to take up employment, and the Act gives 12 examples of steps employers are expected to take. These include making adjustments to premises and altering working hours. Employers with fewer than 20 people are exempt from this part of the Act. The Disability Rights Commission which used to be responsible for administering the Act has been replaced with the Equality and Human Rights Commission which came into existence following the Equality Act 2006.

Education Act 1996

The Education Act 1996, like many Acts of Parliament, is long and complex. It covers practically all aspects of education. Its ten parts include sections on the statutory system of education, local authority schools, grant maintained schools, special educational needs and the curriculum. It is essential that practitioners are familiar with those parts of the Act that relate to their work. Part 4 concerns special educational needs. It states that a child has 'special educational needs' if he has a learning difficulty that calls for special educational provision to be made for him. It goes on to say that a child has a 'learning difficulty' if: (a) he has significantly greater difficulty in learning than the majority of children his age; (b) he has a disability that either prevents or hinders him from making use of educational facilities of a kind generally provided for children of his age in schools within the area of the local education authority or (c) he is under the age of 5 and is, or would be if special educational provision were not made for him, likely to fall within paragraph (a) or (b) when over that age.

A child must not be regarded as having a learning difficulty solely because the language (or form of language) in which he is, or will be, taught is different from the language (or form of language) which has at any time been spoken in his home. The Act also states that a child with special educational needs should normally be educated in a mainstream school. The Secretary of State is required to issue a Code of Practice giving guidance concerning special educational needs. Schools and settings must have regard for the Code of Practice and should have a written special educational needs policy. It is essential that all practitioners have access to a copy of this document and are aware of their role in working within it.

School Standards and Framework Act 1989

The School Standards and Framework Act 1989 covers educational provision from nursery education through to further education. Part 5 of the Act relates to nursery education, which it defines as 'full or part time education suitable for children who have not yet attained compulsory school age'. This is the Act that governs exclusions from school, it also outlaws corporal punishment for all pupils and requires head teachers to take measures to prevent all forms of bullying.

Human Rights Act 1989

The Human Rights Act 1989 is based on the European Convention of Human Rights. This is a European charter that deals with civil and political rights. The Act came into force on 2 October 2000. The Act is based on a series of articles listing the various rights, including:

Article 2 – Right to life;
Article 3 – Prohibition of torture;
Article 4 – Prohibition of slavery and forced labour;
Article 5 – Right to liberty and security;
Article 7 – No punishment without trial;

Article 8 – Right to respect for private and family life;
Article 9 – Freedom of thought, conscience and religion;
Article 10 – Freedom of expression;
Article 11 – Freedom of assembly and association;
Article 12 – Right to marry;
Article 14 – Prohibition of discrimination;
Article 16 – Restrictions on political activity of aliens;
Article 17 – Prohibition of abuse of rights;
Article 18 – Limitation on use of restriction of rights.

The Act also states under Part II of the first protocol:

Article 2 – Right to education

The Act affects all public authorities and states that 'it is unlawful for a public authority to act in a way that is incompatible with a Convention right'. A public authority is defined as 'a court or tribunal and any person certain of whose functions are of a public nature'. Public authorities could include health authorities, central and local government agencies, local authorities and private agencies if they are carrying out a public function.

Care Standards Act 2000

The Care Standards Act established the National Care Standards Commission. This no longer exists. The Care Quality Commission is now responsible for regulating health and adult care services in England, whether they are provided by the NHS, local authorities, private companies or voluntary organizations. They also protect the rights of people detained under the Mental Health Act. The Office for Standards in Education (Ofsted) is responsible for regulating and inspecting childcare and children's social care. They assess children's services in local areas, and inspect services for looked after children, safeguarding and child protection. The Care Standards Act also established the General Social Care Council and the Care Council of Wales, which are responsible for maintaining a register of social workers. Part 6 of the Care Standards Act 2000 becomes part 10A of the Children Act 1989.

Race Relations (Amendment) Act 2000

The Race Relations (Amendment) Act 2000 says it is 'an Act to extend further the application of the Race Relations Act 1976 to the police, and other public authorities'. It states that 'It is unlawful for a public authority in carrying out any functions of the authority to do any act which constitutes discrimination'.

It covers the work of public bodies such as the police, NHS, local education authorities, and any private or voluntary agency carrying out a public function. There are, however, some authorities that are exempt from the Act, and they are listed in the Act. Those authorities that are required to comply with the Act 'shall in carrying out its functions, have due regard for the need: (a) to eliminate unlawful racial discrimination; and (b) to promote equality of opportunity and good relations between people of different racial groups.

Special Educational Needs and Disability Act 2001

This Act states that it is an amendment to Part 4 of the Education Act 1996 to make further provision against discrimination on grounds of disability in schools and other educational establishments and for connected purposes. The Act makes it unlawful for schools to discriminate against disabled pupils and prospective pupils. It says that there is a duty to educate children with special educational needs in mainstream schools unless: (a) 'it is incompatible with the wishes of parents and (b) the provision of efficient education for other children'. The Act also says that 'The LEA must arrange for the parent of any child in their area with special educational needs to be provided with advice and information about matters relating to those needs'.

Education Act 2002

The Education Act 2002 updates the National Curriculum introduced in the Education Reform Act 1988. Part 6 of the Act deals with assessment arrangements and attainment targets for the key stages in the curriculum. It says ' "attainment targets," in relation to a key stage, means the knowledge, skills and understanding which pupils of different abilities and maturities are expected to have by the end of that stage'. It goes on to say that the curriculum for a maintained school or maintained nursery school satisfies the equipments of this section if it is '(a) balanced and broadly based curriculum which promotes the spiritual, moral, cultural mental and physical development of pupils at the school and of society and (b) prepares pupils at the school for opportunities, responsibilities and experiences of later life'. This is also the requirement of the curriculum for any funded nursery education where ever it takes place.

Race Relations 1975 (Amendment) Regulations 2003

These regulations have updated the Race Relations Act 1976. It defines harassment as 'violating that other person's dignity or creating an intimidating, hostile, degrading, humiliating or offensive environment for him' on grounds of race, ethnic or national origins. The Act also states that it is unlawful for employers to harass a person employed or who has applied for employment, and that for some jobs, 'being of a particular race or of particular ethnic or national origins is a genuine and determining occupational requirement'.

Disability Discrimination Act 2005

The Disability Discrimination Act 2005 has updated the Disability Discrimination Act 1995. The Act states: 'It is unlawful for a public authority to discriminate against a disabled person in carrying out its functions.' It defines discrimination as treating a disabled person less favourably than they treat others and that they cannot show the treatment is justified. The Act also places a general duty on public authorities to: (a) eliminate discrimination that is unlawful under the Act; (b) to eliminate harassment of disabled persons that is related to their disabilities; (c) to promote equality of opportunity between disabled persons and other persons; (d) to take steps to take account of disabled persons' disabilities, even where that involves treating disabled persons more favourably than other persons; (e) the need to promote positive attitudes towards disabled persons and (f) the need to encourage participation by disabled persons in public life. The Act defines a public authority as any person certain of whose functions are functions of a public nature.

Children Act 2004

The Children Act 2004 has had a major impact on all those who work with children and young people. It brought with it many new developments and it is the Act that underpins and provides legal force to the 2003 Green Paper, Every Child Matters.

'Every Child Matters' contained the 'Outcomes for Children' that are the aims for every child, from birth to the age of 19, whatever their background or circumstances. To have the support they need to:

> Be healthy;
> Stay safe;
> Enjoy and achieve;
> Make a positive contribution;
> Achieve economic well-being.

This means that everyone working with children and young people must work towards these outcomes. This includes health visitors, nurses, nursery practitioners, school staff, childminders, foster carers, residential workers, college staff in whatever sector they are employed whether it is the public, private, voluntary sector or a registered charity.

It is important that all practitioners are aware of what the outcomes are and how they can ensure they are providing for them. One way to remember the five outcomes is to use the word 'SHEEP' as each letter stands for one of the outcomes. Safe, Healthy, Enjoy and achieve, Economic well-being, Positive contribution.

The outcomes in full are as follows:

Be Healthy

Physically healthy, mentally and emotionally healthy, sexually healthy, healthy life-styles, choose not to take illegal drugs. *Parents, carers and families promote healthy choices.*

Stay Safe

Safe from maltreatment, neglect, violence and sexual exploitation, safe from acci-dental injury and death, safe from bullying and discrimination, safe from crime and anti-social behaviour in and out of school, have security, stability and are cared for. *Parents, carers and families provide safe homes and stability.*

Enjoy and achieve

Ready for school, attend and enjoy school, achieve stretching national educational standards at primary school, achieve personal and social development and enjoy recreation, achieve stretching national educational standards and secondary school. *Parents, carers and families support learning.*

Make a positive contribution

Engage in decision making and support the community and environment, engage in law abiding behaviour in and out of school, develop positive relationships and choose not to bully and discriminate, develop self-confidence and successfully deal with significant life changes and challenges, develop enterprising behaviour. *Parents, carers and families promote positive behaviour.*

Achieve economic well-being

Engage in further education, employment or training on leaving school, ready for employment, live in decent homes and sustainable communities, access to transport and material goods, live in households free from low income. *Parents, carers and families are supported to be economically active.*

From: www.dcsf.gov.uk.everychildmatters. 2009.

The Act also established a role of Children's Commissioner. There is a Children's Commissioner in each of the four nations – England, Wales, Scotland and Northern Ireland. The role of the Children's Commissioner is to promote awareness and the views and interests of the children of each nation and then report on this annually to Parliament. Specifically in England, there is a duty for children's services to promote co-operation between agencies, relevant partners, and other persons or bodies in order to improve the well-being of children. The Act also places a duty on key agencies to safeguard and promote the welfare of children as well as set up Local Safeguarding Boards. This means that Area Child Protection Committees no longer exist. One part of the Act that made headlines in the media at the time it received Royal Assent was Part 2, section 12, which is the part of the Act that relates to the introduction of information databases which will contain the following information on every child up to the age of 18:

> (a) his name, address, gender and date of birth; (b) a number identifying him; (c) the name and contact details of any person with parental responsibility for him (within the meaning of section 3 of the Children Act 1989 (c. 41)) or who has care of him at any time; (d) details of any education being received by him (including the name and contact details of any educational institution attended by him); (e) the name and contact details of any person providing primary medical services in relation to him under Part 1 of the National Health Service Act 1977 (c. 49); (f) the name and contact details of any person providing him services of such description as the Secretary of State may by regulations specify; (g) information as to the existence of any cause for concern in relation to him; (h) information of such other description, not including medical records or other personal records, as the Secretary of State may by regulations specify.

This allows for better sharing of information, although who will be able to access information will be controlled. The Data base is to be known as 'Contact Point'. The Act also required each local authority to draw up a Children and Young People's Plan and keep it under review. Local authorities are also required to appoint a Director of Children's Services and a lead member who will be responsible for services related to children which include social services, education and other services relating to children and young people as required. The last two areas of major implications of the Act are the inspection framework that requires those inspecting children services to work together and the conduct 'Joint Area Reviews' (commonly known as JARs), to assess how the local area is progressing in improving outcomes. The Act also makes several provisions concerning foster care, private fostering and the education of children in care, including promoting the educational achievement of looked after children. The Common Assessment Framework (CAF) and Integrated Working (IW) have also come out of the Every Child Matters agenda and is outlined in the Children Act 2004. The Department for Children Schools and Families (Dcsf) say CAF is 'a standardised approach to conducting assessments of children's additional needs and deciding how these should be met'. It can be used by practitioners across children's services in England. The CAF promotes more effective, earlier identification of additional needs, particularly in universal services. It aims to provide a simple process for a holistic assessment of children's needs and strengths, taking account of the roles of parents, carers and environmental factors on their development. Practitioners are then better placed to agree with children and families about appropriate modes of support. The CAF also aims to improve Integrated Working by promoting coordinated service provisions. Every practitioner, wherever they work will need to be familiar with the common assessment framework and integrated working.

A Chance to Think 1.9

The Outcomes for Children

Your manager has asked you to give a presentation to the staff team on the outcomes for children. You want your colleagues to be able to name the outcomes and understand what they mean to them in practice.

What will you include in your presentation?

Compare your answers to the sample answers in Appendix 1.

Education Act 2005

This Act states that its purpose is

> to make provision about the inspection of schools, child minding, day care, nursery education and careers services; to make other provision about school education; to make provision about the training of persons who work in schools and other persons who teach, about the supply of personal information for purposes related to education and about the attendance of children at educational provision outside schools; and for connected purposes.

It states that there is a 'Duty to inspect certain schools at prescribed intervals'. This Act also brings into being the Training and Development Agency for Schools which was formerly known as the Teacher Training Agency. The objectives of the new training and development agency for schools are to:

> (a) to contribute to raising the standards of teaching and of other activities carried out by the school workforce, (b) to promote careers in the school workforce, (c) to improve the quality and efficiency of all routes into the school workforce, and (d) to secure the involvement of schools in all courses and programmes for the initial training of school teachers.

The Act goes on to say that the Agency should have regard in particular to ensuring the school workforce is well fitted and trained to: '(a) to promote the spiritual, moral, behavioural, social, cultural, mental and physical development of children and young people, (b) to contribute to their well-being, and (c) to prepare them for the opportunities, responsibilities and experiences of later life.' The Education Act 2005 makes further amendments section 79N to the Children Act 1989. It now says that the Chief Inspector of Schools has general duty to keep the Secretary of State informed about:

> (a) the quality and standards of child minding and day care provided in England, (b) how far child minding and day care provided in England meet the needs of the range of children for whom they are provided, (c) the contribution made by child minding and day care provided in England to the well-being of the children for whom they are provided, and (d) the quality of leadership and management in connection with the provision of day care in England.

Equality Act 2006

We saw earlier in this chapter, when looking at the Sex Discrimination Act 1975, The Race Relations Act 1976 and the Disability Discrimination Act 1995, mention of the Equality Act 2006 and the formation of the Commission for Equality and Human Rights which brings together the work of the now disbanded Equal opportunities Commission, the Commission for Racial Equality and the Disability Rights Commission. The Equality Act 2006 is a wide-reaching Act and is

> An Act to make provision for the establishment of the Commission for Equality and Human Rights; to dissolve the Equal Opportunities Commission, the Commission for Racial Equality and the Disability Rights Commission; to make provision about discrimination on grounds of religion or belief; to enable provision to be made about discrimination on grounds of sexual orientation; to impose duties relating to sex discrimination on persons performing public functions; to amend the Disability Discrimination Act 1995; and for connected purposes.

The Commission has a wide-ranging role in encouraging and supporting the development of a society in which:

> (a) people's ability to achieve their potential is not limited by prejudice or discrimination; (b) there is respect for and protection of each individual's human rights; (c) there is respect for the dignity and worth of each individual; (d) each individual has an equal opportunity to participate in society and (e) there is mutual respect between groups based on understanding and valuing of diversity and on shared respect for equality and human rights.

The Commission will exercise its powers to:

> (a) promote understanding of the importance of equality and diversity; (b) encourage good practice in relation to equality and diversity; (c) promote equality of opportunity; (d) promote awareness and understanding of rights under the equality enactments; (e) enforce the equality enactments; (f) work towards the elimination of unlawful discrimination and (g) work towards the elimination of unlawful harassment.

The Commission is also tasked with promoting understanding of the importance of good relations between members of different groups and others, as well as working towards the elimination of prejudice against, hatred of and hostility towards members of groups, and working towards enabling members of groups to participate in society. The Act defines 'group' as a class of persons who share a common attribute this can be age, disability, gender – proposed, commenced or completed reassignment of gender (within the meaning given by section 82(1) of the Sex Discrimination Act 1975 (c. 65)) – race, religion or belief, and sexual orientation. The Act also makes it unlawful to discriminate against people on the grounds of religion or belief, and it says 'The Secretary of State may by regulations make provision about discrimination or harassment on grounds of sexual orientation'. It also inserts a new section into the Sex Discrimination Act putting an additional duty on public authorities to promote equality of opportunity.

Childcare Act 2006

The Childcare Act 2006 is the first piece of legislation to be only about early years and childcare. It takes forward the commitments from the Ten Year Childcare Strategy that was published in 2004. The Act is in four parts. Part 1 – Duties on local authorities in England. Part 2 – Duties on local authorities in Wales. Part 3 – Regulation and inspection arrangements for childcare providers in England. Part 4 – General provisions.

The duties it imposes on English local authorities are to: (a) improve the well-being of young children in their area and (b) reduce inequalities between young children in their area. Well-being is taken to relate to: physical and mental health and emotional well-being; protection from harm and neglect; education, training and recreation; the contribution made by them to society and social and economic well-being.

The Act also imposes the duties on local authorities: To secure sufficient childcare for working parents and to provide a better parental information service. Another requirement of the Act is that local authorities and relevant parties work together with the duty to secure prescribed early years provision free of charge 'for such periods as may be prescribed for each young child in their area who: (a) has attained such age as may be prescribed, but (b) is under compulsory school age.' They also have a duty to provide information, advice and training to childcare providers. Another change the Act has made is that changes the system for regulation and inspection. The Office for Standards in Education (Ofsted) now holds two registers of providers. The early years register and the Childcare register. Childcare providers who care for children from birth to 5 must register on the early years register and deliver the EYFS, for example, childminders and day nurseries. There are some exemptions to this. The Childcare register has two parts to it: a compulsory part and a voluntary part. Providers must register on the compulsory part if they care for children from the 1st September following their 5th birthday up to the age of 8. The voluntary part of the register is for providers who want to provide care that does not need to be registered, for example, nannies. Ofsted will also inspect settings. They must make a report in writing on: (a) the contribution of the early years provision to the well-being of the children for whom it is provided; (b) the quality and standards of the early years provision; (c) how far the early years provision meets the needs of the range of children for whom it is provided and (d) the quality of leadership and management in connection with the early years provision. Sections 39–48 of the Act introduce the EYFS replacing all documentation that went before. From September 2008 it has been mandatory for all schools and early years providers in Ofsted registered settings attended by young children to deliver the EYFS. Settings must meet the learning and development requirements, and must comply with the welfare requirements. The learning and development requirements are made up of three elements:

> The early learning goals – the knowledge, skills and understanding which young children should have acquired by the end of the academic year in which they reach the age of 5.

The educational programme – the matters, skills and processes which are required to be taught to young children.

The assessment arrangements – the arrangements for assessing young children to ascertain their achievements.

The six areas covered by the early learning goals and the education programme are:

- Personal, Social and Emotional Development;
- Communication, Language and Literacy;
- Problem Solving, Reasoning and Numeracy;
- Knowledge and Understanding of the World;
- Physical Development;
- Creative Development.

All the areas of learning and development overlap and interlink and all are equally important. By the end of the EYFS some children will have exceeded the early learning goals, other children will still be working towards some of them.

Settings must also comply with the welfare requirements. There are five welfare requirements:

- Safeguarding and promoting children's welfare;
- Suitable people;
- Suitable premises, environment and equipment;
- Organization;
- Documentation.

Each of the welfare requirements is set out in three sections: The overarching (1) general legal requirements, (2) specific legal requirements (3) statutory guidance. This is the first time that everyone, early years schools, nurseries, childminders, out of school provision and anyone working with children from birth to the end of the academic year in which a child has their fifth birthday, has been working within the same statutory framework. The very first sentence in the statutory framework of the EYFS says 'every child deserves the best possible start in life and support to fulfil their potential'. Its overarching aim is to help young children achieve the five Every Child Matters outcomes. There several ways that the EYFS will do this one of them being: 'providing for equality of opportunity and anti-discriminatory practice and ensuring that every child is included and not disadvantaged because of ethnicity, culture or religion, home language, family background, learning difficulties or disabilities, gender or ability'. The EYFS is built on four guiding themes. Each theme has a principle that underpins it. Each of the four themes is then further broken down into four commitments making a total of 16 commitments in all. Settings need to ensure they are working within all four themes and the 16 commitments. The Themes and Commitments of the EYFS.

The EYFS pack contains 5 items that will help and support practitioners deliver it. These are the statutory framework booklet that contains all the information about the legal requirements of the EYFS. The Practice guidance booklet that gives useful information to support the delivery of the areas of learning and development. The wall poster shows visually the themes, principles and commitments in the EYFS. The 24 principles into practice cards give more information about each commitment and the six areas of learning, and the CD-Rom contains the information in the pack as well as links to other resources. Equality of opportunity underpins and runs through the EYFS. It can be found in all parts of it. Some examples of this are:

THEME	PRINCIPLE	COMMITMENTS			
A UNIQUE CHILD	Every child is a competent learner from birth who can be resilient, capable, confident and self-assured.	Child Development	Inclusive Practice	Keeping Safe	Health and Well-being
POSITIVE RELATIONSHIPS	Children learn to be strong and independent from a base of loving and secure relationships with parents and/or a key person	Respecting Each Other	Parents as Partners	Supporting Learning	Key Person
ENABLING ENVIRONMENTS	The environment plays a key role in supporting and extending children's development and learning	Observation, Assessment and Planning	Supporting Every Child	The Learning Environment	The Wider Context
LEARNING AND DEVELOPING	Children develop and learn in different ways and at different rates, and all areas of learning and development are equally important and inter-connected.	Play and Exploration	Active Learning	Creativity and Critical Thinking	Areas of Learning and Development

From the EYFS poster.

The Statutory framework says: 'All children, irrespective of ethnicity, culture or religion, home language, family background, learning difficulties or disabilities, gender or ability should have the opportunity to experience a challenging and enjoyable programme of learning and development'. It runs thought the early learning goals for example, one of the goals for personal, social and emotional development is 'having a developing respect for their own cultures and beliefs and those of other people'.

The welfare requirement on safeguarding and promoting children's welfare requires providers to 'have and implement an effective policy about ensuring equality of opportunities and for supporting children with learning difficulties and disabilities'.

The welfare requirement on organization requires that 'providers must plan and organise their systems to ensure that every child receives an enjoyable and challenging learning and development experience that is tailored to meet their individual needs'.

The welfare requirement on documentation requires providers to keep data that includes a child's ethnicity which can be collected on a voluntary basis.

The Principles into Practice card 1.2. Inclusive practice says 'the diversity of individuals and communities is valued and respected. No child or family is discriminated against'.

How to implement the learning and development requirements in a practical way will be discussed in greater detail in Chapter 4.

A Chance to Think 1.10

Early Years Foundation Stage

Anti-discriminatory practice needs to be thought about and embedded in day-to-day practice for all 16 of the EYFS commitments. Think about commitment 1.1. Child Development.

What are some of the things that practitioners need to be aware of that can influence how a child develops and becomes an individual? Compare your answers to sample answers in Appendix 1.

Education and Inspections Act 2006

This Act has a wide ranging scope and is concerned with the organization of primary, secondary schools, further education and training and inspection of children's services. It puts five new duties on local authorities, one of which is the duty to promote high standards and the fulfilment of every child's educational potential. Another is to identify children not receiving education. The Act also says that a parent can request that their child be excused from religious worship in a maintained school. This Act brought into being the new Ofsted – the Office for Standards in Education, Children's Services and Skills, and it became responsible for inspecting or regulating a wider range of settings including fostering and adoption and residential settings.

Racial and Religious Hatred Act 2006

This Act makes it an offence to stir up hatred against a person on racial or religious grounds. Religious hatred means hatred against a group of persons defined by reference to religious belief or lack of religious belief.

Mental Health Act 2007

The Mental Health Act 2007 amends four previous Acts. These are the Mental Health Act 1983, the Domestic Violence, Crime and Victims Act 2004, Mental Capacity Act 2005 and section 40 of the Mental Capacity Act 2005. The Act provides a single definition of mental disorder as 'any disorder or disability of the mind'. The Act says that 'hospital managers ensure that patients aged under 18 admitted to hospital for mental disorder are accommodated in an environment that is suitable for their age (subject to their needs)'. It is important to remember that children are not isolated individuals but have family and friends and it is possible for anyone to have or be related to someone with a mental health issue.

Children and Young Persons Bill 2007–08

We saw earlier in this chapter that children who are 'looked after' do not achieve as well as other children. This Bill is about ensuring that those children who are 'looked after' are able to achieve their potential and it proposes to reform the statutory framework for the care system. It seeks to ensure greater consistency of placements and to improve educational attainment.

Special Educational Needs (Information) Act 2008

This Act amends the Education Act 1996 in relation to the provision and publication of information about children who have special educational needs. It has two key areas in it. The first is to find and highlight the support of children with special educational needs which is of both high quality and done with efficiency, and to publish this information. The second is to help with the roll-out of good practice to improve the well-being of children in England with special educational needs.

Education and Skills Act 2008

This Act makes it a requirement for young people to remain in education or training until the age of 18 or until achieving a level 3 qualification if earlier. It also requires local education authorities and employers to enable and support young people to do this.

Children and Young Persons Act 2008

The Children and Young Persons Act 2008 amends Parts 2 and 3 of the Children Act 1989. It has five parts to it. Part 1 is about the delivery of social work services for children and young persons. Part 2 is about the functions in relation to children and young persons. Part 3 is concerned with adoption and fostering. Part 4 relates to orders under part 2 of the 1989 Act, and part 5 is supplementary, general and final provisions.

Equality Act 2010

This Act strengthens and streamlines the legislation relating to equality. It 'will harmonise and in some cases extend existing discrimination law covering the "protected characteristics" of age, disability, gender reassignment, marriage and civil partnership, pregnancy and maternity, race, religion or belief, sex, and sexual orientation'. The Act gives definitions of all the protected characteristics. It defines Disability as '(1) A person (P) has a disability if – (a) P has a physical or mental impairment, and (b) the impairment has a substantial and long-term adverse effect on P's ability to carry out normal day-to-day activities'. Race includes: (a) colour; (b) nationality; (c) ethnic or national origin. It goes on to define direct and indirect discrimination. Some of the key areas it addresses are that it

> Clarifies protection against discrimination by association, for example in relation to a mother who cares for her disabled child. Extends protection from discrimination on the grounds of gender reassignment to school pupils. Creates a unified public sector duty which is intended to promote equality in public policy and decision-making with existing provisions being extended to the protected characteristics of sexual orientation, age and religion or belief, and proposes a new public sector duty related to socio-economic inequalities and provides for legislation requiring that employers review gender pay differences within their organisations and publish the results.

This Act is going to have far-reaching effects, and practitioners need to be aware of its existence and implications.

Child Poverty Bill 2008–2009

This bill enshrines in law a duty to eradicate child poverty by 2020. It has four income targets to be met by 2020 which will define the eradication of child poverty. These are: Relative poverty; Material Deprivation; Persistent poverty and Absolute low income. The Secretary of State has a duty to publish a UK child poverty strategy which must be revisited every three years.

Apprenticeships, Skills, Children and Learning Act 2009

This Act received Royal Assent in November 2009. One of the key elements of the Act is that it continues the reform of education and training for the 14 to 19 age group and it creates a right to an apprenticeship for suitably qualified 16–18-year-olds. It establishes the Young People's Learning Agency for England and the Office of Qualifications and Examinations Regulation (Ofqual) as a new independent regulator of qualifications and assessments. The Qualifications and Curriculum Authority (QCA) continues as the non-regulatory body with the new name of the Qualifications and Curriculum Development Agency (the QCDA). Part 9 of the Act concerns Children's Services. It provides for the establishment of Children's Trust Boards with part of their role being to prepare a 'Children and Young People's Plan', and it places a new duty on Local Safeguarding Children Boards to produce and publish an annual report on safeguarding and promoting the welfare of children in its area. The last requirement in part 9 of the Act requires children's services authorities to arrange for sufficient numbers of children's centres in their area to meet local need, and make provision for the inspection of children's centres.

Children's Schools and Families Bill 2009–2010

This bill aims to provide guarantees for parents and pupils so that they are clear about what they can expect from the school system. It reforms the primary curriculum and introduces a new licensing scheme for teachers. The Bill has 3 parts and 5 Schedules: Part 1 Children and Schools; Part 2 Family Proceedings and Part 3 Miscellaneous and Final Provisions. The Bill makes Personal, Social, Health and Economic Education (PSHE) a statutory requirement and ensures that all young people receive at least one year of sex and relationship education.

United Nations Convention on the Rights of the Child 1989

The UN Convention on the Rights of the Child was ratified by the United Kingdom in 1991. It has no legal standing but is known internally as an ethical code. The convention contains 54 articles. Many relate to anti-discriminatory practice. Article 2 says:

> State parties shall respect and ensure the rights set forth in the present Convention to each child within their jurisdiction without discrimination of any kind, irrespective of the child's, or his or her parent's or legal guardian's race, colour, sex, language, religions, political or other opinion, national, ethnic or social origin, property, disability, birth or other status.

Article 14 states: 'state parties shall respect the rights of the child to freedom of thought, conscience and religion.' Some practitioners, dependant on their role, may also need to be aware of the following regulations:

- The Sex discrimination (gender reassignment) regulations 1999.
- The Employment Equality (Age) Regulations 2006.
- The Employment Equality (Sex Discrimination) Regulations 2005.
- Employment Equality (Religion or Belief) Regulations 2006.

It is important to remember that new legislation is constantly being introduced. Practitioners need to keep up to date with it and be aware of how it affects their day-to-day working practices.

Approaches to work

We have seen that legislation requires workers to be aware of many different things when working with children, parents, colleagues and others. It is important that practitioners aim towards good practice, that they reflect on and evaluate rather than just doing what is necessary or required by law. Different settings will have different ways of working, which may be influenced by the amount of time children spend in the setting, the physical layout of the building or the support and direction from the management of the setting. Some early years settings have a particular philosophy which they follow, for example, Frobel, Montessori, Steiner or High Scope approach. Whatever approach is taken, it is important that the welfare of the children is central to it and that settings meet the individual needs of each child. All children need to feel that they are respected as individuals and that their needs are been catered for.

One very specific philosophy and approach is that of Reggio Emilia which is a model of childcare and education named after the area in northern Italy where it began and is still practiced. It is a system designed for children from birth to 6 years of age. The approach views children as competent, resourceful, curious, imaginative and possessing a desire to interact and communicate with others. The curriculum builds on the interests of the child and teachers then works together with children to consider the possible directions of a project exploring what resources are needed and how parents and the local community can be involved. Reggio Emilia integrates and utilizes the '100 languages of children' and uses multiple forms of representation, such as print, art, constructions, drama, music and shadow puppets.

Collaboration between settings, parents and the home school community are considered extremely important. The role of the teacher is that of a learner along with the children. Teachers work together in pairs. They listen, observe and document children's work in the classroom and help to stimulate the children's thinking, guiding children and supporting them to work together with their peer group. Teachers document children's work using a portfolio approach of photos, videos, the children's words to describe what they are doing, as well as examples of the children's work. They follow children's interests and do not undertake formal focused input in reading and writing. Teachers continually reflect on and evaluate their work, and ongoing development is seen as important. There is no hierarchical structure among the teachers. All are seen as equal. The Reggio Emilia approach believes that children learn through interaction with others, including peers, parents, family and the community in a friendly learning environment. Programmes are very family centred and parents are fully involved in decision making in the school, and are kept up to date with their child's progress as well as being involved in helping with activities and projects.

The environment is considered very important and is considered the 'third teacher'. The first teacher being the parents and the second teacher being the classroom teacher. Teachers spend a great deal of time organizing the environment, ensuring there is space for large and small group work and a common space where children from different classes can come together. The aesthetics of the environment are seen as very important. Children's work is displayed at both child and adult eye level. Working within an anti-discriminatory framework is important for everyone, not just children. The document *A Fairer Future, The Equality Bill* says:

> Equality is not just a right in principle, it is necessary for:
>
> Individuals: everyone has the right to be treated fairly and the opportunity to fulfil their potential. To achieve this we must tackle inequality and root out discrimination. The economy; a competitive economy draws on all the talents and ability – it's not blinkered by prejudice and Society: a more equal society is more cohesive and at ease with itself.

A Chance to Think 1.11

Approaches to Work

Many pre-school settings have information leaflets that they hand out to people who are interested in the setting. Three different leaflets collected from settings in London describe the approaches they have for working in the settings. Settings 1 described itself as multicultural. Setting 2 said it took an anti-racist, anti-sexist approach. Setting 3 said it worked within an anti-discriminatory framework.

What are the differences in these three approaches?

Which one do you feel ensures that all the groups that go to make up the society in which we live are reflected in it?

Compare your answers with the sample answers in Appendix 1.

All children learn that we live in a diverse society, and they need to learn to acknowledge and to respect that diversity. All groups are included in an anti-discriminatory framework because all are equally important, although not all groups are equally visible in society. Some groups are discriminated against, and it is important for practitioners to recognize that discrimination exists and work to help children, parents and colleagues to acknowledge this and try to develop strategies to prevent it.

Our society comprises of people of different races, religions, cultures, languages, disabilities, abilities, ages, gender, sexual orientation, ethnic origin, nationalities, economic status, legal status, colour, to list but a few. Some individuals may belong to more than one group and it is important for people to be recognized as individuals with their own needs, which may, or may not, be the same as another individual from the same group. Indeed, there may be as many differences between groups as there are within groups. Some practitioners may feel uncomfortable addressing some of the issues that are raised by particular groups, for example, addressing the issue of sexual orientation may be uncomfortable for some people. Practitioners need to be aware of the issues they feel uncomfortable with as this affects their work with children and families. Some of the children in the setting may be living and growing up in lesbian and gay homes. Colleagues may be lesbian or gay. It is important that practitioners to recognize that working within an anti-discriminatory framework might raise issues for them that need to be addressed. This will be discussed further in the sections on parents, families and colleagues.

A child is an individual, but also part of a family whose members may belong to some or many of the different groups mentioned above. Children need to be helped to develop within this framework. An anti-discriminatory framework will help children value and respect themselves, and individuals and groups that go to make up the society in which we live. This is not just something that can be done on special occasions or for special events, but it is something that should be integrated and ingrained into everyday practice. In Chapter 4 we shall look at how anti-discriminatory practice can be incorporated into children's play, but there is much more to anti-discriminatory practice than that. It includes being aware of issues and attitudes, planning to meet issues before they arise, incorporating them into policies, procedures and practices, reflecting on and evaluating practice, addressing issues as they arise and keeping up to date with new developments. The whole environment, which includes the social environment, the emotional environment, the cognitive environment and the physical environment needs to be taken into account when working within an anti-discriminatory framework. All are equally important; they all overlap, interlink and have an impact on how people feel coming into settings. The social environment is about relationships and interactions between people. The emotional environment is about how people feel and their ability to express themselves. The cognitive environment is about how people learn and the stimulation provided, and the physical environment is about the layout of the setting and how it is used. Everyone, children, parents, colleagues and visitors are affected and influenced by the environment of a setting. Everyone needs to feel welcome and that they are a part of the setting.

A Chance to Think 1.12

Part of the Whole
Think about your own setting and the social, emotional, cognitive, communication and physical environments as a whole.
Does everyone – children, parents, colleagues and visitors feel included in your setting?
Do they feel welcome and part of the whole setting and able to contribute as they would like to, or only feel included in parts of the setting?

Sometimes it is not easy to work within an anti-discriminatory framework. It requires practitioners to think about their own attitudes and abilities. It can sometimes be uncomfortable, challenging or frustrating as the environment continues to give out discriminatory messages to children and adults. It is important that practitioners try not to become disillusioned or so worried that they do nothing for fear of upsetting people, but continue to provide and anti-discriminatory environment for all who use the setting.

A Chance to Think 1.13

Disability
You are visiting the library with a group of 5-year-olds. When you get there, a father is choosing a book with his daughter, who has Down's syndrome. Some of the children in your group start to make comments about the girl and ask you why she 'has a funny face'. Both the father and daughter have heard the comments.
How would you feel in this situation? What would you do?
Compare your answers to the sample answers in Appendix 1.

Parents and families

People who work with young children also work with parents and families, for children are not isolated units. Parents are generally the most important and influential people in a child's life and they usually have more information about their child than anyone else. Some children live with both birth parents, some with one parent. Some children live in reconstituted families or extended families and some children live with foster carers or in residential settings, and a number of children are adopted. This means that not all children will see their birth parents on a daily basis. A number of children may have parents who have died. Some children have other adults in their lives who have 'parental responsibility' for them for example, a court-appointed guardian or a stepparent. Whatever contact may be had with parents, be it daily, weekly or less often it is still imperative to continue to recognize parents as important and influential people in their children's lives. An anti-discriminatory framework is as necessary in work with parents as with children. Working with parents requires many different skills, and some practitioners many find this threatening, especially if this is the first time they have worked with parents. Likewise, some parents may also feel threatened by what they see as 'professional childcare practitioners'. Practitioners should be sensitive to the needs of all parents as parents may have differing needs and wants from the setting. Parents should be fully informed about the setting. Some settings have websites and others have information books for parents that contain information about the setting, including staffing, the setting's routine, polices and procedures and other important information. Indeed it is a legal requirement that certain information be provided to parents, as laid down by the welfare standards in the EYFS. The Children Act 1989 stresses the need to work in partnership with parents. The EYFS that was introduced with the Childcare Act 2006 states in its purpose and aims:

> close working between early years practitioners and parents is vital for the identification of children's learning needs and to ensure a quick response to any area of difficulty. Parents and families are central to a child's well-being and practitioners should support this important relationship by sharing information and offering support of extending learning in the home.

It goes on to offer further information and advice on the Principles into Practice card 2.2. 'Parents as Partners' where it starts by saying 'Parents are children's first and most enduring educators. When parents and practitioners work together in early years settings, the results have a positive impact on children's development and learning'. The style of working with parents can vary between settings depending on the setting and the needs of particular parents. For example, childminders and nannies will have more detailed daily contact with parents than will practitioners in a school reception class. It is important that whatever style of working settings may have, parents are treated as equal partners. Treating all the same is not treating parents equally, or valuing or respecting them as individuals. Practitioners need to be aware of the needs of parents, which may be influenced by many things. These may include: hours or patterns of work; family composition, for example, lone parent family, lesbian or gay family or extended family; child rearing practices; racial, religious, cultural or linguistic needs of parents; parental attitudes; special needs of parents and the particular needs of mothers and fathers. These are discussed in greater detail below.

A Chance to Think 1.14

Relationships with Parents

Think about your own setting and the relationships you have with parents. Look at the entrance to the setting, and observe how parents are greeted on arrival and interaction during the time they are in the setting.

Is the entrance welcoming and, if it has posters and notices, are they accessible to all parents?

Are all parents made to feel welcome, valued and respected, and how does this happen?

Do all parents feel they can express their views about the setting and that they feel they have a role to play in it?

Relationships with parents begin from the very first contact they have with a setting. This may be on the phone when parents ring up to enquire about the setting. Even though it is not possible to see people over the phone, voices can make people feel welcome and at ease, or feel uncomfortable and make them not want to visit the setting. It may happen when parents first step through the door on their first visit to the setting. It is important that this is as positive as possible, as parents will begin to form an opinion about the setting and the practitioners who work there from this first contact. It is also important that all parents, whatever their background, religion, sexual orientation, language or any other aspect that makes them the person they are, are made to feel welcome in the setting. Entrances should be kept clean, attractive and accessible. In settings with notice boards, boards providing information to parents, or display boards, these should be accessible and up to date (for example, notices could include photos of the staff and information about what is happening that day) (see Figure 1.1). A smile is one of the best ways of showing parents they are

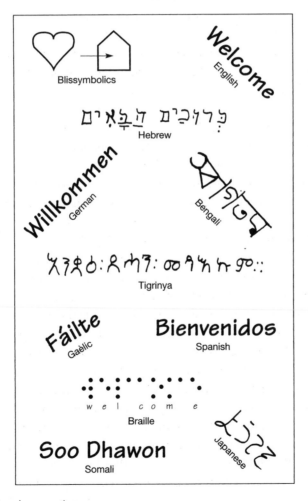

Figure 1.1 A welcome notice

welcome in the setting, as is allowing parents time to talk, or just be with their children. The first visit to a setting can sometimes feel threatening for practitioners and parents, as they may feel they are 'on show', but the more time parents spend in the settings, the less threatening their presence becomes for everyone. It also shows parents that their presence in the setting is welcome and that they are seen as having a valuable contribution to make to the setting and to the care of their children. Spending time with parents and getting to know them as individuals will, it is to be hoped, ensure that a relationship and partnership is being built where parents feel able to voice their views and suggestions about the setting, and where practitioners can ask parents for information or raise issues on which they may need help or advice.

For parents who work, their hours or patterns of work will influence the type of contact that may be developed between practitioners and parents. Parents who work full time or during the night may be unable to come into the setting on a regular basis. They may only have time to drop off their child and then rush to work. They may have a nanny or childminder who brings and collects their child from a setting. It is important that parents are kept up to date with their child's progress and that they have a chance to communicate with practitioners. This may need to be done through day books, where what has happened during the day is written up (what the child has eaten, what and whom they have played with, etc.). Letters, telephone, texts, blogs and emails are another way of communicating, but it is still important for face-to-face contact to be established and maintained. Appointments may need to be made or a special time set aside that is convenient for both parent and practitioner. Some settings may have parent's evenings or open days, where parents can discuss issues relating to their child or the setting.

Family composition is another changing area in today's society. The publication Families in Britain: an evidence paper in December 2008 by the Cabinet Office found: A quarter of families use grandparent childcare each week. Stepfamilies are one of the fastest growing family forms in the UK. In 2005, 10 per cent of families with dependent children were stepfamilies. Since the 1980s, the proportion of children being born to older mothers has increased as women postpone having children until later in life. In 2007 the proportion of lone parents as heads of households (12%) was treble that of 1971 (4%).

No longer are families made up of a mum, dad and two children. Families may consist of a mum and dad and three, four or more children. They may be lone parent families where both parents are still alive, with mother or father bringing up the children on their own with a lot of contact or sometimes, limited or no contact with the other parent. They may be a lone parent who is widowed and having to come to terms with the death of their partner.

With more people getting remarried or forming new relationships, stepparents and stepfamilies are on the increase. Families may be made up of children from previous marriages or partnerships, and children may spend time with both birth parents. Some children are brought up in lesbian or gay families, some children live with foster parents or residential settings, some are adopted, other children are brought up in extended families, with brothers, sisters, aunts, uncles and grandparents being fully involved in the care of the children, including bringing them to, and picking them up from the setting. This means that the setting may not see the parents on a daily or even weekly basis, but it may be seeing members of the extended family or other carers employed by families. Many children have grandparents who play an active part their day-to-day lives. Other children may not see their grandparents. Whatever the composition of the family, workers need to be aware of it, as this will help them understand the needs of the parents and the children. For example, many families of lesbian women and gay men face discrimination and homophobia. Lesbian and gay parents may not find it easy to be involved in a childcare setting. They may be reluctant to share information with practitioners until they know and trust them. Foster carers and practitioners who work in residential settings may also face issues around sharing information with other settings for legal reasons. Another group of people who often face issues in settings are fathers. Fathers have an enormous role to play in their child's life, and research shows that children who have strong father figures in their lives are less likely to get into crime, grow up with mental health problems or struggle to form relationships. Fathers may sometimes feel like the invisible parent in a setting and fathers may not often visit settings because of work commitments or because they do not feel comfortable there or they do not feel the need to visit the setting. In many families the father is the main carer and responsible for the day-to-day child care. This can have its own challenges in a society where the majority of child care is undertaken by women. Indeed, a father who is the main carer of his child, took his son to see a doctor recently as the little boy was ill. He explained what was wrong with his son and that he was his son's carer. The doctor listened to dad until his female partner walked in the door and the doctor then started addressing all her questions to mum. Mum explained that she did not know what the matter was as she had not been there, and that the doctor needed to talk to dad. Settings and practition-ers need to evaluate their setting to see how 'father friendly' it is. Do dads feel welcome in the setting and is the environment father friendly? Are dads actively encouraged to come into the setting? What images do they see of males working with, or caring for, children? What support is offered to dads? Do practitioners understand and value the important role dads have in their children's lives? Do practitioners feel confident talking to, and interacting with, all dads? Does the information being sent home by the setting relate to dads? Is the commitment to working with dads reflected in the setting's policies, procedures and practices? When settings actively engage with fathers they will see the benefits to the child, the father, the family and the setting. It is important for practitioners to remember that dads are unique individuals: no two dads are the same. Some may be young, others older. Some may be working and some unemployed. Some may be the primary care giver for their children, others may not. Some may be lone parents, others gay parents, and some may be in a relationship with their children's mother, married or in a civil partnership, some may be separated and not see their child every day. Dads have all kinds of backgrounds and it is important to remember that they are very important people in their children's lives.

A Chance to Think 1.15

Working with Parents

You have a new child called Claire starting in your setting and you are going to be Claire's key person. Claire and her parents have been to visit the setting, but unfortunately you were away sick on the day of their visit. The manager has told you the visit went well and that Claire appeared to be happy to be starting at the setting, as some of her friends are already there. The manager has given you all the background information you need, including the family compositions. Claire's mother and her partner are both women. This is the first time you have worked with a lesbian family.

How would you feel about this and how would you deal with these feelings?

How would you ensure you work in partnership with Claire's parents?

Other children in the setting are aware that Claire is being brought up by two women and are beginning to ask questions. What would you say to them?

Compare your answer to the sample answers in Appendix 1.

It is essential that practitioners do not make assumptions about parents, families and family structures. Practitioners need to continually evaluate their practice and work in a way that is welcoming and non-threatening to all parents and families. This can be done by showing non-judgemental attitudes towards parents and taking time to communicate with parents and build up relationships with them. The setting also needs explicit polices and procedures for working with parents that all practitioners are aware of and working within. Practitioners need to discuss and evaluate these policies and procedures as a team and support each other with this area of work. As well as differences in family composition there also may be differences in child-rearing practices taking place in families who attend the setting. These may be followed for social or cultural reasons. David and Anne Woollett say in their book , 'Different cultures have somewhat different ideas about children, how they what them to grow up and the activities in which it is considered that children should engage'. Practices followed may include picking up children every time they cry; letting children eat what and when they want; allowing children to fall asleep when they are tired and then putting them to bed; breast-feeding children up to the age of 5; babies and children sleeping in the parent's bed or in the same room as parents.

These may or may not be the same as the child-rearing practices followed by practitioners in a setting, but that does not mean they are bad or wrong. There is no one right way of bringing up children and there are many different books published on how to bring up children, all giving differing advice. People generally learn how to bring up children by remembering how they were brought up, observing how other parents are bringing up children and trying to do what they think is right. Most parents want to do the best that they can for their child and help them make the most of the opportunities that are available to them. It is important for practitioners to recognize that there are a variety of ways of brining up children that are influenced by culture, religion, family traditions and many other things, and not to be judgemental about the ones that do not correspond with how they think a child should be brought up. Asking parents in a sensitive way is the best way of finding out about cultural variations in child-rearing practices. Practitioners may be asked to provide advice and guidance about bringing up children, and if this happens they need to make it clear that it is their opinion being given, and why they think this is valid. It must be remembered that for the majority of the time parents are able to bring up children appropriately without help. However sometimes parents themselves do not have a good role model to follow for bringing up children, or they may be following what they define as 'cultural practices' that are harmful to children and should not be condoned, and may be illegal and must be reported following the settings safeguarding policies and procedures, (e.g. female genital mutilation, which will be disused in more depth in Chapter 5). Sometimes parents do not have the skills to bring up children appropriately with the result that these parents may be bringing up their children inappropriately, and if practitioners think this is the case they need to be very clear as to why they think that, and what to do to help. Some children and parents may be attending settings so that parents can learn parenting skills. If this is so, parents need to be encouraged and respected for taking part in parenting skills classes. Differences in child-rearing practices will be discussed in more depth in Chapter 2. Parents may have specific needs relating to their racial, religious, cultural or linguistic backgrounds.

Some parents wish to keep their children with them for religious festivals and assume practitioners realize that is what is happening, or phone in on the day their child is going to be away. If practitioners know when religious festivals take place they will be aware of when some of the children in their setting may be absent. Parents may also not be able to attend the setting for events on particular days of religious significance, (for example, Muslim parents may go to the mosque on Fridays). Practitioners also need to be aware of parents' dietary restrictions, perhaps for religious reasons, if they are organising an event with food or drink provided, or if parents are helping on an outing when food is being eaten. Religion is discussed in more detail in Chapters 2 and 3.

A Chance to Think 1.16

Language

A new child, Fasil, is starting in your setting. Fasil's parents do not speak English. They are also not literate in their own language, which is Amharic.

How will you make Fasil's parents feel welcome in the setting?

How will you try to ensure that they receive the information that they need and are able to feel valued and respected?

Compare your answers to the sample answers in Appendix 1.

Britain is a multilingual society and some settings will be working with parents who do not speak English and who do not have English as their first language. It is important that practitioners develop ways of communicating with parents who do not speak English. A friendly smile of welcome and, if possible, knowledge of a few words, such as 'Hello' in other languages, will make parents feel they are welcome in the setting. Interpreters may be needed on occasions, particularly when a child first starts in a setting, so that parents are clear about what is happening and are able to ask any questions they may have and to express their points of view. Local Authorities should be able to put practitioners in touch with interpreters and translators. If possible, notices and letters should be translated for parents. Settings should use interpreters whom parents trust. Often friends, relatives and older children are used as interpreters and translators. Sometimes this will not be appropriate because parents might not wish people close to them to be involved in interpreting for them, as issues of a personal nature may be being discussed, and it also raises issues of confidentiality.

Some parents may not be literate and may be embarrassed to tell practitioners this. Practitioners need to be aware of parents' feelings and needs concerning the fact that they cannot read or write, and make time to ensure that they talk to parents and tell them what is happening in the setting. Sometimes practitioners may not know that parents cannot read or write. Practitioners should not assume parents can, or do, read notices on notice boards or newsletters that are sent home. These should all be secondary to personal contact. It is still important to use notice boards and practitioners need to make sure that these are up to date and as accessible as possible. Practitioners also need to ensure the setting is meeting the needs of, and working with parents with disabilities. Some parents with disabilities may feel vulnerable coming into a setting. It is important that practitioners treat parents with disabilities as individuals and do not make assumptions about them. Practitioners should try and find out what a disabled parent needs in order to help them attend and feel comfortable and valued in the setting. For example, a parent with a visual impairment may, or may not, need help getting around the building, and if they have a guide dog, practitioners need to be aware of this. A few parents may not be able to attend the setting and practitioners need to develop channels of communication with them. It is possible to take photos of the children in the setting so that parents can visualize how they are spending their time. Some settings will have access to a camcorder and be able to make DVDs of how children are spending their time and their achievements in the setting. When taking photos or other recordings it is essential that practitioners get permission from parents and use the equipment that belongs to the setting. The best way to find out about parents' needs is to ask them. It is important that parents are seen as parents first, and as disabled parents second, and that practitioners are sensitive to their needs. Some parents may feel very happy to come into the setting and voice their opinions and share information with practitioners. Other parents may feel shy about doing so, or may be lacking in confidence, either in themselves, their parenting skills or of talking to practitioners. Others may feel awkward about being in the setting depending on why their child is attending. For example, a parent who is having to attend the setting because he or she is required to may feel deskilled and resentful. Every parent is different and practitioners need to respond to them and work with them accordingly. Practitioners, by the very nature of their job and place in the setting, are in an extremely powerful position. All parents are having to 'come into' the setting; they are the ones who are entering into what at first may be a new experience for them. This can create a situation where the practitioner is in a position of power and authority. Practitioners need to be aware of the power dynamics that arise and so work with parents sensitively. One way to change the power dynamics is to undertake home visits and visit parents and children in their own homes. If settings are going to undertake these visits, they need to be planned and thought about carefully so that both parents and practitioners are clear about the aims and purposes of them. These need to be explained carefully to parents who have the right to refuse them if they wish. If they are not explained carefully, then parents may feel that practitioners are coming to make judgements about them and their home. One of the hardest things that practitioners may have to cope with is to work in partnership with parents who have very different attitudes to themselves, particularly if these attitudes are prejudiced or stereotypical. Parents need to be aware of the ethos and aims of the setting. This can be done by giving parents copies of the settings policies and procedures, statements of acceptable behaviour and talking to parents about the setting and what is acceptable and what is not, so that parents are aware of this right from the beginning and they can make an informed choice about whether or not to use the setting. Words on paper are not enough on their own. Settings need to develop ways of working with parents that allow parents to recognize and deal with their own attitudes. This may be a difficult and challenging piece of work and training and support may be needed for both parents and practitioners. It is not always an easy task, and practitioners need to be confident about tackling this issue with parents.

A Chance to Think 1.17

Attitudes

You are facilitating a parents' group. One of the group, Jane, is pregnant. She is white and the father of the child is black. The parents are talking together about pregnancy and childbirth. You are also involved in the conversation, when one of the mothers says to Jane, 'It's nice when anyone is having a baby. It's such a shame that your child will be a mongrel'.

What would you do in this situation?

Compare your answers with the sample answers in Appendix 1.

Colleagues

We have seen throughout this chapter that working within an anti-discriminatory framework can sometimes be difficult, challenging, frustrating, and, it is to be hoped, in the end, rewarding. All practitioners have attitudes and values and it is important to recognize this and be aware of how they may influence behaviour. In 2010 was published called 'A review of the measures to prevent the promotion of racism by teachers and the wider workforce in schools'. It 'reviewed the existing measures in place in maintained schools in England to prevent the promotion of racism and intolerance'. It found that 'all agree that behaviour that promotes racism is incompatible with membership of the teaching profession' and

> that evidence from the review does not support the profound measure of barring members of the teaching profession, or the wider workforce, from membership of organizations that promote racism and intolerance because: 1. It would be disproportionate to the level of risk/prevalence. 2. The relationship between racist behaviour and membership is not necessarily causal. 3. There is no consensus about where to 'draw the line' if a ban were considered.

Practitioners need to examine their own attitudes, values and behaviour and the setting must develop ongoing ways of supporting and evaluating the practice of the people working within it. People who work alongside others, or in a team setting, have each other as a valuable resource to do this. Staff meetings, if managed well, can be very supportive. They can be used to discuss how and why teams are going to approach issues, and how people feel about things. They can provide an opportunity to discuss situations practitioners have found difficult and to discover how colleagues might have dealt with them. Sometimes working in a team can be difficult and challenging. It is not always possible to agree with every member of the team, and disagreements may occur because, although each team member is following the policies and procedures laid down in the settings, they are also individuals with their own opinions and attitudes about things. Sometimes practitioners will need to 'agree to disagree' while continuing to work to the same objectives and within an anti-discriminatory framework. It is good practice for teams and individuals to revisit and evaluate polices and procedures to ensure they are up to date, that practitioners are working within them and to ensure they meet the requirements of the setting and comply with legal requirements. All polices and procedures should reflect and state a commitment to anti-discriminatory practice and should just not be pieces of paper in a file, but living working documents. Effective communication between individuals and in teams allows all workers to be human and to recognize that no single person has the answer to every problem. It allows practitioners to recognize that everybody makes mistakes and to learn from them. Some settings have supervision sessions, where practitioners get the opportunity to discuss issues with their manager or a colleague. Supervisory relationships, like any relationship, have power dynamics in them, as seen, for example, in the case of a young practitioner supervising someone older than themselves. Those taking part in supervision need to be aware of these dynamics and how they affect working relationships. Anti-discriminatory issues arising from supervision and day-to-day practice need to be addressed and resolved by all those involved. It is possible, and indeed highly likely, that practitioners and colleagues will have differing opinions about many things, including attitudes and approaches to work and childcare. We have seen that everyone possess attitudes and values. Individuals working in childcare are first of all 'people' before they are 'practitioners', and so will have formed attitudes and values that they bring with them to their work. Some practitioners will also be parents and have attitudes stemming from their role as a parent. It is to be hoped that most of these attitudes and values will be positive, allowing practitioners to be open to reflection, evaluation and self-development. On the other hand, some of the values and attitudes held by workers may be stereotypical and discriminatory, for example, it is possible for practitioners to be sexist and homophobic. It is essential that all practitioners are given support in dealing with the issues that working within an anti-discriminatory framework raises for them as individuals and how it may affect and influence their work with children, parents, colleagues and others. Isolated practitioners, or people who work on their own, such as childminders, nannies and foster carers also need support in dealing with these issues which may arise for them in working within an anti-discriminatory framework. This might come from attending mutual support groups where practitioners have the chance to get together with other practitioners in the same line of work. Childminders might also receive support from the National Childminding Association. Some settings may have students working in them. Settings need to have clear polices and procedures about the roles and responsibilities of students, their placing agency and the setting. They may be spending only half a day in the setting or they may be on a long term placement. Students will need to be supervised and, as discussed earlier in this section, there are many issues to be aware of in a supervisory relationship. As with all practitioners, students are individuals from diverse backgrounds. Settings need to be clear about how they can meet the needs of students as well as the children, families and practitioners in the setting.

A Chance to Think 1.18

Students

George is a trainee in your setting. On his first visit to the setting the manager explained that although the setting did not have a uniform, it did have certain expectations about the way individuals dressed when at work. Practitioners and students were expected to dress in a way that would allow them freedom of movement when they were with the children, and not to wear anything dangerous to themselves or the children, such as long dangly earrings or large belt buckles. Practitioners were also asked to dress in a way that would not be considered offensive to other practitioners or parents. After George had been in the setting for about a month he informed his supervisor that he was a transvestite, and asked if it would be Ok for him to wear a dress to the setting.

What would you do if you were George's supervisor?

How do you think this situation should be handled?

Compare your answers with the sample answers in Appendix 1.

For some individuals or groups of practitioners, a specific issue may arise on account of who other people perceive them to be, or because they are thought to belong to a particular group. For example, older members of a team may not feel their experience is being valued; younger members may feel they are not being taken seriously; gay and lesbian practitioners may feel isolated or unable to share their life experiences with the team. Practitioners who practise a particular religion may feel that it is not respected if they are being asked to undertake tasks that conflict with their beliefs, for example, Jehovah's Witnesses do not celebrate birthdays.

One particular group of practitioners have found many issues raised for them in working with children and families are male practitioners, as the majority of practitioners in this field are women. The research by Claire Cameron titled: 'Men in the Nursery Revisited; issues of male workers and professionalism', found:

> men in non-traditional occupations, particularly those involving young children, often encounter queries about their status expressed as surprise at their presence, disbelief in their abilities or suspicion about their motives. Such reactions may have the effect of keeping men out of the early years workforce and stem from both cultural unease about men as paid carers for young children and from men's 'token' presence.

Much research has been undertaken into issues faced by male practitioners and researchers have found that it is often difficult for male practitioners to find employment. Childcare is still seen as 'women's work' and childcare as a largely 'female environment'. Male practitioners are constantly aware of the need to protect themselves and the children in their care in case there are allegations of child abuse. Some of the male practitioners say they face prejudice and suspicion from both female colleagues and parents. The Cameron study mentioned earlier found that 'although male workers were widely welcomed, their experience was often one of marginalisation'. Male practitioners are very much needed in the childcare field, and there are many befits for everyone in having male practitioners in settings. They can help balance the team, ensure children see positive male role models, give children a chance to learn to communicate with both men and women, and provide a chance for children to develop a healthy relationship with both men and women. In January 2009 research by the Children's Workforce Development Council found that 55 per cent of parents say they want a male childcare worker for their nursery-aged children. In order to attract and retain male practitioners in childcare settings, employers have a responsibility to acknowledge that male practitioners face issues that their female colleagues do not. Employers need to address areas of concern not just for male practitioners but for all practitioners in order to recruit, retain and support male practitioners. This can be done by: (a) ensuring recruitment procedures are in place and followed; (b) put in place a high quality induction; (c) provide ongoing support and supervision for all practitioners; (d) develop effective communication strategies and build a team so that everyone feels part of the team and is able to contribute to it; (e) provide ongoing support for all staff around attitude development and anti-discriminatory practice and; (f) constantly monitor and evaluate all areas of work.

A Chance to Think 1.19

Male Practitioners

James is a practitioner in your setting. Throughout his career James has been aware that some people think it is strange for a man to be working in a childcare setting. He is also aware that a few parents may have concerns about a man looking after their children, particularly when it comes to the area of supervising children in the bathroom and changing children. Because he is aware of these feelings and concerns, James has always ensured that he tries to deal with them and reassure parents. Lalita is an 18-month-old Hindu girl who is in the process of learning to use the potty. James is in the bathroom helping Lalita when her father arrives to collect her. Lalita's father says to James that he does not want him changing Lalita, as it is not right; he says he wants only female practitioners to supervise his daughter in the bathroom.

How would you feel if you were James in this situation?

How do you think this situation should be handled?

Compare your answers with the sample answers in Appendix 1.

All practitioners need to continue to receive relevant training and development that will help support their work in all areas. Everyone is continually learning and developing; individuals grow and change; new things happen in settings and changes take place in the sector that need to be taken on board. Training and development can be attending a course or undertaking some e-learning, but it does not have to be. It can include visiting another setting to see how they address a particular issue. It may include visiting the library or searching the internet to get some background information, or it could involve reading or attending a support group, or talking to a colleague who has a particular skill or experience that you can learn from. It may even involve taking on a new role in the setting that provides a development opportunity, or undertaking a new qualification. Nevertheless, it goes without saying that traditional courses and conferences are still important. Practitioners get the chance to hear people considered to be experts in their field, and they have the added value of meeting practitioners from other settings and exchanging information and experiences. Sometimes it is possible to arrange for a trainer to attend the setting to address a particular issue with the whole team.

Team meetings provide an important time to reflect on and evaluate practice

We have seen how new legislation is continually coming into force. Good practice issues also change, as do teams, individuals and the children and families practitioners are working with. Practitioners themselves change. They learn new skills, gain fresh insights and acquire new knowledge or qualifications, become more confident in themselves as individuals and as a member of a team. Through day-to-day work, meeting new people, encountering new and different situations and experiences, practitioners are constantly having to reflect on, evaluate and develop their practice. This may be a difficult or uncomfortable experience for some individuals. It can be hard to work with change and recognize the impact we have on situations, and that the situations have on us; but if we are to grow and develop as individuals and practitioners in any setting, not just in childcare settings, it is an essential part of life. Personal and professional reflection and evaluation are necessary in order that practitioners understand both their own role and impact, and the role and impact of others in their day-to-day work. Practitioners are constantly having to think about their own attitudes and the impact they have on others. New initiatives appear all the time and practitioners have to assimilate constant change. This requires the development of new knowledge, understanding, skills and attitudes or the refining of existing ones.

A Chance to Think 1.20

Teamwork

Everyone is part of a team. This can be a team in a setting. For workers, who may work mainly on their own on a day-to-day basis, such as childminders, nannies or foster carers, their team may include other professionals involved in their work such as advisers, speech therapists, social workers and many others.

Think about the team and what you value and respect about your team members.

Now think about what you would like your colleagues to value and respect about you.

Lastly think about the needs of your colleagues and try to evaluate how sensitive you are to those needs.

References and useful resources

Abbot, L. and Moylett, H. (1997). *Working with the Unders-3's; Responding to Children's Needs*. Open University Press.

Aldgate, J., Jones, D., Rose, W. and Jeffery, C. (2006). *The Developing World Of The Child*. Jessica Kingsley Publishers.

Alibhai-Brown, Y. (2001). *Who Do We Think We Are? Imagining the New Britain*. Penguin Books.

Alibhai-Brown, Y. (2001). *Mixed Feelings: The Complex Lives of Mixed Race Britons*. The Women's Press.

Arnot, M. and Mac an Ghaill, M. (2006). *The Routledge Falmer Reader in Gender and Education*. Routledge.

Biddulp, S. (1997). *Raising Boys*. Thorsons.

Blackmore, J. E., Laure, A. A. and Olejuik, A. B. (1979). 'Sex appropriate toy preferances and the ability to conceptualise toys as sex related', *Developmental Psychology* 15, 341–2.

Brighouse, H., Howe, K. R. and Tooley, J. (2010). *Educational Equality.* Continuum.

Brown, B. (2007). *Unlearning Discrimination in the Early Years.* Trentham Books.

Cabinet Office, The. (2008). *Families in Britain: An Evidence Paper.* The Cabinet Office.

Cameron, C. (2006*).* 'Men in the Nursery Revisited; issues of male workers and professionalism', *Published in Contemporary Issues in Early Childhood,* 7 (1), 68–79.

Campenni, C. E. 'Gender Stereotyping of Children's Toys: A Comparison of Parents and Non Parents', in *Sex Roles* volume 40, Numbers 1–2 January 1999.

Caruso, J. and Temple Fawcett, M. (1999). *Supervision in Early Childhood Education: A Developmental Perspective.* Teachers College Press.

Chakrabati, M. and Hill, M. (2000). *Residential Child Care: International Perspectives on Links with Families and Peers.* Jessica Kingsley Publishers.

Children's Workforce Development Council. (2009). *Parents Demand More Childcare Workers.*

Children's Workforce Development Council. (2009). *Common Assessment Framework: Managers' Guide.*

Children's Workforce Development Council. (2009). *Common Assessment Framework: Practitioners' Guide.*

Christiensen, P. and James, A. (2008). *Research with Children Perspectives and Practices Second Edition.* Routledge.

Crabb, P. B. and Bielawski, D. 'The social representation of material culture and gender in children's books', *Sex roles.* Volume 30, numbers 1–2, January 1994.

Curtis, A. and O'Hagan, M. (2008). *Care and Education in Early Childhood: A Students Guide to Theory and Practice.* Routledge.

Dare, A. and O'Donovan, M. (2002). *Good Practice in Caring for Young Children with Special Needs, Second Edition.* Nelson Thornes.

Dfee. (2000). *Education of Young People in Public Care.*

Dfes. (2001). *Special Educational Needs Code of Practice.*

Dfes. (2003). *Aiming High: Raising the Achievement of African-Caribbean Pupils – Guidance.*

Dfes. (2003). *Aiming High: Raising the Achievement of Gypsy-Traveller Pupils – A Guide to Good Practice.*

Dfes. (2003). *Aiming High: Raising the Achievement of Minority Ethnic Pupils.*

Dfes. (2004). *Understanding the Educational Needs of Mixed Heritage Pupils.*

Dfes. (2006). *Priority Review: Exclusion of Black Pupils 'Getting it. Getting it right'.*

Dcsf. (2007). 'Care Matters Time for Change'. White paper.

Dcsf. (2007). *Confident, Capable and Creative: Supporting Boys' Achievements.*

Dcsf. (2008). *Early Years Foundation Stage.*

Dcsf. (2009). *United Nations Convention on the Rights of the Child Prioritiesfor Action.*

Dcsf. (2009). *Care Matters Ministerial Stocktake Report 2009 – Young Persons Version.*

Dcsf. (2009). *Care Matters Ministerial Stocktake Report 2009.*

Dcsf. (2009). *Guidance on Managing Staff Employment in Schools.*

Dcsf. (2009). *Segmentation of Children and Young People.*

Dcsf. (2009). *Segmentation of Parents and Carers.*

Dcsf. (2009). *Childcare and Early Years Survey of Parents 2008.*

Dcsf. (2009). *Disproportionality in Child Welfare – The Prevalence of Black and Minority Ethnic Children within the 'Looked After' and 'Children in Need' Populations and on Child Protection Registers in England.*

Dcsf. (2009). *Influences and Leverage on Low Levels of Attainment – A Review of Literature and Policy Initiatives.*

Dcsf. (2009). *United Nations Convention in the Rights of the Child, Priorities for Action.*

Dcsf. (2010). *Maurice Smith Review.*

Derman Sparks, L. (1989). *Anti-bias Curriculum: Tools for Empowering Young Children.* National Early Years Network.

Elfer, P., Goldschmied, E. and Selleck, D. (2003). *Key Persons in the Nursery.* David Fulton Publishers.

Council for Europe. (2000). *European Convention on Human Rights.*

Fahlberg, V. I. MD. (2001). *A Child's Journey through Placement.* Published by British Agencies for Adoption and Fostering (BAAF).

Fog Olwig, K. and Gullov, E. (2003). *Children's Places. Cross Cultural Perspectives.* Routledge.

Goldschmied, E. and Jackson. S. (1997). *People under Three.; Young Children in Day Care.* Routledge.

Government Equalities Office. (2009). *A Fairer Future the Equality Bill and Other Action to Make Equality a Reality.*

Government Equalities Office. (2010). *An Anatomy of Economic Inequality in the UK – Summary. Report of the National Equality Panel.*

Gurian, M. (2002). *Boys and Girls Learn Differently.* Jossey-Bass.

Jossey-Bass, Harrison, R. and Wise, C. (2005). *Working with Young People.* Open University in association with Sage Publications.

James, A., Jenks, C. and Prout, A. (2002). *Theorizing Childhood.* Polity.

Kehily, M. J. and Swann, J. (2003). *Children's Cultural Worlds.* Edited by Open University.

Lindon, J. (2007). *Understanding Children and Young People Development from 5–18 years.* Hodder Arnold.

Livingston, T. (2005). *Child of Our Time.* Random House.

Loreman, T. (2009). *Respecting Childhood.* Continuum.

Maccoby, E. E. (1998). *The Two Sexes. Growing Up Apart Coming Together.* Belknap Harvard.

Maclean, I. and Maclean, S. (2008). *From Birth To Eighteen Years. Children and the Law.* Kirwin Maclean Associates.

MacNaughton, G. (2000). *Rethinking Gender in Early Childhood Education.* Paul Chapman Publishing.

Maximé, J. E. (1993). 'The therapeutic importance of racial identity in working with black children who hate'. In *How and Why Children Hate. A Study of Conscious Sources.* Jessica Kingsley Publishers.

Myers, K. and Taylor, H. with Adler, S. and Leonard, D. (2007). *Genderwatch – Still Watching*. Trentham Books.

National Children's Bureau. (2008). *Human Rights Are Children's Rights: A Guide to Ensuring Children and Young People's Rights are Respected*.

National Institute For Health And Clinical Excellence. (2010).Draft Guidance. *The Physical and Emotional Health and Wellbeing of Looked-after Children and Young People*.

Newberger, E. H. (2001). *Bringing Up a Boy: How to Understand and Care for Boys*. Bloomsbury Publishing.

Newell, P. (1991). *The UN Convention and Children's Rights in the UK*. National Children's Bureau.

Ofsted. (2004). *Achievement of Bangladeshi Heritage Pupils*.

Ofsted. (2009). *Care and Prejudice*.

O, Hagan, M. and Smith, M. (1999). *Early Years Child Care and Education: Key Issues*. Bailliere Tindall.

Okitikipi, T. (2005). *Working with Children of Mixed Parentage*. Russell House Publishing.

Owen, C., Cameron, C. and Moss, P. (1998). *Men as Workers in Service for Young Children: Issues of a Mixed Gender Workforce*. Institute of Education.

Paechter, C. (2007). *Being Boys Being Girls Learning Masculinities and Femininities*. Open University Press.

Palmer, S. (2009). *21st Century Boys How Modern Life is Driving Them Off The Rails and How We Can Get Them Back*. Orion Books.

Parker, D. and Song, M. (2001). *Rethinking 'Mixed Race'*. Pluto Press.

Pomerleau et al. (1990). 'Pink or blue: Environmental gender stereotypes in the first two years of life'. *Sex Roles*, volume 22, numbers 5–6, March 1990.

Sax, L. (2006). *Why Gender Matters*. Broadway Books.

Sirota, E. and Bailey, L. (2009). 'The impact of teachers' expectations on diverse learners' academic outcomes'. *Childhood Education*, 85 (4), 253–57.

Siraj-Blatchford, I. and Clarke, P. (2000). *Supporting Identity, Diversity and Language in the Early Years*. Open University Press.

Smidt, S. (2009). *Key Issues on Early Years Education*. Routledge.

Sure Start. (2004). *Promoting Race Equality in Early Years*.

Thompson, N. (2003). *Promoting Equality Challenging Discrimination and Oppression Second Edition*. Palgrave Macmillan.

Walker, G. (2008). *Working Together for Children: A Critical Introduction to Multi-Agency Working*. Continuum.

Welch, S. and Jones. P. (2010). *Rethinking Children's Rights Attitudes in Contemporary Society*. Continuum.

Wheal, A. (1999). *Positive Approaches for Working with Young People*. Russell House Publishing.

Wheal, A. (1999). *The RHP Companion to Foster Care*. Russell House Publishing.

Wood, E. (2008). *The Routledge Reader in Early Childhood Education*. Routledge.

Wright, M. A. (2000). *I'm Chocolate, You're Vanilla: Raising Healthy Black and Biracial Children in a Race-Conscious World: A Guide for Parents and Teachers*. Jossey-Bass.

Useful websites

www.cqc.org.uk – Care Quality Commission.

www.dfe.gov.uk – Department for Children, Schools and Families.

www.fatherhoodinstitute.org – Fatherhood Institute.

www.ofsted.gov.uk – Office for Standards in Education.

www.opsi.gov.uk – Office of Public Sector Information.

www.parliament.uk – the website of parliament.

Useful DVDs

Celebrating Diversity Inclusion in Practice by Team Video Productions.

Race, Religion and Culture

Race, religion and culture are represented in, and go to make up, the society in which we live. This chapter will give an overview of what is meant by race, religion and culture. It will examine some of the issues involved, and, I hope, allow practitioners to explore their feelings concerning these issues and how they may affect working practices. Individual religions will be examined in more depth in Chapter 3.

We saw in Chapter 1 that there are many different pieces of legislation that workers need to be aware of and work within that refer to race religion and culture. The Children Act 1989 requires practitioners to take into account a child's racial, religious, linguistic and cultural needs. The Education Reform Act 1988 says that schools must offer a curriculum that promotes the spiritual, moral, cultural, mental and physical development of pupils, the school and society. The Childcare Act 2006 brought us the Early Years Foundation Stage (EYFS) that says in its purpose and aims: 'that every child is included and not disadvantaged because of ethnicity, culture or religion, home language, family background, learning difficulties or disabilities, gender or ability'.

The EYFS early learning goals, a statutory requirement, say children should:

> Have a developing respect for their own cultures and beliefs and those of other people. Understand that people have different needs, views cultures and beliefs, that need to be treated with respect. Understand that they can expect others to treat their needs, views, cultures and beliefs with respect.

In order to be able to promote anti-discriminatory practice, practitioners need to have an understanding of the terminology used. This chapter will use the definitions given by the Concise Oxford Dictionary:

- race: 'each of the major divisions of humankind, having distinct physical characteristics; a tribe, nation and so on, regarded as of distinct ethnic stock';
- religion: 'the belief in a superhuman controlling power, especially in personal God or Gods entitled to obedience and worship';
- culture: 'the customs, civilizations and achievements of a particular time or people';
- faith: 'firm belief, especially without logical proof; a system of religious beliefs; beliefs in religious doctrines';
- spiritual: 'of or concerning the spirit as opposed to matter; concerned with sacred or religious things; holy; divine; inspired'.

A Chance to Think 2.1

My Background

It is important that people working with young children are secure in their knowledge of themselves. Practitioners need to explore how they feel about various issues, including race, religion and culture. Think about yourself.

How would you define your racial background?

Would you say that you hold any religious views or that you are religious?

How would you define your cultural background?

Are these things the same?

How does your background play a part in your work with young children?

Race

Race can be quite an emotive subject. Many people feel uncomfortable about talking about it because they do not know what words to use, or they feel awkward, or worried about saying the wrong thing. Some people express strong feelings when discussing the issue of race. Often these can be negative or discriminatory views. Practitioners need to work towards providing and anti-discriminatory environment so that all children can develop positive self-images and identities. This will be discussed further in Chapter 5. It is also important that practitioners continue to work towards developing a setting where attitudes and issues about race are addressed and reflected on. This is not just about working with children, but also parents, colleagues, visitors, other professionals, anyone coming into the setting, the community the setting is based in and the wider community. As well as being good practice this is also a legal obligation. The Children Act 1989 says that practitioners must take into account a children's racial origin when caring for children. The Equality Bill 2009 says: 'Race includes – Colour Nationality Ethnic or national origin'.

The Race Relations Act 1976, and the Race Relations (Amendment) Act 2000, Equality Act 2006 and the Equality Bill 2009 all work towards the elimination of racism and discrimination on racial grounds. The report Race equality in education by Ofsted 2005 examined several issues including how standards and achievements have improved with reference to the Race Relations (Amendment) Act 2000 (RRAA) and how race equality concepts were incorporated into the school curriculum. It found:

> The RRAA has provided a formal structure to guide and stimulate work that was already underway to tackle attainment gaps between groups of pupils.' and 'in effective schools, race equality concepts enrich the curriculum as a whole, contribute to effective teaching and learning and support pupils' attainment.

Chapter 1 provides more details on the major pieces of legislation that practitioners need to be working within. We saw in Chapter 1 that research shows that young children recognize and put values on different skin colours, and these values can be racist and discriminatory. Children have learnt that people with white skin are seen as having more powerful positions in society than people with black skin. These views are perpetuated throughout society at large, including the media, language and literacy.

A Chance to Think 2.2

Race

Earlier in this chapter we saw a definition of the word 'race' and how the Equality Bill 2009 defines race. We know that there is, in fact, only one race the human race. Some people think that classifying people according to racial grounds can be harmful and lead to generalizations, prejudice and stereotyping.

What is your opinion on this and why?

Racism exists, and can be very damaging to everyone. Practitioners have a duty to recognize its existence and work towards its elimination. Racism occurs when one race is perceived to be superior to another. At one time science and psychology tried to justify such perceptions. As long ago as the 1950s UNESCO pronounced that 'available scientific knowledge provides no basis for believing that groups of mankind differ in their innate capacity for intellectual or emotional development'. Practitioners working with children and families need to acknowledge that racism and racial prejudice exist at many levels in society. The Stephen Lawrence Inquiry report by Macpherson in 1999 following the death of the black teenager Stephen Lawrence said 'Racism in general terms consists of conduct or words or practices which disadvantage or advantage people because of their colour, culture, or ethnic origin. In its more subtle form it is as damaging as in its overt form' and that

> Unwitting racism can arise because of lack of understanding, ignorance or mistaken beliefs. It can arise from well intentioned but patronising words or actions. It can arise from unfamiliarity with the behaviour or cultural traditions of people or families from minority ethnic communities. It can arise from racist stereotyping of black people as potential criminals or troublemakers. Often this arises out of uncritical self-understanding born out of an inflexible police ethos of the "traditional" way of doing things. Furthermore such attitudes can thrive in a tightly knit community, so that there can be a collective failure to detect and to outlaw this breed of racism.

Racism and racial prejudice, and the behaviour resulting from them, are harmful and impact on individuals, groups and the wider society. Racism can happen anywhere and anyone can be racially prejudiced. Sometimes racism is intentional, for example, use of offensive words to describe someone, or not employing an individual because of their colour or ethnic background. Sometimes it is unintentional for example, using resources before evaluating them effectively to see what images or messages they contain. Both of these result in individuals and groups being disadvantaged and hurt and it also has implications for the society in which we live. Training, development, evaluation and reflection are needed by practitioners in order that they can address the issue of race and its impact on themselves, the setting and society. All practitioners like to think that all children, families and colleagues are being treated equally, but this, sadly is often not the case. In many studies where practitioners' practice has been observed, workers have been found to be spending more time with white children; saying that Asian children are disadvantaged and criticizing black children more often than white children. This has a huge impact on all children.

The Ofsted report Achievement of Bangladeshi heritage pupils in May 2004 found that: 'compared with pupils nationally, Bangladeshi pupils have below average attainment at the end of each key stage, but achievement is improving, especially among Bangladeshi girls.' It also found that, 'The attainment of Bangladeshi pupils at key stage 1 is considerably below the national average and the same pattern is shown at key stage 2 and 3'. One of the recommendations it makes to help raise the achievements of Bangladeshi pupils is that 'the school ethos is one that recognises and celebrates diversity and takes a firm stand on racism'. It is important for practitioners to recognize that this is happening. There are many reasons why it may be difficult to recognize this and act on it. Sometimes things are done unconsciously without realizing it; sometimes it is hard to talk about this area of work with colleagues; sometimes individuals do not have enough knowledge about what is happening; sometimes individuals feel that it is the job of someone else to deal with it. It is the role of every practitioner to work in a way that promotes and provides for racial equality.

A Chance to Think 2.3

Inspection

On visiting a setting in a rural area an inspector was told, 'we only have two children here from minority ethnic backgrounds so we do not need to address issues of race. Anyway they do not notice colour and we treat all children the same'.

What do you think about this statement?

Why does this setting need to address issues of race?

How can it begin to address these issues?

Compare your answers with the sample answers in Appendix 2.

Children of mixed parentage / dual heritage have parents from two different races. For some children this can be a very positive experience. Other children receive confusing messages about their identity. Some children may feel torn between two races. This may mean that children have difficulty in developing a sense of identity and high self-esteem. Children need to receive positive messages about their racial identity from both home and the setting they attend. The development of self-esteem is discussed further in Chapter 5.

Whatever setting practitioners are in, it is important to give everyone in the setting an understanding of, and respect for, the different races that make up society. Children and parents need to know that this is an integral part of the ethos of the setting; that their racial background will not just be acknowledged, but respected and valued. In many settings the ethos of the setting is written down in the form of a mission statement that is available for all to see. Settings should also have policies and procedures on how issues are dealt with on a day-to-day basis. The welfare requirements in the statutory framework of EYFS require that: 'all providers must have and implement an effective policy about ensuring equality . . . .'

It also says: 'providers must maintain records, policies and procedures required for the safe and efficient management of the settings and to meet the needs of the children'.

It requires that settings record a variety of data including a child's ethnicity and it says: 'this data can be collected on a voluntary basis. A child's ethnicity should only be recorded where parents have identified the ethnicity of their child themselves.'

The Race Relations Amendment Act 2000 requires that settings in or run by the Local Authority have to have regard to it. This means having a race equality scheme in place, including having a race equality impact assessment. This is a tool to help settings embed equality into practice and to ensure that the setting is treating everyone equally. It is also good practice for all settings to have a race equality policy and procedure that is actively used and implemented. It is important that these are not just pieces of paper for show or brought out for inspections purposes, but that workers incorporate issues of race into their day-to-day work. The incorporation of race into the curriculum and daily activities is discussed in Chapter 5.

A Chance to Think 2.4

Policies, procedures and practice

Both legislation and good practice demand that all settings are required to have polices and procedures relating to racial equality. Think about your own setting and try and find all the paperwork you can that relates to racial equality.

What written work does your setting have in relation to race equality and how it is embedded into practice?

How did you find out about it?

How often is it monitored and evaluated and who is involved in doing this?

What happens if someone disagrees with the policy or other documentation?

Religion

Individuals may be born into a religious family and brought up in the religion held by their family. As individuals grow older, they will have to make their own personal decision as to whether they continue to follow that religion. Some people chose not to enter formally or follow the religion in which they were brought up, though they may still follow some if its customs. Some individuals make a decision to follow a different religion from the one in which they were brought up. The Universal Declaration of Human Rights says 'People should be able to practice their religion wherever they live and have the right to change their religion if they want to. No one should be persecuted because of their religious belief'. At present, Christianity is the dominant religion in British society. However, many other religions are represented in society and practised by many people. Practitioners need to acknowledge and be aware of this. Religions have given the world many great things, including sacred scriptures, literature, art, music, symbols and architecture. Some terrible things have also been done in the name of religion, with communities being torn apart by religious conflict.

Religions are treated by the media as news. The way religions are portrayed by the media influences the way people view them, especially if this is the only contact people have with the particular religion portrayed. Sometimes stereotypical attitudes towards particular religious groups are perpetuated by the media, and issues are often sensationalized in the interest of readership or viewing figures. The internet can also provide both useful and unhelpful information about religions. When reading or watching anything it is important to remember that all information given has a bias and to be aware of it.

Religion has a long history. Some religions stretch back to the dawn of humanity and are recognized throughout the world as having firmly established beliefs and traditions (see Figure 2.1). Other religions are relatively new and may not be as firmly established, or as widely recognized, as the major world religions. Religions incorporate many things in their practices and some may include guiding principles on dress and dietary rules that an individual may follow. Everybody has a racial and cultural background and some people also have religious beliefs that influence how they live their lives. Children, families and colleagues may have a religious background that practitioners need to be aware of. Although practitioners cannot know every detail of every religion, and indeed, individuals may interpret religious guidelines in different ways, practitioners should have some general knowledge of the many different religions practised in society today and be aware of where they can obtain

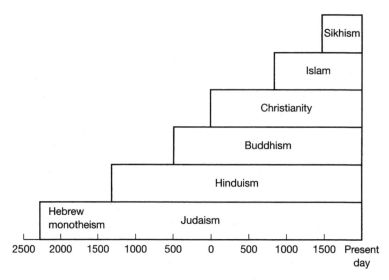

Figure 2.1 Ages of major religions

further information from. Some practitioners may work in a setting that is affiliated to a particular religion. Some may work in settings where not many religions are represented, and other settings may have many different religions represented in them. Some parents may tell practitioners that they belong to a religion; other parents may not share this information with practitioners. Whatever setting practitioners are in, it is important to give all the children in the setting an understanding of, and respect for, the different religions in society. Children and parents also need to know that doing so is an integral part of the ethos of the setting.

A Chance to Think 2.5

Religion

Think about your own setting, and the children, families and colleagues that make it up. How many different religions are represented in the setting and what are they?

How much do you feel you know about the different religions represented in your setting?

How do you show that you acknowledge, value and respect people's religious backgrounds?

Compare your answers with the sample answers in Appendix 2.

Religions have very different beliefs, which may clash with each other. Practitioners need to develop policies and procedures concerning religion. These will help address the issue of how the setting is going to meet the needs of children, families and practitioners in the setting, including how to avoid becoming involved in activities that compromise their religious beliefs. Just as some of the children and families attending settings will come from different religious backgrounds, so do some of the individuals who work with the children. Childcare practitioners are likely to disagree with some of the beliefs of the different religions because there are so many different religions. Some have a core of beliefs that overlap, while others have differing and conflicting beliefs. Although practitioners may not agree with some aspects of people's beliefs, it is important to recognize that people have the right to those beliefs and try and respect the way they feel about them. Some practitioners may find that there is a conflict between their own personal beliefs and those of their colleagues or the families with whom they work. If this situation arises, it is important to deal with it, if possible through discussion with a senior colleague. For example, people who are Jehovah's Witnesses do not celebrate festivals such as birthdays. A worker who is a Jehovah's Witness may have a personal conflict over the celebration of festivals in the workplace. Discussion with a senior colleague and reference to relevant polices and procedures should allow for a successful resolution to the matter that is acceptable to both parties. Practitioners who work on their own (e.g. childminders and nannies) may be unable to do this. However they may be able to talk to other practitioners in the same or a similar situation. Childminders may have the opportunity to discuss these issues with a support officer from the local authority or with the National Childminding Association. It is important to remember that everyone is an individual. People may observe all, some or none of the guidelines of their religion. It is important not to make assumptions about what families attending the setting, or colleagues we work with, believe or observe. One of the best ways of trying to make sure we have the right information is to ask parents or colleagues in a sensitive way about their religious backgrounds. By doing this, we are acknowledging the validity of people's religious background, and placing them in the position of being the most knowledgeable individual about their own beliefs. Parents and colleagues may also be able help to gather more information and resources to be able to help practitioners understand a particular religion. Settings need to think about and plan how to acknowledge and ensure that the requirements of religions, and how families follow them, are incorporated into the setting.

This means more that acknowledging festivals. It is about incorporating them into the day-to-day life of the setting. It is also about helping children to learn about religions other than their own and what this may mean to individuals on a daily basis who belong to a religion. It is important to recognize that some people may not have any religious beliefs or belong to a particular religion. These people may class themselves as either agnostics or atheists.

Agnostics

We need to remember that not everybody belongs to a recognized faith. There are people who have no religious beliefs. People who belong to a religion may acknowledge that a god, or several gods, exist. There are also people who are not sure if they believe in a god or not. However, those with no religious beliefs may follow guiding principles of daily living.

People who are not sure whether they believe in the existence of a god are called agnostics. People who are agnostics question the existence of a god. This is because no one can prove whether a god exists or not. The Concise Oxford Dictionary defines 'agnostic' as 'a person who believes that nothing is known, or can be known, of the existence or nature of God or anything beyond material phenomena'.

Some families and colleagues in the setting may be agnostics. Practitioners should be sensitive to the feelings of people who feel they do not belong to any religion.

Atheists

Many people in the world have some sort of religious faith. However, there are also many people who have no religious faith. Some people believe there is no god. Unlike agnostics, who are not sure whether a god exists, atheists are quite sure there is no such thing as a god in any shape or form. The words 'atheist' comes from the Greek word *a-theos,* which means 'without god'. The Concise Oxford Dictionary defines the word 'atheism' as: 'the theory or belief that God does not exist'.

Humanism

Many people call themselves 'humanists'. Humanism encompasses both atheism and agnosticism and humanists try to live their life following a code of conduct for the good of humanity which they believe is right, and that helps both them and their fellow human beings and promotes human welfare, happiness and fulfilment. Humanists mark important events with Humanist ceremonies that are occasions filled with words, music and warmth and conducted by a celebrant. These include naming ceremonies, weddings and partnership celebrations and funerals and memorials. It is important to remember that people have a right to these beliefs. Practitioners should not make judgments about people just because some people do not believe in the existence of a god.

Culture

Practitioners need to take into account cultural backgrounds of everybody in the setting. Cultural background is different from racial background, but as with race, individuals have no control over the cultural background into which they are born. It is important to remember that everyone inherits a culture and cultural background. Culture is not 'exotic' but something that can affect and influence all areas of a person's life, often without people realizing it. Every family and every setting has its own particular culture and ways of doing things.

Culture is not static, it is dynamic, always changing and evolving. Individuals move and introduce new things to the place they move to. Families move or come together, change and develop their own traditions and practices. The culture of settings change as new legislation is introduced and practitioners reflect and develop new practices. The families using the setting may also influence and change the culture of the setting. The changes in the way individuals communicate using technology, and the way information is now disseminated so rapidly, all influence and affect the culture of the moment. No one culture is more important that another.

A Chance to Think 2.6

Culture

We saw earlier in this chapter how culture can be defined, but there is much more to culture than simple definitions. A person's cultural background can have a profound effect on the way a person lives. Think about culture and write down all the things that may in be included in this that influence a person's life.

Why will culture have an effect on the things that happen in childcare settings?

Compare your answers with the sample answers in Appendix 2.

Melvin Konner in the book *Childhood* said: 'Children are vessels for the passing on of culture. They soak it up, find it impossible to avoid.' Cultural background plays a very important role in child-rearing and has a large impact on the way a child develops. Each culture has its own set of values and ways of bringing up children. These vary greatly. It is also important to remember that in every culture there are subcultures and groups that have variations on different things such as dress and language. Some of the things that may vary between, across and within cultures are:

Size of family and family make up;
Language;
Diet, food and ways of eating;
Dress;
Hair care;
Discipline and how to help children manage their behaviour;
Customs and traditions;
Religion;
Expectations of children;
Child rearing practices;
Child development;
Music;
Values;
Access to information;
Attitudes.

Sociologists and psychologists have long recognized the effect of culture on child-rearing practices and child development. In some cultures it is unacceptable to leave babies to cry; they will be picked up and comforted. In other cultures it is thought that children must learn they will not be picked up every time they cry.

In some cultures children sleep in their parents' room, or in their parent's bed until they decide they want to sleep alone. There is some interesting research undertaken into culture and sleep. Mckenna (2000) found that 'much of the advice given by paediatric health workers on transitional objects, and cosleeping may be unknowingly biased towards traditional Euroamerican views on childrearing'. He reports that cosleeping is practised in many cultures including Asian, Guatemalan Japanese Vietnamese and Chinese cultures. He looks at a study conducted in Australia where a Vietnamese mother was interviewed and said, when talking about cosleeping, 'babies are too important to be left alone with nobody watching them'. He also reported on studies that found that both males and females who coslept with their parents had higher self-esteem than those who did not. Cosleeping might include 'sharing parents' beds, futon cosleeping or infants sleeping alongside, but not on the same surface, as the mother'. Jennie and O'Connor (2005) in their research titled 'Children's Sleep; An Interplay Between Culture and Biology', discussed a recent study that found that Italian parents 'reported that it was customary and preferable to have infants sleep in their rooms with them irrespective of the availability of separate rooms and considered the American norm of putting children to bed in separate rooms to be "unkind"'. They went on to find that bedtime routines also varied across and between cultures, with some cultures, including American families, having set betimes rituals and routines, and other cultures having less structured and more fluid approaches, including Italian, Spanish and Greek families. They go on to say that in other cultures 'the wake-to-sleep transition of children is not a culturally "marked" event . . . and that infants and young children simply fell asleep when they were sleepy, usually in someone arms'. They found this pattern in the community in Mayan families in Guatemala. Breastfeeding is another aspect of child rearing that varies across and between cultures and individuals. The reasons for this may include personal preference, economic status, family support and medical reasons, for example, a mother who knows she is HIV positive may seek help and advice on how to protect her baby when breastfeeding. Indeed the World Health Organisation (WHO) issued guidance on this in 2009. In many cultures children are breastfed until they are 4 or 5 years old and in others even longer. For some children breastfeeding ceases early their life. The WHO recommends that mothers exclusively breastfeed for the first 6 months of a child's life. Research across cultures has found that children will wean themselves when they are ready. It is important to remember that there will be differences within cultures and practitioners should not generalize about cultures and practices. Not all babies will be breast fed some will be bottle fed. The decision parents make about whether to breast or bottle feed should be respected by practitioners and supported. Mothers who are breastfeeding may need somewhere that they can feed their baby while in the setting. They may also need somewhere to store milk they have expressed ready for their baby for when they are not there. Another area of child rearing that may vary across and between cultures is that of toilet training and the use of nappies. Research by Horn, et al., into the beliefs about the appropriate age for initiating toilet training found that 'caucasian parents believed that toilet training should be initiated at a later age (25.4 months compared with both American parents (18.2 months) and other races (19.4 months)' In many parts of the world children never wear nappies and parents may start toilet training children before a child is a year old. This is done as parents get to know their baby. They recognize the signs given by them when they are going to urinate or defecate. When parents see this sign the parent will lift the child over a receptacle and as the child passes a motion the parent will make a vocal sign that the baby eventually comes to associate with 'going to the toilet'. Mary Exton, a mother from China married to an American, describes her experiences of toilet training her two children. The first born in China and the second born in America. She says:

> one month after Elizabeth was born my mother suggest we toilet train her . . . Chinese toilet training means to hold a baby gently by the hips over a potty or the edge of the road and whistle softly to imitate the tinkle of urine. Chinese babies don't wear diapers at all, . . . instead they wear open-crotch pants . . . just as my mother said Elizabeth was toilet trained when she was seven months old.

Mary goes on to say her son who was born in America was still wearing nappies at 21 months of age. She says 'cultural conflicts can create quite a challenge. In many ways they are an asset. You can only gain strength and skills as you work through them'. Another aspect of child-rearing that varies across cultures is childcare. In some cultures mothers play very little part in caring for their child. Children may be cared for by childcare workers, extended family or by their fathers. There is also difference across cultures in what is expected of children. Some cultures expect children to be quiet and obedient and show respect for adults. Children may be expected to take on responsibility and help in the home from a very early age, and to look after their brothers and sisters. In some cultures children are expected to work to help to support the family. Children are seen as people, and childhood is not seen as a separate stage of development. In other cultures childhood is very much seen as a distinct stage of development where children can have fun, grow, learn and develop without any of the responsibilities they will be expected to take on when they become adults. The way children develop is guided by many things including their genes and the opportunity to practise their behaviour and skills. These will be influenced by the culture in which they are brought up, as can be seen from Piaget's theory of children's learning. He said that there are four stages to children's learning:

- Sensori-motor stage (birth to 2 years);
- Pre-operational stage (2 to 6 or 7 years);
- Concrete operations stage (7 to 12 years);
- Formal operations stage (12 years plus).

Psychologists have researched this theory across cultures to see whether all stages appear in the same order. They found that in non-literate adults the formal operations stage (12 years plus) was rare, leading them to conclude that this stage represented a culturally specific course of development in Western society. Cross cultural research has also been undertaken into Piaget's theory of conservation of volume. This is where children see water in a tall narrow glass and it is then poured into a short wide glass. Piaget says that until children are between 7 to 11 years of age, most Western children will say the tall narrow glass holds the most water. However children in other cultures who are used to working with water say that both amounts are the same. We can see that Piaget's stages follow a linear or chronological pattern, that is, they all follow each other and are not interlinked in any way. A psychologist who put forward a theory that was not linear or chronological was Brofenbrenner. He developed a theory known as the 'Social Ecological Systems Theory'. This theory links the four different systems that influence an individual, with the individual at the centre of all the systems rather like a system of stacking Russian dolls (see Figure 2.2).

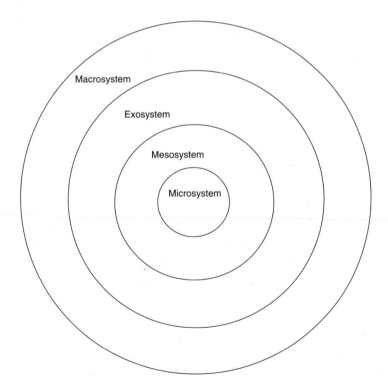

Figure 2.2 Bronfenbrenner's Model

The Microsystem is about a child's daily experiences in the family, home, peer groups, places of worship and setting. A child may have many Microsystems.

The Mesosystem shows how two or more of the Microsystems work together and interact.

The Exosystem is about the social systems that affect the child but in which the child is not directly involved. These could include the media, transport, informal social networks, parents friends and work.

The Macrosystem is the outside circle furthest from the centre. This includes broad social structures such as laws, belief systems, cultural values and economic systems.

At first glance it may be difficult to see how all link together and influence each other. Let's take law as an example from the macrosystem. We have the Every Child Matters (ECM) agenda receiving legal status through the Children Act 2004. This directly affects the exosystem in that it has been publicized in the media and government agencies have been funding projects related to the ECM agenda. This then impacts in the mesosystem as parents, children and settings all interact together, which takes us to the child at the heart of the microsystem who will be attending a setting, or have parents using the facilities of a setting, working to meet the outcomes in the ECM agenda. Bronfronbrenner also recognized that time and place have an important part to play in a child's development, for example, children born in 2010 in Adigrat in Ethiopia, Washington in the United States , or London in the United Kingdom, will all have very different experiences that affect and impact on their development. He also spoke about 'Within child' differences. This approach fits very well within an anti-discriminatory framework as it encourages practitioners to look at all the aspects which influence children and their development and places the child at the centre of this. When examining any research it is important to remember that researchers are also a product of their own culture and research also takes place in a cultural context. Examination of child development across cultures allows us to see some of the similarities between cultures. These include a similarity in the sequence of sensory-motor development, smiling and the degree of distress at separation from parents. Also constant across a large variety of cultural groups is the development of language. This will be discussed in greater depth in Chapter 5.

Another important finding for childcare practitioners is that children learn more, can perform tasks better and find more meaning in activities using culturally appropriate material. This has implications for the type of equipment and resources needed in settings, as well as the way activities are carried out. This was shown in a piece of research looking at children's memory. When asked to remember things of which they had no previous knowledge, children had a great deal of difficulty. In their own home, and using objects with which they were familiar, the same children could use their memory well. Some aspects of development and behaviour may also be related to the cultural context in which children are brought up. Practitioners need to acknowledge that there are cultural differences in the way children are brought up and the experiences they have, for example, we saw earlier in this chapter potty training can vary greatly between cultures, with some cultures starting potty training early and others leaving it until a child is around 3 years of age. Some child rearing practices may be harmful to children, for example, some forms of disciplining children that may be said to be undertaken for cultural reasons. It is important not to condone these, and not to accept child rearing practices that may be both illegal and not good practice. With those exceptions in mind it is generally not a case of one culture being right or wrong, and unless they are harmful to children, practitioners should value and respect cultural variations in child rearing and be sensitive to them.

A Chance to Think 2.7

My Setting

Think about your own setting and the children, families and colleagues that make it up.

How many different cultures are represented in the setting, and what are they?

How much do you feel you know about the different cultures represented in your setting?

How can you show that you acknowledge value and respect people's cultural backgrounds?

Compare your answers with the sample answers in Appendix 2.

There may also be different opinions about child rearing practices between practitioners in a setting. It is important to remember that just as children's and families' values, practices and attitudes are influenced by their cultural backgrounds, so too will those of practitioners. Different opinions about childcare issues should be discussed, with special emphasis on how they affect the setting. Some children whose culture is not the same as that of the setting may feel torn between two cultures. Children and parents need to know that as an integral part of the ethos of the setting, their cultural background will be acknowledged, respected and valued. How to incorporate such acknowledgment and respect into daily working practices will be discussed in Chapters 4 and 5. All settings have their own culture and no two settings will ever be the same. Indeed every setting will be constantly changing and evolving, and a setting that has been in existence for many years may have a different culture now than it did when it was first established. The culture of a setting is influenced and shaped by where it is; the training, qualifications and values of the practitioners working there; the ethos of the setting; who attends the setting; legislation; funding available and many other things. Practitioners may chose to work in a setting where they feel the culture, ethos and values are similar to their own. However it is important that all practitioners continue to reflect, evaluate and develop their own practice.

A Chance to Think 2.8

Culture of the Setting

All settings have their own culture and ways of doing things. This can be influenced by where it is based; the training of the staff; its ethos and values; the people who attend, and may other things. Think about the setting you work in.

How would define the culture of your setting?

How do you influence the culture of the setting and how does it influence you?

It is important to remember that the concept of culture is always changing and evolving. Language changes and evolves; the toys children play with change; there is now much more use of technology and access to the internet. Research brings with it new knowledge that changes practice; families develop their own customs and traditions; people move around more that they used to; economic circumstances alter and change how people do things. All of these things impact on and change cultures.

Influences on child protection / child abuse

It is the role of all adults, including parents and practitioners, to safeguard children, to look after them and protect them. Child abuse can, and does, happen in any family and in all cultures and in all religions. Child abuse takes place when a person harms a child, either deliberately or by not keeping them safe from harm. Local authorities and agencies working in the safeguarding / child protection area have many technical definitions of what child abuse is. Abuse can be defined under four headings

- Physical abuse;
- Sexual abuse;

- Emotional abuse;
- Neglect.

Practitioners need to be aware of, and working within, the policies and procedures of their settings. They must also follow the guidelines set out in the document 'What to do if you are worried a child is being abused' and know about their Local Safeguarding Children Board.

Practitioners work with children who have different skin colours and skin tones. All children bruise themselves and practitioners need to be able to recognize bruises and how they age and change while healing with different skin colours and skin tones. A bruise will look different on a child with white skin than a child with black skin. If practitioners are not sure how bruises of differing ages look like, then it is a good idea to watch one as it heals the next time you are bruised. Some black children and children of mixed parentage may have a birthmark that looks like a bruise. This is called a Mongolian blue spot. It is a naturally occurring mark, and is sometimes found at the base of the spine. It is useful for practitioners to know whether children have any birthmarks, as sometimes they may wonder what they are when they first see them. Parents will be able to provide practitioners with this information. Practitioners also need to be aware of some cultural traditions that are considered abuse and are illegal in Britain. One of these is female genital mutilation, also known, incorrectly, as female circumcision. The World Health Organisation (WHO) says:

> the causes of female genital mutilation include a mix of cultural, religious and social factors within families and communities. An estimated 100–1140 million girls and women are living with the consequences of female genital mutilation. It is mostly carried out on young girls sometime between infancy and age 15 years. The practice is most common in the western, eastern, and north-eastern regions of Africa, in some countries in Asia and the Middle East, and among certain immigrant communities in North Africa and Europe.

Although it is illegal in Britain, some girls are still at risk. It may take place in Britain or young girls may be taken abroad for the procedure, often with no anaesthetic and with basic instruments. The WHO says female genital mutilation can be classified into four major types:

1. Clitoridectomy; partial or total removal of the clitoris (a small, sensitive and erectile part of the female genitals) and, in very rare cases, only the prepuce (the fold of skin surrounding the clitoris).

2. Excision: partial or total removal of the clitoris and the labia minora, with or without excision of the labia majora (the labia are 'the lips' that surround the vagina)

3. Infibulation: narrowing the vaginal opening through the creation of a covering seal. The seal is formed by cutting and repositioning the inner, or outer, labia, with or without the removal of the clitoris.

4. Other: all other harmful procedures to the female genitalia for non medial purposes, for example, pricking, piercing, incising, scraping and cauterizing the genital area.

Neglect happens when adults fail to care for children appropriately and to meet their essential needs. This is often difficult to define, as everyone has different standards of care. These may be influenced by the way people themselves were brought up, their parenting skills, cultural expectations, level of income and the environment in which they live. As we saw in the section on hygiene routines, everybody has different ways of doing things but practitioners need to be guided by the policies and procedures in their setting and follow them. Child abuse and child protection is a complex and sensitive subject and practitioners should discuss any concerns they have with their line manager or relevant professional. Practitioners also need to receive help, support and ongoing training when working with issues around child abuse, child protection and how to safeguard children.

A Chance to Think 2.9

Safeguarding

Child protection and safeguarding work can be unsettling and raise many emotions in practitioners. We have seen that there are four main categories of child abuse and it is known that abusers can be male or female.

What other issues do practitioners need to be aware of when thinking about anti-discriminatory practices in child protection work?

Compare your answers with the sample answers in Appendix 2.

Influences on the calendar

A calendar is a system of naming and marking periods of time. The Gregorian calendar is the calendar that is used in the West as the civil or international calendar, with 1 January being the first day of a new year. A calendar followed by an individual or group of people may be influenced by many things, including religion and culture. One person may use many different calendar systems at a time, for example, the Gregorian calendar to agree dates with others, a financial calendar for business purposes, the academic calendar if working in an educational establishment and a religious calendar showing when festivals are celebrated. The calendar a person follows will tell when the year starts its length. For example, the Ethiopian year starts in September and is made up of 13 months – 12 months of 30 days each and 1 month of 5 (6 days in a leap year). It is 7 years and 8 months behind the Gregorian calendar so that the 11 September 2010 will be, the 1st day of 2003 in the Ethiopian calendar. Among other calendars that differ from the Gregorian calendar in the date of the new year are; (1) the fiscal or financial year. In the United Kingdom the financial year starts on the 1 April. Other countries may follow a different financial year. (2) The academic year, the year followed in educational establishments, can also vary between countries. In Scotland it starts in August and ends in late June or early July. In Northern Ireland the academic years starts in September and finishes the end of June. In England and Wales academic year starts in September and ends in July. (3) The Chinese calendar follows the lunar calendar which is based on the cycles of the moon. This means that the date the new year falls on changes every year. It can fall between the end of January to the middle of February. (4) Legal calendars. Many religions have their own calendars that tell when the year starts and when festivals occur. For example, the Baha'i calendar is made up of 19 months, each containing 19 days and begins in March. The calendars followed by religions will be discussed in more detail in Chapter 3.

Practitioners need to be aware of the many different calendar systems and where to find out information about them. Indeed many practitioners themselves may be following several of the different calendars. It is useful to know when different dates fall and when important events occur; as parents and children may be observing them. Settings may also wish to acknowledge events on particular dates as it may influence when a setting is open or closed for holidays.

Influences on customs and traditions

There are many origins to customs and traditions. Customs are a particular way of behaving and traditions are customs, opinions, beliefs and behaviours that have been established over time and passed from generation to generation. Many religions have customs that are part of the religion. Many of these relate to important events in the religious calendar or events in people's lives, for example, naming ceremonies, marriage and funeral rites. These customs and traditions can include when to hold an event, what to wear, what order to do things in, and so on, Some of these are discussed in Chapter 3 which looks in more detail at religions. Many customs and traditions that started as part of a religion have now become embedded in day-to-day life for example, Halloween. As well as customs arising from religions, customs and traditions may arise from cultures, settings, families and events in a person's life, especially around events that mark something important in a person's life. For example, some families develop customs and traditions around birth, naming ceremonies, birthdays, first day at school, losing the first baby tooth and anniversaries. Other families may develop customs and traditions around holidays, storytelling, special celebration meals and many other things. It is difficult for practitioners to be aware of all the many different customs and traditions that individuals may follow, particularly as many will be very specific to an individual family. It is especially important to talk to parents and children so that they feel comfortable sharing their customs and traditions with the setting if they wish to.

Influences on diet

Race, religion and culture can impact upon the diet and personal care routines followed by individuals. The requirements laid down by religions will be discussed further in Chapter 3.

Food plays an important part in people's lives and a person's background can affect an influence their diet. This can include such things as what people eat and drink and when, how people eat and drink and how they cook and prepare food. The way food is presented and how it is eaten may be influenced by a variety of factors, the main one being how individuals are brought up and how they see food presented and eaten. We have seen that everybody inherits a culture and each family has its own culture and ways of doing things. Some families eat their meals sitting round a table, with the meal being the focal point for a social occasion. Other families eat their meals in front of the television. In some families people eat meals at different times.

A Chance to Think 2.10

Mealtimes
We all eat our different food in different ways. Think back over all the meals you have eaten in the past week.
   Where were you when you ate and what did you use to eat with?
   Did you eat with your fingers, with chopsticks or with a knife and fork?
   What influences the way you eat your food?

Most cultures have some food that is eaten with the fingers. Some children will eat all of their food with their fingers if this is the way that food is eaten at home. Children who then stay for lunch in the setting where knives and forks are laid out on the table may be unsure what to do with them and may need support to learn how to use them effectively. Practitioners need to value the experience and skills the children bring with them to the setting, whether it is eating with their fingers or with other implements, such as chopsticks, or a spoon and fork. The setting should try and be flexible and allow children to eat with their fingers or with the implements they are used to using at home in this way. The other children in the setting can also learn the skill of eating with fingers or other implements. Children who are unfamiliar with knives and forks will need to learn how to use them and they will soon learn the new skill with encouragement from the practitioners in the setting, and by observing the other children using them. It is important that children learning how to use new implements are not made fun of or ridiculed. This will make them feel their experiences are not valued and will give the message to the other children in the setting that only one way of eating is correct. Mealtimes provide a valuable chance for children to interact together and learn from each other. They can learn about the way that food is prepared, cooked, served and eaten and how this varies between and within cultures. When doing this with children or talking about it with them, it is important to provide positive images of both males and females preparing food, cooking and clearing up.

A Chance to Think 2.11

Ways of eating

Mealtimes are a good time for practitioners to ensure that children experience a variety of foods from different countries and cultures and different ways of eating. Sarah works in a nursery where the children often have curry and naan bread for lunch. So that the children can fully experience how this can be eaten, Sarah has brought in thali dishes for the children. This means the meal can be served in the thali dishes and the children can be encouraged to use their fingers to eat the meal. This has been discussed with the parents and staff, who have all agreed that they would like this to take place.

What benefits do you feel that the children and adults in the setting will get from this experience?

Compare your answers to the sample answers in Appendix 2.

Influences on dress

A person's choice of dress may be influenced by a variety of things including religion, culture and social and personal reasons for example, some babies may be swaddled, others may not. Indeed the clothes practitioners wear to work are influenced by the culture of the setting they work in. Practitioners may spend part of their day carrying out activities that involve handling, or talking about, children's clothes or the way they are dressed. One question that practitioners may need to consider in relation to dress is under what circumstances it is appropriate to help children to alter or remove articles of children's clothing or jewellery. Reasons for doing this may include when a child is too hot; for safety reasons (e.g. if a child wears clothes that constantly get caught up in equipment); making the child more comfortable or allowing the child to take part in an activity such as swimming. Before you alter a child's clothing or jewellery it is important to consider when it is not appropriate to do this and discuss this with parents. Practitioners need to be aware of, and to respect, the religious, cultural and social reasons that determine a child's or adult's dress. When they take children swimming, for example, practitioners need to consider that in some religions and cultures it is not considered appropriate for young girls or women to show parts of their bodies in public.

A Chance to Think 2.12

Swimming

Shelan works in a day nursery. The manager of the nursery has decided that the children should go swimming once a week. It has also been decided that the staff should take it in turns to supervise the sessions and go swimming with the children. The staff and parents have not been consulted about this. Shelan is a Muslim, and observes the guideline that she should cover her hair and body in public. Shelan feels that she is unable to go into the swimming pool with the children, but she is happy to accompany the group to the pool and help with the session.

If you worked with Shelan, how would you feel about this?

How would you support Shelan during this time?

Compare your answers with the sample answers in Appendix 2.

One of the best ways for practitioners to be aware of what is appropriate with regard to children's clothing, and what is not, is to ask their parents. Practitioners need to be aware of individuals' dress codes as they might have implications for the planning of outings, such as swimming, or during play activities, such as dressing up.

How children are dressed can be influenced by culture, religion and personal preferences

Some religions have guidelines about how a person should dress. Individuals may follow this differently. Some people follow all, or some, of the guidelines; others do not follow any. The only way practitioners can be sure is not to make assumptions or judgements, but to ask the individuals in a way that will not make them feel awkward or embarrassed. Further details of dress guidelines given by religions is given in Chapter 3.

Influences on hair care

We have seen that individuals have different general hygiene routines that may be influenced by religion and culture. Individuals may also have different hair care routines. Chapter 3 will give more information about the guidelines that different religions have about hair care. Some religions have guidelines that hair should be covered. They are Orthodox Christianity, Islam, Judaism, Rastafarianism and Sikhism. Some individuals may follow these guidelines and others may not, but practitioners may have children in their setting, both boys and girls, who will keep their hair covered. Rastafarian men and women may grow their hair into dreadlocks. This happens when the hair is left uncombed and allowed to matt into locks. Although the hair is not combed it is still cared for and groomed, and covered to ensure that dirt does not come into contact with the hair. Many Sikh men and women grow their hair long and do not cut it for religious reasons. It is traditional for some cultures to put oil, grease or fragrant oils in their hair for religious or cosmetic reasons, or to keep the hair in good condition. Practitioners need to acknowledge and respect this. If individuals do put oil or grease in their hair it means that some things may stick to it, such as sand. It may be that the setting thinks about providing hats for children to wear when playing in the sand. This should be done in a positive way with all children being able to wear hats if they want to, and not as a way of making children feel awkward or singled out.

It is important for practitioners to be aware of the needs of the children in the setting regarding hair care. All practitioners are involved hair care in some way and there are some activities in the setting that can have an effect on a child's hair, for example, going swimming, or playing in the sand.

A Chance to Think 2.13

Hair care

Amarjit is a 4-year-old Sikh boy who attends your setting. He wears his hair uncut and plaited in a jura (bun) on the top of his head. This is covered by a white cloth. One day, by accident, the cloth comes off and Amarjit's hair comes down. Some of the other children notice this and start teasing Amarjit, saying that because he has long hair he is a girl. Amarjit is very upset by both the teasing and the fact that his hair has been uncovered.

What would you do in this situation?

Compare your answers with the sample answers in Appendix 2.

Influences on helping children manage their behaviour

There are many variations in how parents help children manage their own behaviour. These are linked to child rearing practices across cultures, religions and families. The way parents often learn their parenting skills is from their own parents. Many aspects of parenting get passed between generations without people realizing it, including attitudes, beliefs and values concerning how children should behave and the parent's role in guiding this. Some individuals consciously try to do things that same way their parents did if it was good practice, and others try to do things differently from their parents if they had a negative experience as a child. The way parents expect their children to behave, and how they help them to achieve this can vary greatly between families and cultures. We have seen that eye contact between children and adults can vary between cultures. Some cultures may place emphasis on conformity and others on independence. Some cultures expect children to look after younger siblings and help in the home. Others do not. The way a child behaves in one family, setting or culture may not be acceptable in another family, setting or culture. Many of the strategies used by parents to help children manage their behaviour work well and are helpful to children, others may not be acceptable and may lead to instances of abuse which is discussed later in this chapter. There is much information available for parents about helping children to manage their behaviour, for example, books and many different programmes on television. Sometimes these can be helpful to parents but sometimes they can confuse parents. There are also many parenting classes run by a variety of organizations that parents can attend. When working with parents and children, practitioners need to reflect on how they support parents to help their children manage their behaviour. Practitioners also need to reflect on the culture of their setting and how this can influence and support children to manage their behaviour.

Influences on hygiene routines

Everyone's hygiene routine is based on, or influenced by, a variety of things. Children's routines will be influenced by the adults they have contact with, as well as their own independence skills. Adults' hygiene routines may be influenced by religious or cultural guidelines as well as personal preference and access needed to facilitate hygiene routines. A family living in bed-and-breakfast accommodation, and having to share a bathroom with several other families, may have a different hygiene routine from a family with its own bathroom and washing machine.

A Chance to Think 2.14

Hygiene routines

Everyone has a personal hygiene routine. Things pertaining to this may include keeping teeth clean, flossing teeth, keeping hair clean and tidy, shaving, using the toilet, having a shower, washing or bathing, washing clothes and keeping them clean and tidy. Think about your own hygiene routine. What does it consist of?

How often do you do these activities?

How would you feel if you could not carry out any of these activities?

Sometimes individuals may have what practitioners consider to be different or inappropriate standards of hygiene, (e.g. some families may wear clean clothes every day, others wear the same clothes for more than one day.) Some people may wash their hair daily, others less often. It is important that practitioners do not make judgements about individuals solely because they do not follow the same personal hygiene routines as themselves. Practitioners need to be aware of the needs of the children in the setting regarding hygiene routines. All children should have a hygiene routine appropriate to their individual needs that allows them to remain healthy. If, and when, it is apparent that a child's health or welfare is suffering owing to a poor hygiene routine, then practitioners may need to discuss hygiene routines with parents in a non-judgemental manner. For example, if a child in the setting is coming in the same clothes all week, and they have not been washed and are starting to smell, the other children or parents may make negative comments about the child. This is not a situation that anyone would ask to be in, but it is important for practitioners to approach it in a sensitive manner by talking to the parents and trying to help them as may be appropriate. The child may, or may not, be aware of the situation, and some parents may not realize that this is an inappropriate hygiene routine. It may be that the family does not have access to a washing machine or many changes of clothes. Practitioners may be able to suggest ways of helping parents to be aware of their children's needs and hygiene routines. There may be occasions that if having worked with parents, practitioners still have concerns, or if parents are neglecting a child, that a referral may have to be made using the child protection procedures of the setting. All practitioners need to be aware of all the policies of the setting and how to use them in practice. Some hygiene routines are influenced by religious or cultural tradition, for example, some Sikhs, Muslims and Hindus consider having a bath in a bath tub as not being clean, because of sitting in water that contains dirt that has just been washed off. For this reason, many individuals prefer having a shower. Settings, particularly residential settings, that are involved in this part of a child's hygiene routines need to ensure that children are able to take showers. If this is not possible, then a bowl of water should be provided to that water can be poured over the body. Some Sikhs, Muslims and Hindus traditionally use the left hand for washing and the right hand for eating.

Influences on language

Language is constantly changing and evolving. New words are introduced, for example, new words in the Concise Oxford English Dictionary eleventh edition include: 1) 'crunk' which is a 'type of hip-hop or rap music characterized by repeated shouted catchphrases and elements typical of electronic dance music, such as prominent bass'; and 2) 'hoody' (also 'hoodie') defined as 'a person, especially a youth, wearing a hooded top'. Some words go 'out of fashion' and others stop being used altogether. Some words change their meaning over time, for example 'awful' originally meant 'full of awe'; it now means 'unpleasant' or 'horrible'. Other words can have different meanings for different people or be used in different ways, for example, a 'mouse' can be a mouse used on a computer or a small rodent. The word 'chip' is used in both British English and American English but has different meanings. In British English it means 'deep fried potatoes' and in American English it means 'crisp'. In both languages and cultures it can mean a computer chip. Sometimes the same object can be called different things for example the vegetable 'courgette' can also be called 'zucchini'. Everyone uses language. Some people use a spoken language, some people use sign or symbol languages or other language systems. Everybody uses body language. Language is part of culture and culture is part of language; they cannot be separated and both influence each other. How a person uses and understands language is ingrained in their cultural background. Some phrases are very culturally specific and people need to be aware of the meaning behind the phrase to understand it, for example, 'It's raining cats and dogs' means 'it is raining hard', not that it is literally raining cats and dogs. People need to have an understanding of the culture of technology to understand the context of the word 'bluetooth' – a device enabling wireless communication between technological artefacts such as mobile phones.

All settings have their own culture, and when at work practitioners use language that relates to the culture of childcare, and in particular their own setting. Practitioners may talk in 'shorthand' or jargon. This can be useful as it forms a shared understanding and bonds practitioners and teams, but it can also make new team members feel excluded or uncomfortable if they do not understand the 'shorthand', or have different meanings for the jargon used, for example, the initials CAF are commonly used by practitioners in settings, and this can understood in at least two different ways. It could mean the Common Assessment Framework or Common Assessment Form. It is important that practitioners and teams check how they are using 'shorthand' and jargon so all practitioners in the setting are clear and understand the terminology being used. The way practitioners use language, both spoken language or other language systems, and body language, can help parents feel welcome and comfortable in the setting or feel unwelcome and uncomfortable in the setting. It is important to remember that body language and non verbal communication varies a great deal across, between and within cultures. Some cultures greet people with a kiss on the cheek, some shake hands, others press noses or bow. In many cultures it is considered disrespectful for children and young people to look at adults when they are talking, and in others it is considered rude if they look away and do not look at the person speaking to them. The concept of personal space and how close people feel comfortable having others near to them also varies across cultures with some cultures needing a larger amount of personal space than others. Even something people do without thinking, such as shaking the head, can mean different things in different cultures and situations, with the same movement meaning 'no' in some cultures and 'yes' in others. Body language is discussed further in Chapter 5. Like all areas of work it is important that practitioners do not make assumptions about what individuals mean when using body language and non verbal communication. For everyone it happens unconsciously and has been learnt and developed without people realizing it through the culture that they have been brought up in. Practitioners should always ask people for clarification when a misreading of body language or non verbal communication has happened or may happen. Many people speak more than one language and this will be discussed in Chapter 5 but many people are monolingual, that is they speak one language. As we saw earlier, there are many differences, even in one language, with the same word having different meanings between cultures and countries. Another thing that everyone has in common, but may also be different is that everyone speaks with a dialect (relates to vocabulary) and accent (relates to pronunciation). These may vary depending on the country or region a person grew up in, or a person's age or gender. No dialect or accent is better than another and they are part of a person's cultural and individual identity.

Another area of language that practitioners may use and hear others using is 'code switching'. This is when people change or move between variations of language in the same conversation. For example, a child who speaks more than one language may start a sentence in one language and finish it in another. Code switching can also occur when speakers switch between dialects in the same conversation. Children and adults can also use different language styles when speaking to different people and in different situations. Children may have different language styles when with family, friends, when talking to practitioners, or when playing. Parents may use different language styles when talking to practitioners and when talking with their child. Practitioners also change language styles to suit the occasion and the people they are with. For example, using a style for playing with the children, a 'phone voice', a different style for talking to other practitioners and many others. This happens as individuals want to 'fit in' with others and language styles are a part of an individual's identity, image and role. A child paying with their peers outside in a setting with no adults involved has a different role and behaviour to the same child talking with their parents. It is also important to consider the impact that religions have had on language. There are many words originating in religions that are now used by people outside that religion. Many religions use a particular language, for example Islam uses classical Arabic, Hinduism uses Sanskrit and Judaism uses Hebrew. Books relating to the religion may be written in these languages and worship conducted in them. Some parents and children may use these languages as part of their worship. Some children may attend lessons in order to learn the language and study the religion.

A Chance to Think 2.15

Use of body language

As a practitioner the role you play has a powerful impact on how people feel in your setting. Think about your own body language and non verbal communication and the messages they give out.

How do people know they are welcome in your setting just by reading your body language and non-verbal communication?

What messages do you think you are giving out through your body language and non verbal communication and are these the messages that people are picking up? Have you ever had an occasion when someone misread your body language and non-verbal communication or you misread someone else's body language and non-verbal communication?

What happened and how did you resolve the misunderstanding?

Influences on play

Play is hugely influenced by race, religion and culture. Play and how it is defined and used in settings will be discussed in Chapter 4. What children play with, how and when they play, are all influenced by the background of a child and the family in which they are brought. Adults may place different values on play with some adults thinking it is not important or of any benefit to children. They may not provide children with play materials, preferring that they engage in 'academic' activities instead. Some adults may view play as something to do when 'learning' or 'work' has been finished. Other adults may view play as very important and provide time, space and resources for play. They may also play with their child. How children play, and views about play, also change over time. The games played by children even ten years ago are different from the games children play now. The equipment and resources also differ. Children now have a greater range of manufactured toys and technological toys than ever before. These can be of great benefit if used well, but they can also lead to children spending more time playing on their own with technology rather than with other children. How children use resources also differs between children and their past experiences. Some children may arrive in a setting not knowing how to do a jigsaw or hold a book, as there are none of these at home and so they have not used them before. Other children may not know how to paint or play with clay as parents view these as activities that children should play with in settings as they are too messy to play with at home. Some parents may not make and use dough with children as they believe that playing with food is wrong. Children may also use resources in different ways over time. For example, settings often put play phones out with imaginative play such as in the home corner or with the hairdressing set. Five years ago children would have used the phone just for making phone calls. Now children can be seen using the phone imaginatively to text, take photos on, and for the older children, pretend to access the internet. It will interesting to see how children will be playing with phones and other resources in another five years' time. Practitioners need to be aware that every child will be coming to the setting with their own experiences of play and that these will vary between children. Every child's experience will be different and may not be the same as that provided in the setting. Practitioners need to support each child with play according to their individual needs. The role of the adult in play is discussed in greater detail in Chapter 4.

References and useful resources

Bell, A., Bryson, C., Barnes, M. and O'Shea, R. (2005). *Use of Childcare Among Families from Minority Ethnic Backgrounds.* Sure Start/The National Centre for Social Research.

Concise Oxford English Dictionary (2009). Oxford University Press.

Dcsf. (2008). *Early Years Foundation Stage.*

Dcsf. (2006). *What to Do if You Are Worried a Child Is Being Abused.*

Derman-Sparks, L. and Brunson Phillips, C. (1997). *Teaching / Learning Antiracism: A Developmental Approach.* Teachers College Press.

Derman-Sparks, L. (2004). 'Early Childhood Anti-Bias Education in the USA' in Van Keulen, A. (ed.) *Young Children Aren't Biased Are They? How to Handle diversity in Early Education and School.* B.V. Uitgeverji SWP.

Draycott, P. and Robins, L. (2005). *Say Hello To – A Multi-faith, Multi-cultural Resource to Aid Learning in the Early Years.* RE today.

Equality Bill. 2009. Exton, M. (n.d). *The Cultural Conflict Over Toilet Training.* http://oz/plymouth.edu/~megp/webct/culturalconflict.htm (accessed April 2010).

Fog Olwig, K. and GullØv. (2003). *Children's Places Cross-cultural Perspectives.* Routledge.

Government Offices for the English Regions. (2009). *Guidance for Safer Working Practice for Adults Who Work with Children and Young People.*

Horn, I. B., Brenner, R., Rao, M. and Cheng, T. L. (2006). 'Beliefs about the appropriate age for initiating toilet training'. *Journal of Paediatrics* 149 (2), 151–2.

James, A., Jenks, C. and Prout, A. (1998). *Theorizing Childhood.* Polity.

Jenni, O. G. and O'Connor, B. B. (2005). 'Children's Sleep: An Interplay between Culture and Biology'. *Paediatrics* Vol 115, No 1 January 2005, 204–16.

Kehily, M. J. and Swann, J. (2003). *Children's Cultural Worlds.* Open University.

Konner, M. (1991). *Childhood.* Little, Brown, and Company (Canada) Ltd.

Lane, J. (2008). *Young Children and Racial Justice. Taking Action for Racial Equality in the Early Years – Understanding the Past, Thinking about the Present, Planning for the Future.* National Children's Bureau.

Lindon, J. (1999). *Understanding World Religions in Early Years Practice.* Hodder & Stoughton.

McKenna, J. J. (2000). 'Cultural Influences on Infant and Childhood Sleep Biology, and the Science that Studies it; Towards a More Inclusive paradigm'. In J. Loughlin, J. Carroll, C.Marcus (eds) *Sleep and Breathing in Children; A Developmental Approach.* 199–230.

Ofsted. (2004). *Achievement of Bangladeshi Heritage Pupils.*

Ofsted. (2005). *Race Equality in Education.*

Siraj-Blatchford, I. and Vlarke, P. (2000). *Supporting Identity, Diversity and Language in the Early Years.* Open University Press.

Stead, K. (2003). *Culture.* Early Years Educator.

Sure Start. (2004). 'Promoting Race Equality in Early Years'.

Taylor, J. (2006). 'Start with a difference: Promoting race equality in the early years – a Jewish perspective'. The Jewish Council for Racial Equality.

Wood, E. (2008). *The Routledge Reader in Early Childhood Education.* Routledge.

World Health Organisation. (2009). *HIV and Infant feeding: Revised Principles and Recommendations.*

World Health Organisation. (2010). *Female Genital Mutilation.*

Publications for children

Cooling, W. (2005). *All The Colours of The Earth.* Frances Lincoln Children's Books.

Fuller, R. (2008). *Let's Dress.* Tango Books.

Fuller, R. (2007). *Let's Eat.* Tango Books.

Global Baby Fund for Children. (2008) *Global Babies.* Charlesbridge Publishing.

Kindersley, B. and Kindersley, A. (1995). *Children Just Like Me.* Dorling Kindersley.

Kindersley, B. and Kindersley, A. (1998). *Children Of Britain Just Like Me.* Dorling Kindersley.

Kubler, A. (1995). *Come Eat With Us.* Child's Play (International) Ltd.

Kubler, A. (1995). *Come Play With Us.* Child's Play (International) Ltd.

Kubler, A. (1995). *Come Ride With Us.* Child's Play (International) Ltd.

Kubler, A. (1995). *Come Home With Us.* Child's Play (International) Ltd.

Lester, J. (2005). *Let's Talk About Race.* Amistad.

Petty, K. (2007). *Hair Around The World.* Frances Lincoln Publishers.

Petty, K. (2007). *Playtime Around The World*. Frances Lincoln Publishers.

Petty, K. (2007). *Home Around The World*. Frances Lincoln Publishers.

Rattigan, J. K. (1993). *Dumpling Soup*. Little, Brown, and Company.

Swain, G. (1999). *Eating*. Small World.

Swain, G. (1999). *Celebrating*. Small World.

Tarpley, A. N. (2004). *I Love My Hair*. Little, Brown, and Company.

Useful websites

www.blackrefer.com/beauty4.html – provides information about black hair and skin care.

www.festivalshop.co.uk – resources and equipment to support festivals, information about religions and diversity.

Useful DVDs

Festivals 1 and 2 by Child's Eye Media.

Major Religious Beliefs 3

This chapter examines the major religions that make up the society we live in today. It gives an overview of each religion, including a short history, the beliefs held by the adherents of the religion, the major festivals celebrated, symbols that have meaning or are important, and dress and dietary requirements of the religion. In this chapter it is only possible to provide an overview of some of the major religions. It is not possible to include every religion or to go into great detail about them. The aim of the chapter is to provide readers with some information so that they have a basic understanding of the different religions. For readers wanting further information, useful addresses and a reading list are given at the end of the chapter. The order of the religions in this chapter does not imply any order of importance: they are listed in alphabetical order.

Baha'i

History and beliefs

The Baha'i faith was founded in Persia in about 1844 by Siyyid Ali-Muhammad, who was known to his followers as the 'Bab'. The word *bab* means gate. The Bab was killed n 1850, and his work and teachings were taken forward by Mirza Husayn Ali, who changed his name to Baha'u'llah. He lived for a time in Bagdad (Iraq) but spent the end of his life in Haifa (Palestine). Haifa is now a holy place for Baha'is.

Baha'is believe in one God and one religion. They believe that all religions come from God and are passed through messengers who live at different times. Jesus was one messenger, Baha'u'llah another, and Baba'is believe that God will Send another messenger in the future to build on the work that has already been done. There are no leaders in the Baha'i faith; every Baha'i is thought of as a teacher and Baha'i also believe that everyone is equal and part of the world family. The holy book of the Baha'i faith is called the Kitab-i-Aqdas. It is a book of laws and scriptures written by the Baha'u'llah. Baha'i worship in a holy place called a temple. One of the features of the temple that it has nine sides and nine entrances.

Major festivals

The Baha'i calendar is made up of 19 months, each containing 19 days. The year Baha'i starts in March. There are 11 holy days in the year (see Table 3.1).

Table 3.1 Major Baha'i festivals

Month	Festival	Background information
March	*Naw-Rúz*	Baha'i new year. A day of celebration and festivities with music and a feast to celebrate the end of the 19 day fast. Gifts may be given.
April / May	Ridvan	A 12 day period commemorating Baha'u'llah declaration of his mission.
May	*Ascension of Bahá'u'lláh*	The anniversary of the death Bahá'u'lláh the founder of the Baha'i faith. A day of rest. Individuals may read or chant from the scriptures.
July	*Martyrdom of the Báb*	A day to remember the events surrounding the death of the Báb in 1850. A day of rest. Prayers are said.
October	*The Birth of the Bab*	May be celebrated with a social gathering and readings from the scriptures.

Baha'i Symbols

A nine-pointed star is used as symbol of faith by the Baha'is. The number nine is important in the Baha'i faith. It is seen as the highest single digit that symbolizes completeness.

Dietary requirements

Table 3.2 Dietary requirements

May eat / drink	May not eat/ drink	Fasting
No food is forbidden	Alcohol	19 days just before the Baha'i new year

Dress guidelines

Baha'is do not follow any particular dress code.

Buddhism

History and beliefs

Buddhism is based on the teachings of Siddhartha Gautama. People who follow his teachings are called Buddhists. They believe that Siddhartha Gautama was a Buddha. This means that he was an 'enlightened one'. Buddhists divide into two main types. The oldest form of Buddhism is practised by the Theravada Buddhists who follow closely the teachings of the Buddha based on his doctrines. The Mahayana Buddhists follow a newer form of Buddhism and now make up the majority. The Mahayana branch of Buddhism contains within it the Zen Buddhists. Siddhartha Gautama was the son of a rich man. He was born in the Himalayas in what is now Nepal, in 563 BC, and lived his life there. His father was worried about all the cruelty and suffering that happened in the world. He tried to protect Siddhartha from it by bringing him up inside a palace so that he would not see what happened in the outside world. When Siddhartha Gautama grew up he married a princess, and they had a baby son. When he was about 30 years old Siddhartha left the palace walls and saw four people. The first person was an old man; the second was a sick man; the third man was dead and the fourth man was a holy man. The holy man looked happy and peaceful. After seeing these four people, Gautama decided he had to do something. He thought there must be a way to ease people's suffering. In order to try and find some answers to these deep questions that would not go away, Gautama left his life in the palace. He went to live with a group of wandering beggars and shared their life. Although he lived the life of a poor man for six years, he did not find the answers to his questions. Gautama decided to leave the group of beggars and look elsewhere for answers to his questions. He lived on his own as an ascetic and meditated focusing his mind. Meditation is an important part of Buddhist life. After meditating and living alone for about six years, Gautama believed he had found the answers to his questions. He believed that he had found how to help people live their lives in a way that would help them to avoid suffering. Gautama called this way of living *the middle way*. It is called this because it involves living between the extremes that are in life. Gautama wanted to share his new knowledge and enlightenment with others. He wanted to tell them about his new beliefs and way of living. He did this by preaching a sermon to the people he had lived with. As a result of this they became his disciples. In his sermon, Gautama explained the Four Noble Truths that he believed were in life:

(1) The truth of suffering: all life contains suffering.
(2) The cause of suffering: we cause our suffering.
(3) The cessation of suffering: we can stop suffering.
(4) The way that leads to the cessation of suffering: by avoiding the extremes in life.

Gautama said that suffering can be avoided by following the Eightfold Path in daily life:

(1) Right understanding;
(2) Right intentions;
(3) Right speech;

(4) Right conduct;

(5) Right occupation;

(6) Right endeavour;

(7) Right contemplations;

(8) Right concentration.

Through understanding the Four Noble Truths and following the Eightfold path, individuals may reach the goal of existence called Nirvana. Nirvana, or transcendant state, is freedom and peace. Achieving it may take years, or even more than one lifetime. Buddhists believe that by transmigration, or being continually reincarnated, it is possible to achieve Nirvana.

Gautama taught for 40 years and died when he was 80 years old. At first his teachings were not written down. Eventually they were written down in a holy book called the *Tripitak,* or the Three Baskets. The language used to write the *Tripitaka* was Pali, an ancient language spoken by the Buddha. The *Tripitak* is made up of 31 books in three sections. The *Vinaya Pitaka* is about the monastic discipline. The *Sutra* (or *Dharma*) *Pitaka* contains the Buddha story, the Precepts and other doctrines. The *Abhidarma Pitaka* contains advanced doctrine and philosophy. The Four Noble Truths and the Eightfold Path are contained in the *Dhammapada.* This is separate from the *Tripitaka.*

Siddhartha Gautama also gave Buddhists the Five Precepts. These are rules that should be followed every day. They are:

(1) Do not kill or harm living things.

(2) Do not steal, but give to others.

(3) Do not misuse your senses.

(4) Do not speak wrongly.

(5) Do not use drink or drugs.

Buddhists do not worship a god, but the Buddha did not say there was not a god. He said that god could not be defined, described or explored.

The place where Buddhists meet is called a temple, or Vihara. No one day of the week is considered more holy than another, and Buddhists will go to the temple on any day.

Major festivals

The Buddhist calendar is based on the lunar calendar, which is determined by the movements of the moon. Each month has a full moon, which is celebrated in different ways according to the branch of Buddhism followed and the country lived in. Different countries may have a festival to mark the full moon of each month, and may not be mentioned here. The major festivals are centred on the events in the Buddha's life and his teaching (see Table 3.3). The Buddhist calendar starts in the month of May with Vesakha.

Table 3.3 Major Buddhist festivals

Month	Festival	Background information
May	Vaisakha Puja / Wesak	A Theravada festival. Celebrates the birth, enlightenment and death of the Buddha. Mahayanists celebrate these events on separate days. Homes may be decorated with garlands of flowers and lanterns. Some people may release or free birds as symbols of compassion and help.
June	Poson / Dhamma Vijaya	A Theravada festival. Celebrates the preaching and spread of Buddhism from India to other countries.
July	Asala	A Theravada festival. Celebrates the first sermon of the Buddha where he talked about the Middle way, the Four Noble Truths and the Eightfold path to enlightenment.
October	Kittika	A Theravada festival. Celebrates the monks leaving the Buddha to spread his word in India.
December	Bodhi Day	A Mahayana festival. Celebrates the Buddha's achieving enlightenment.
February	Parinirvana	A Mahayana festival. Commemorates the death of the Buddha.

Buddhist symbols

There are many different statues of the Buddha in the world. The ways in which the Buddha is represented in statues have different meanings. If the Buddha is shown with his fingers near his heart and palms touching, this symbolizes him preaching his first sermon. If the Buddha is shown with his right hand pointing down, this symbolizes him resisting temptation.

Dietary requirements

Some Buddhists are vegans. This means they will not eat any animal or animal product. Some Buddhists are vegetarians. Vegetarian and vegan food and non-vegetarian food must not come into contact with each other. Practitioners should use separate utensils in the setting to serve vegetarian and non-vegetarian food. If this is not possible, utensils should be washed between serving of the different foods.

Table 3.4 Dietary requirements

May eat / drink	May not eat / drink	Fasting
Eggs (by some people) Cheese (vegetarian) Yogurt (vegetarian) Milk (soya) Fruit Vegetables	Meat Fish Shellfish Animal fat Alcohol	Some Buddhists fast

Figure 3.1 A Statue of the Buddha

Dress guidelines

Some Buddhists may cover their hair. Jewellery may be worn from personal choice.

A Chance to Think 3.1

Buddhism

A child of a family who follows the Buddhist religion is starting in your setting and you are going to be her key person. You do not know very much about the Buddhist religion.

How and where can you get information that may help you become aware of the needs of the child and the family?

Compare your answers with the sample answers in Appendix 3.

Christianity

History and beliefs

Christians believe there is one God who created the world and then sent his Son, Jesus to teach people about God. The word 'Christian' comes from the name of Jesus Christ. The word 'Christ' is a title that in Greek means 'anointed one'.

Christians believe that Jesus was born in Bethlehem to a Jewish couple, Mary and Joseph. When Jesus was 30 years old he was baptized by a man called John the Baptist in the river Jordan. Jesus then called 12 people together, called his disciples, to help him teach others about the kingdom of God. For three years Jesus and the disciples travelled the country telling people about God. Christians believe that Jesus performed miracles, such as turning water into wine, healing the sick and even raising the dead.

At the age of 33 Jesus was put to death by the Roman authorities in power at the time, at the insistence of Jewish religions leaders who accused him of blasphemy. He was crucified on a cross outside the city walls of Jerusalem. He was taken down from the cross and placed in a tomb. After three days some women followers went to anoint the body, but it was gone. They asked a gardener where the body had gone when suddenly they realized they were talking to Jesus. Christians believe that Jesus died on the cross, but after three days he rose again and appeared to his disciples on many occasions for a period of 40 days. He then ascended to heaven, having told his disciples to preach his gospel of salvation to the world.

Christians believe that Jesus rose from the dead, and so they believe in a living Christ. After his death, Jesus' disciples continued to teach people about God and salvation and so Christianity spread throughout the world and became accepted as a religion.

Christians were persecuted by the Roman emperors. In AD 312 Emperor Constantine was converted to Christianity and Christianity became the official religion of the Roman Empire. Because Rome was the capital of the empire, the Bishop of Rome (later called the Pope) was the most important bishop in the church. When Emperor Constantine moved his capital to Constantinople the power within Christianity shifted, and in AD 451 the Bishop of Constantinople was given the same powers as the Pope. In 1054 they had a power struggle over the leadership of the church. This resulted in a major split to form two different branches of the Christian Church. These became known as the Eastern Church and the Western Church. Both branches of the Church believe in the same basic tenants, but they have different ways of interpreting them and celebrating them.

The Eastern branch of the church now contains what is known as the Orthodox churches. These include the Russian Orthodox, Greek Orthodox, Eastern Orthodox, Ethiopian Orthodox and Egyptian Orthodox churches. These churches have their own rules and leaders or patriarchs. The person to whom all the Orthodox churches look to for leadership and guidance is the Patriarch of Constantinople. The Orthodox churches follow the Julian calendar with Christmas (the celebration of the birth of Jesus) being celebrated on the 6 January.

The Latin, or Western branch of Christianity, was first made up of Christians who looked to the Pope of Rome as the head of the Church. In 1517 a German monk called Martin Luther split with Rome to form a branch of the church known as the Protestant church. A further split came in 1536, when, in England, Henry VIII also split from the Church of Rome. This branch of the church is known as the Anglican church. Further divisions ensued with branches or denominations including Baptists, Methodists, Quakers, Presbyterians, Plymouth Brethren and Congregationalists all coming into existence. The Catholic (Roman) and Protestant churches follow the Western Christian calendar (Gregorian), with Christmas being celebrated on the 25 December.

All Christians follow the teachings of Jesus, which are written down in four Gospels, a part of the holy Christian book called the Bible. The Bible is divided into two parts. The Old and New Testaments. Each Testament is made up of books written by different authors. The Old Testament contains different chapters on the creation of the world, guidelines on how to live, prophecy and Jewish history, all written before the birth of Jesus. The New Testament contains writings that took place after the birth of Jesus, including writings by some of the disciples about the life of Jesus.

The Christian holy day is Sunday. This is day when Christians meet to pray, sing, think, read the Bible and worship God. Different branches of Christianity have different ways of worshiping together. The places they meet are holy or special and have many different names including cathedral, church, chapel and meeting hall.

All the branches of the church have special ceremonies where sacraments are celebrated. These are services at which Christians show others that they are practising their faith. The first is where individuals formally join the Christian church. This is called Baptism and may take place either when individuals are children or adults. All branches of the Church celebrate the Eucharist, which is when people take part in a communion ceremony commemorating the death and life of Jesus Christ. These two sacraments are called the Dominical sacraments because Jesus (the Lord or Latin *Dominus*) ordered that they should take place. The Roman Catholic and Orthodox churches have five other sacraments called confirmation, penance, extreme unction, holy orders and marriage.

Major festivals

All the major Christian festivals are centred on events that happened in the life of Jesus or the early church. The Christian year begins in November with Advent Sunday. Some festivals happen on the same day each year, for example, Christmas always falls on the same day, the 25th December for the Western Church and the 6th January for the Orthodox church (see Table 3.5). Other festivals change their date and are dependant on the first fasting day of Lent. This falls on the Friday of the first full moon of the spring equinox.

Christian symbols

The main symbol of the Christian church is the cross on which Jesus was crucified. It reminds Christians that Christ died on the cross. Protestant and Orthodox churches generally (but not always) have an empty cross to show that Jesus rose from the dead. Different branches of Christianity have different designs of crosses. Churches of a Catholic or 'High Church' tradition may have a symbol called a crucifix. This is a cross with the body of Jesus Christ still crucified on it. This is to remind them of the agony that Jesus endured for them.

Dietary requirements

The different Christian denominations may have different dietary guidelines. Generally no food is forbidden. Some Christians may abstain from meat and fish on Fridays.

Table 3.5 Major Christian festivals

Month	Festival	Background information
November	Advent	Advent begins with the four Sundays before Christmas. It is the time when Christians prepare for the coming of Jesus Christ on Christmas day. It may be celebrated by the making of an Advent wreath. This has one candle for each of the four Sundays in Advent and one candle in the centre to represent Christmas day. A candle is lit on each of the Sundays to show the coming of Christ at Christmas.
December and January	Christmas	Christians celebrate the birth of Jesus Christ. The Catholic and Protestant churches celebrate this day on the 25th December. The Orthodox churches celebrate on the 6th January. Christians may give each other presents and exchange cards. They may have special foods such as Christmas cake and mice pies and may decorate their houses with Christmas trees and coloured lights.
January	Epiphany	Marks the visit of the kings to the baby Jesus. This is celebrated 12 days after Christmas.
February, March or April	Lent	Lent is the 40 days leading up to Easter remembering Christ's fast in the desert. Some Christians fast at this time and others may give up something they enjoy. The date of Lent changes every year. Lent begins for the Catholic and Protestant church on Ash Wednesday. The Orthodox churches begin Lent on Clean Monday.
March or April	Palm Sunday	Celebrates Jesus' entry into Jerusalem. Palm crosses are usually given out at church on this day.
March or April	Maundy Thursday	The day of Jesus' last supper with his disciples.
March or April	Good Friday	The day Jesus was crucified.
March or April	Easter and Easter Sunday	Easter begins on Easter Eve Saturday. The day when Christ rose from the dead. Easter is the most important day in the Christian calendar. Easter lasts for 40 days. Christians may give each other Easter eggs to show Easter is a sign of new life. The date of Easter is set by the date of the start of Lent.
May	Ascension	Takes place 40 days after Easter Sunday. Celebrates the day Jesus rose to heaven. The last day of the Easter season.
June	Pentecost or Whit Sunday	Pentecost is the day when the Holy Spirit visited the followers of Jesus in order to give them strength to spread the word of God.
August	Assumption	Celebrated by the Orthodox and Catholic churches. A feast day to remember the day when Mary the mother of Jesus was received into heaven.

Table 3.6 Dietary requirements

May eat / drink	May not eat / drink	Fasting
All foods	No foods are forbidden. Some Christians may not drink alcohol	Some Christians may fast on some holy days or during Lent. Some Christians may give up certain foods in Lent

Figure 3.2 Plain, Celtic and Ethiopian Crosses; and a Crucifix.

Dress guidelines

There are no formal guidelines laid down on dress. Some Orthodox Christian women may keep their hair covered. Generally wedding rings are worn on the left hand by people who are married. Some individuals wear jewellery that has religious significance, such as a cross or crucifix. Other jewellery may be worn from personal choice.

A Chance to Think 3.2

Christianity

The setting you working in wants to take a group of children aged 4 and 5 to visit local religious buildings, shops, houses, flats, fire station and a hospital as part of a theme on buildings. One of the places the setting plans to visit is a church, where the vicar will show the children round.

What do you think about this idea?

What are some of the things you will need to take into account when organizing this trip?

What sort of things would you do with the children before the trip takes place?

How would you follow up the trip on your return?

Compare your answers with the sample answers in Appendix 3.

Christian Science

History and beliefs

People who call themselves Christian Scientists belong to a church called the Church of Christ, Scientist. It was founded by Mary Baker Eddy, who was born in Bow, New Hampshire in the United States. She married three times and spent her life looking for peace (by reading the Bible), and for healing (for which she looked to homeopathy for the answers). She found the answers to all her questions when in 1866 she believed she was healed from an injury by reading the Bible.

Mary Baker Eddy believed that prayer could heal people. She began to teach people about this and formed the Church of Christ, Scientist, and wrote a book called *Science and Health with the Key to the Scriptures*.

Christian Scientists believe in one God. Bible study is an important part of their beliefs, as is reading and studying the *Christian Science Monitor*. This is a publication started by Mary Baker Eddy. Christian Scientists have their own churches and reading rooms. The main church is based in Boston in the United States.

Major festivals

Christian Scientists are an unorthodox branch of Christianity and so largely follow the festivals in the Christian calendar although many will only celebrate them by worshiping together if they fall on a Sunday (see Christianity). The one festival that is observed by Christian Scientists, especially in the United States is Thanksgiving which is regarded as a religious holiday (see Table 3.7).

Table 3.7 Major Christian Scientist festivals

Month	Festival	Background information
November	Thanks giving	Marked by church services, Bible lessons and personal healing testimonials.

Christian Scientist symbols

Christian scientists use the same symbols as Christians

Dietary requirements

Individuals make their own decisions regarding diet.

Table 3.8 Dietary requirements

May eat	May not eat / drink	Fasting
Everything	No restrictions	Individuals make their own decisions regarding fasting

Dress guidelines

There are no particular guidelines on dress.

Confucianism

History and beliefs

Confucianism is a Chinese moral, ethical, philosophical and political system sometimes seen as a philosophy, and sometimes as a religion. It is based on the teachings and thoughts of the Chinese philosopher Confucius who described himself as a 'transmitter of knowledge'. K'ung Fu Tzu, known in the West as Confucius, was born in China in 551 BC. His father died when he was 3 and he was brought up by his mother. Confucius spent part of his life travelling, and at one point he was a government minister. One of the key moral rules he lived by was, 'What you do not want done to yourself, do not do unto others'. He died in 479 BC, aged 72. He lived at the same time as Buddha. The teachings of Confucius were not accepted during his lifetime and it was not until after his death that his teachings were formalized and written down into the texts known as 'The Analects'. These are a collection of his discussions with his disciples and they contain an overview of his teachings. The major life stages of birth, marriage and death are marked. There are currently six different branches or schools of Confucianism who all have no specific place of worship. Confucius said many things that are quoted by many people today, even though they may not know where they originated from, including; 'Respect yourself and others will respect you' and, 'I hear and I forget. I see and I remember. I do and I understand'.

Major festivals

Table 3.9 Major Confucian festivals

Month	Festival	Background information
September 28	Birthday of Confucius.	Observed as a national holiday in China and Taiwan.

Confucian symbols

No standard universally recognized symbol.

Dietary requirements

Food should only be eaten at mealtimes. People should not over eat. Eat food in Season (see Table 3.10).

Table 3.10 Dietary requirements

May eat	May not eat / drink	Fasting
Everything	No food is restricted but Confucius said food should not be eaten if it is rotten or unclean or if its colour had changed	No particular guidelines

Dress guidelines

No particular dress guidelines.

Hare Krishna

History and beliefs

The Hare Krishna movement was founded by Swami Prabhupada, who was a Hindu. He was born in India and spent most of his life there. He left India in 1965 to tell the world about his message.

Hare Krishnas follow the majority of Hindu teachings. They study Hindu scriptures, and believe they are happy, have clear minds and know who they are. To achieve self-knowledge Hare Krishnas chant a mantra. A mantra is made up of words or sounds that are repeated. The mantra used by the Hare Krishnas contains the names of God, such as Hare, Krishna and Rama. Hare means Lord, Krishna is most important name of God, and Rama is one of the other names used by Hindus to represent God. Like Hindus, Hare Krishnas believe in reincarnations. Hare Krishnas follow the holy book, the Bhagavad Gita, and believe that Krishna is the supreme Lord.

Followers of the Hare Krishna movement live in temples. There are four stages to becoming a follower of the Hare Krishna movement:

1. Pre-initiation stage: a person is taught the movement and may live in the temple.
2. Initiation: when people are ready they are given a Hare name and formally join the movement by taking part in a fire ceremony.
3. Brahmin: this usually takes place about six months after the initiation ceremony and is when members are given their own mantra.
4. Sannyasa: this is the last stage, which only a few men get to. They have to promise to practise celibacy, poverty, to preach and to do good things in their life.

Men are considered to be superior to women by the Hare Krishna movement. There are rules that should be followed in daily life, including not playing games and gambling.

Major festivals

Hare Krishna follows the lunar calendar. This means dates of festivals and celebrations vary each year. There are many holidays and celebrations in Hare Krishna (see Table 3.11).

Table 3.11 Major Hare Krishna festivals

Month	Festival	Background information
Every fortnight	Ekadasi	A day of prayer and meditation. May fast or simplify meals and spend time reading the scriptures and chanting.
August / September	Janmashtami	Celebrates Krishna's appearance day.

Hare Krishna symbols

Most followers of Hare Krishna will have a mark on their head called the Tilaka mark. It is made up of two stripes that signify the lotus feet of Krishna and a leaf in the centre which represent holy basil or Tulasi which traditionally adorns Krishna's feet.

Dietary requirements

Most Hare Krishna's follow a vegetarian diet. Cooking food is seen as a devotion to Krishna and eating is a spiritual experience with food being offered to Krishna. Vegetarian and vegan food and non-vegetarian food should not come into contact with each other. Practitioners should use separate utensils in the setting to serve vegetarian and non-vegetarian food. If this is not possible, utensils should be washed between serving of the different foods (see Table 3.12).

Table 3.12 Dietary requirements

May eat	May not eat	Fasting
Cheese (vegetarian) Yogurt (vegetarian) Milk (soya) Fruit Vegetables	Fish Meat Eggs Tea Coffee Alcohol	May fast on festivals and celebrations

Dress guidelines

Monks and priests (men) live in a temple and wear white or saffron robes and shave their heads except for a topknot called a Sikha. Women residents of the temple wear brightly coloured saris. For members of Hare Krishna there are no dress requirements.

A Chance to Think 3.3

Hare Krishna

A new little boy called Krishna is staring in your setting. Krishna's parents have told you they are Hare Krishnas. You are not sure what this means for Krishna's diet.

How can you gather the information you need to ensure you plan appropriate menus, so that Krishna's parents are happy with the diet provided in the setting.

Compare your answers to the sample answers in Appendix 3.

Hinduism

History and beliefs

Hindus believe in one supreme or high god called Brahman. The word 'Brahman' means 'all that is'. Brahman is the high god, but he is represented in the form of many different gods. Hindus believe that God has many parts. Different images of him are needed to show the different parts that make him up, and these illustrate the different aspects of life.

Brahman is the supreme god who made the world. He is then represented as the god Vishnu. The god Vishnu takes care of the world and has appeared in the world in ten different forms to fight evil. One of the forms he took is that of Rama whose story is written in one of the Hindu holy books. Shiva is another important representation of God. He is the god who destroys old life in order to create new life. Like Vishnu, Shiva has different forms. One of these is Kali, who is a goddess with great power.

Some of the other gods worshipped in the Hindu religion are Shakti, a mother goddess; Ganesh, who is the god of new beginnings and is represented as an elephant-headed god; Lakshmi, who is the goddess of wealth; and Saraswati, the goddess of learning and knowledge.

Hinduism is one of the oldest religions in the world, dating from about 1500 BC. Unlike some religions which have a founder, Hinduism does not. It evolved over the course of many years and originated in India. The word 'Hindu' comes from a Persian word which means 'people who live by the river Indus'. There are three main branches within Hinduism. Each of these worships a different representation of God: Vishnu, Shiva or Shakti. The three branches all believe in the same basic things, but may interpret them in slightly different ways.

One of the things that is important in the Hindu religion is the principle of the three truths or three paths:

1. The law of identification: a person searching for his or her true self in relation to God. This can be found in the words written in the ancient language Sanskrit: *Tat twam asi,* which mean 'God and I are one'.
2. The law of Karma: which says that the way in which people behave will influence the form in which they are reincarnated in their next life.
3. The law of reincarnation: this is central to Hindu beliefs. All people are originally part of God, but they became separated from him. People are then caught up in the wheel of rebirth. They are born, live their lives, die and are reborn again. The aim of life is to become one with God again.

There are three paths to be followed that can lead to being reunited with God and so leaving the wheel of rebirth. The first path is to search for knowledge by reading and studying the Hindu religious books. The second path is to practise yoga and meditation, which will help both mind and body.

The third path is to give devotion to God by worshiping, praying and serving him in daily life.

Knowledge can be gained by studying the Hindu religious scriptures. The most sacred and important of these is called the Rig Veda, which is part of the *Vedas* or holy books. The word *veda* means spiritual wisdom. There are four *Vedas*, which were originally written in the ancient language of Sanskrit. They contain the duties of religious life and are called the Rig Veda, the Sama Veda, The Yajur Veda and the Atharva Veda.

The other holy books in the Hindu religion are the Brahmanas, the Upanishads, the Law Codes, the Puranas and the Great Epics. The two great epics are very important. The Mahabharata contains the story of the struggle of two families and the Bhagavad Gita, or the song of God, which describes the three paths to religious realization. The Ramayana contains the stories that explain the Hindu beliefs. One story is about Rama and Sita, and is celebrated during the festival of Divali.

The structure of Hinduism is made up of castes, or social divisions, that people are born into. Hindus believe that these are essential parts of the body (see Table 3.13). All are equally important and cannot work without the other parts that make up the whole. There are also some people who are regarded as lower caste (Harijans) and have therefore experienced discrimination and need anti-discriminatory practices.

Table 3.13 Hindu Castes

People represented	Hindu name	Part of the body likened to
Priests	Brahmin	Head
Nobles or warriors	Kshatriyas	Arms
Merchants / tradesmen and general populace	Vaishyas	Stomach
Craftsmen / labourers and servants	Shudras	Legs

Many Hindus worship god at home. There may be a shrine, a special place dedicated to god, in the home. There is no special day of the week that is considered to be more holy that the others when Hindus join together to worship. The place where Hindus meet together in public to worship is called a temple or Mandir. The Mandir is usually dedicated to one main god, but will also have images of the other gods in it. These may be in the form of pictures or statues. The statues are treated in the same way as people. They are washed, put to bed and woken up again to worship. A food offering, called a prasada, is given.

Table 3.14 Major Hindu festivals

Month	Festival	Background information
April	Chaitra / Varsha-Pratipada	First day of the new year in the Hindu calendar.
April	Rama Navami	The birthday of Rama (one of the forms of Vishnu). Celebrated by reading the Ramayana. Making candles and putting images of Rama in them, which are covered until midday, which is the time Rama was said to have been born.
June	Ratha Yatra	Celebrated mainly in Puri, but also in other places. Honours Lord Jagannath, the Lord of the Universe.
August	Raksha Bandhan	Celebrates Indra, the king of the heavens, and is a festival of protection. Sisters tie a rakhi (or amulet) around their brothers' wrists to protect them from evil. Brothers give sisters gifts.
August	Janamashtami	Celebrates the birthday of Krishna, one of the forms of Vishnu. Some Hindus may fast until midnight, the time Krishna is said to be born. Many people go to the temple and sing and dance and give out sweets.
August	Ganesh-Chaturthi	Celebrates the festival of Ganesh, the elephant-headed god of new beginnings. This celebration lasts for ten days.
September / October	Navaratri/ Durga Puja / Dusserah	This festival has many different names, but all celebrate the same thing. Rama beating the ten-headed king Ravana, and Durga's killing of the buffalo demon; good triumphing over evil. This festival lasts from four to nine days. Special dances and plays are performed.
October	Divali(Deepavali)	The word Deepavali means 'cluster of lights', and Divali is the festival of lights. It celebrates Rama's return to his kingdom after beating Ravana. It is also associates with other gods, depending on the area in which it is celebrated. The festival lasts from two to five days. Special food is eaten. Lamps (divas) are made and cards are given.
January	Makar Sankranti / Lohri	A time for making good neighbours.
February	Vasanta Panchami / Saraswati Puja	Celebration to honour Saraswati, the goddess of knowledge. Also celebrates the start of spring.
February	Mahashivratri	A festival dedicated to Shiva. Prayers may be said all night and celebrations held during the day.
March	Birthday of Sri Ramakrishna	Celebrates the birth of Sri Ramakrishna, a great Hindu teacher.
March	Holi	A celebration of spring. This festival lasts between two and five days. People may throw coloured water and powder over each other. There may also be processions, dances and bonfires.

There is a sacred flame burning in the Mandir. When people enter the Mandir they will take off their shoes as a sign of reverence.

Hindus also believe that there are special holy places. One of these is the river Ganges, which people visit in the form of a pilgrimage.

Major festivals

The Hindu calendar is based on the lunar calendar, which is dictated by the moon's rotation (see Table 3.14). The Hindu new year begins in April.

Hindu symbols

When Hindus go to the temple they chant the word 'om', a sound representing God in Hinduism. The symbol for 'om' is shown in figure 3.3.

Figure 3.3 The symbol for *om*

Dietary requirements

Some Hindus are vegetarians. In the Hindu religion the cow is considered to be a sacred or holy animal, so is not eaten. Eggs are seen as a source of life and are generally not eaten (see Table 3.15). Workers should ensure that vegetarian and non-vegetarian foods so not come into contact with each other. Separate utensils should be used to serve different foods. If this is not possible, utensils should be washed between serving different foods.

Table 3.15 Dietary requirements

May eat	May not eat	Fasting
Cheese Milk Pork (unless vegetarian) Chicken (unless vegetarian) Lamb (unless vegetarian) Vegetables Fruit	Beef Eggs Alcohol	Some Hindus may fast on holy days such as Janamashtami

Dress guidelines

Women should cover their legs, breasts and upper arms. Some Hindu women wear a sari. This is a long piece of material about 5 to 6 meters long, which is wound round the body in a special way. It is usually worn over a blouse and sometimes the midriff may be left bare. Some Hindu women wear a shalwar-kameez. Shalwar are long loose trousers and a kameez is a long tunic with full or half-length sleeves. Some women cover their hair with a long scarf called a chuni or dupatta. Married women may wear colourful clothes, wedding bangles and other jewellery which is generally not removed. Widows generally remove jewellery and wear white. Young girls may also wear bangles and jewellery which should not be removed. Married women may also have a dot on their forehead, called a bindi or chandlo. Some women who have been to a religious ceremony have a dot called a tilak put on their forehead by the priest.

Men should cover themselves between the waist and knees. Some Hindu men wear a kameez and pyjama or dhoti, which is a type of trouser.

A Chance to Think 3.4

Hinduism

You have been asked to organize some activities for the Hindu festival of Divali, the festival of lights.

What do you need to take into account when doing this?

What sort of activities could you do with the children?

Compare your answers with the sample answers in Appendix 3.

Islam

History and beliefs

Islam is the name of the religion followed by Muslims. The word 'Islam' is an Arabic word meaning 'resignation' or 'surrender'. Muslims believe they have to surrender their lives to God. Muslims believe in one God, called Allah. Allah gave his words to the prophet Mohammed, who, Muslims believe, is the last and greatest prophet of God.

The Prophet Mohammed was born in Mecca in about AD 570. His father died when he was very young and he was brought up by close relatives.

He marries his wife, Khedijah, at the age of 25 and had three daughters. Mohammed had been concerned about religious matters for some time and when he reached the age of 40 spent time in a cave on Mount Hira, outside Mecca, meditating. It was here that he was visited by the Angel Gabriel. The Angel Gabriel told him of God's message, that there was only one God and he was to be God's prophet and tell people about him. Mohammed returned to Mecca to tell people what he had experienced. At that time people worshiped many different gods. Most people did not listen to Mohammed, but a few did and became his companions. These were mainly his family, with his wife Khedijah becoming the first Muslim.

In 622 Mohammed decided to leave Mecca because of persecution and travel to Medina. This was a very important date as it is the date taken for the start of the Muslim calendar. While he was in Medina, Mohammed organized both political and religious activities. In 630 Mohammed returned to Mecca with many followers. He went to a place called the Ka'ba, which was a religious site where people worshiped many different gods. Mohammed tore down the statues of the different gods and dedicated the Ka'ba to Allah. The Ka'ba is now the most holy place in the Islamic religion.

At the age of 63, Mohammed died. No one was named to take over the leadership of this new religion, so one of his companions became his successor. He was known as a caliph. At the time of his death, the words Mohammed had received from God were not written down, as Mohammed could not read or write. He memorized what he had been taught. It was only after his death that the third caliph, Uthman, wrote them down in a book. They were written in classical Arabic in a book called the Qur'an. The first authoritative version was compiled in Medina in about AD 650. The Qur'an provides Muslims with an almost complete guide on life. It contains statements on how to pray and keep the pillars of Islamic faith and practice. It is the body of teaching that instructs governments how to treat their subjects and other states. It also contains social teachings that are the basis of law and personal contact in Muslim societies. This is the most holy book in Islam and had 114 chapters.

The second most important book contains writings about the life and times of Mohammed. This is called the Hadith. It contains the example set by Mohammed, which all Muslims should try and follow. The words of The Qur'an and the Hadith put together form the Sunna, which is a guide for Muslims on how they should live their lives and conduct themselves. Eventually the principles of interpretation evolved which hold true in modern times. The sharia or 'highway' of divine commands and guidance is clear, and no aspect of life falls outside it for there are matters that the Qur'an and Hadith cold not deal with, as they did not exist at the time.

After Mohammed's death Islam spread throughout the Middle East. It developed in different ways by interpreting things with differing traditions. There are now two main groups of Muslims in the world. The largest group are the Sunni Muslims, comprising orthodox Arabs and Turks. They follow the Sunna laid down by the prophet Mohammed. The second group comprises the Shi'ite Muslims who have imams or teachers to interpret the word of the prophet Mohammed for them. The Shi'ites are mainly restricted to Iran.

Central to all Muslim beliefs are the Five Pillars of Islam. These are the five tenets that Muslims should hold to:

1. Belief in one god. This is called shahadah, and says 'There is no God but Allah, Mohammed is the prophet of Allah'.
2. Prayer. This is called salah. Prayer is an important part of the Islamic religion. Muslims should pray five times a day and the prayers involve a set of movements. The first prayer takes place at daybreak, followed by further prayers at noon, mid-afternoon, sunset and night. There are special rules laid down about how to pray. Before praying people should wash their hands, arms, face, legs and feet. When they pray they use a special prayer mat and they should face Mecca. People can pray anywhere as long as they face Mecca.
3. Fasting. This is called sawm. Every year, during the month of Ramadan, Muslims fast. This means that between the hours of sunrise and sunset they do not eat, drink, smoke or have sex. Ramadan is a time of self-control and a chance to think and cleanse the body. It lasts for a complete lunar month. Young children and people who are ill or pregnant do not have to fast.
4. Compulsory charity. This is called zakat. Every year Muslims have to give part of their income to charity, usually around 2.5 per cent. The money can be given to the poor, or be used to build hospitals or schools, for example.
5. Pilgrimage. This is called hajj. During their life Muslims should make a pilgrimage to Mecca, the holy city of Islam, if they are able to. During this time they will visit the Ka'ba. Men wear special clothes and women dress modestly.

Islam also contains the Articles of Faith. These are the six things that Muslims believe in:

(1) A belief in one God called Allah. Muslims have 99 names for God and they recite them all. Two of these names are God the Great and God the Merciful.
(2) The Qur'an contains the words of God. The book was written by God and Mohammed was his messenger.

(3) A belief in angels. Angels are God's messengers and it was the Angel Gabriel who spoke to Mohammed to give him the word of God. Angels are made of light. There are also Jinn, who can be good or bad angels.

(4) God sent prophets into the world to tell people about him. There have been many prophets, including Moses, Abraham and Jesus. Muslims believe that Mohammed was the last and greatest prophet. When they say or write his name they also add the words 'peace be upon him'.

(5) God has set a course for people's lives and controls them. People do still have free will that they can exercise, but only within in the course of life that God has set for them.

(6) A Belief in the Day of Judgment and Afterlife when the souls of every person will be judged and a decision made on where they will go – to heaven or hell.

We have already seen that it is possible for Muslims to pray anywhere. There is also a holy building called a mosque where Muslims meet together to pray and worship God publicly. Men and women will pray in separate areas of the mosque. All who enter the mosque must take off their shoes and wash before they pray. There are no statues or pictures of people or artefacts in the mosque as this is forbidden by the Qur'an. The building will be decorated with patterns and Arabic writing from the Qur'an. Muslims consider Friday to be a special holy day. Families may go to the mosque, where a sermon will be preached.

Major festivals

Islam has only two officially recognized major festivals. These are Eid-ul-Fitr and Eid-ul-Adha. However, other events are celebrated (see Table 3.16). The Muslim calendar is based on the lunar calendar. This means that festivals will be celebrated on different days each year. The Islamic year has 12 months, but the months all have 29 or 31 days. This means that they will correspond with different Western months in different years. The Muslim calendar moves forward throughout the secular year. One year Ramadan may be in the winter, another year it may be in the summer. The Islamic year starts with the new year celebrations at the beginning of the 12 months.

Muslim symbols

The moon and the stars are important symbols in Islam. Muslims believe that Islam guides people through life just as the stars and the moon guide people over the desert. The crescent moon symbol is used by the Red Crescent, the Islamic equivalent of the Red Cross.

Table 3.16 Major Muslim festivals

Month	Festival	Background information
Month 1 Muharram	Muharram/Al Hajra	New Year's Day. The life of Mohammed is remembered and greetings exchanged.
Month 3 Rabi'al-Awwal	Milad-an-Nabi	This is remembered by Shi'ite Muslims as the day the grandson of Mohammed died. They may fast on this day. Sunnni Muslims may fast as well.
Month 7 Rajab	Lailat-ul-Isra	The night of ascension. Celebrates the journey Mohammed made to Jerusalem when he spent a night in heaven. The Dome of the Rock is now built on the place where Mohammed ascended to heaven. This is considered a very holy site after Mecca and medina.
Month 8 Sha'abaan	Lailat-ul-Bara'ah	The night of forgiveness. Muslims see this as a preparation for Ramadan and the fast. They may stay up all night to pray. Special food and sweets are prepared and given out.
Month 9 Ramadan	Ramadan Laitat-ul-Qadr	The month of fasting from sunrise to sunset. The fast will be broken every evening with a meal. The night of power celebrated towards the end of Ramadan. Muslims may pray all night and read the Qur'an.
Month 10 Shawwal	Eid -ul- Fitr	A festival to mark the end of the fast. Families may go to the mosque. Special meals may be eaten and presents given.
Month 12 Dhul-Hijjah	The Hajj Eid –ul-Adha	The pilgrimage to Mecca. Celebrates the end of the Hajj pilgrimage. A two to four day celebration. Muslims may sacrifice animals, with one-third of the sacrifice being given to the poor. This is the most important festival of the year.

Figure 3.4 The crescent moon and star

Dietary requirements

There are very strict dietary laws in Islam that are laid down in the Qur'an. Muslims do not eat any products from pigs, as this animal is considered unclean. Any other animals that are eaten must be slaughtered according to Islamic law (see Table 3.17). Correctly slaughtered meat is said to be halal. Workers should ensure that prohibited food is not in contact with non-prohibited food. Separate utensils should be used to serve different foods. If this is not possible, utensils should be washed between serving of the different foods.

Table 3.17 Dietary requirements

May eat	May not eat	Fasting
Chicken (halal) Lamb (halal) Beef (halal) Fish (halal) Shellfish (halal) Animal fat (halal) Fruit Vegetables	Pork or any products from a pig. Yogurt or any other products with rennet in it. Alcohol	Muslims fast during the month of Ramadan

Dress guidelines

Women should keep their bodies covered from head to foot. Any clothes worn should conceal the shape of their body. Some Muslim women wear a shalwar kameez, some a sari, others, clothing depending on their cultural background. Muslim women should cover their hair. Married women may wear wedding bangles which are generally not removed. Other jewellery may be worn that has religious significance or from personal choice. Young girls may also wear bangles and jewellery.

Men should be covered from waist to knees. Some Muslim men wear shalwar kameez and others may wear a gallibaya, again depending on cultural background.

A Chance to Think 3.5

Islam

Your setting is short-staffed and is employing workers from an agency to cover for the week. The worker the agency sends is Fatma, who is Muslim. Fatma prays five times and day, at daybreak, noon, mid-afternoon, sunset and night.

How do you think this will affect the setting?

How will the setting ensure that Fatma is able to pray at the times she is required to?

Compare your answers to the sample answers in Appendix 3.

Jainism

History and beliefs

Jainism is an ancient religion from India. People who follow this religion are known as Jains. Jains believe in the cyclical nature of the universe and that every soul is potentially divine and that humans, plants and animals all have souls. There have been many teachers, known as tirthankara, who, at different times, 'reactivate' the Jain religion.

Mahavira, is the 24th tirthankara and is the person who gave Jainism its current form. Mahavira lived at the same time as Buddha, born in 599 BC in India. He was born a prince in a palace, and his given name was Vardhamana, later to be known as Mahavira. When he was 30 he left his life in the palace and became a wandering ascetic. This means he gave up everything, including his home and possessions, and travelled around. After 12 years of fasting and meditating he achieved enlightenment. He shared his teachings with 12 disciples and built up a following and structured his teachings into the Jain scriptures. The texts containing his teachings are called the 'Agamas', and the scriptures are called the 'Svetambara Jainism'. These were written by his disciples following his death. Mahavira died in 527 BC. In the fourth century Jainism split into two major groups with different interpretations and ways of practicing. The Digambaras (sky clad) believe that possessions hinder the way to liberation, and the Shvetambaras (white clad) believe that detachment is in the mind. The two groups disagree on many issues including the status of women and the scriptures. Both believe in reincarnation and use meditation and yoga as part of their daily life. Jainism does not believe in a creator God and has no priests; it is guided by monks and nuns. Monks and nuns follow a code of conduct and accept the five 'Great Vows', or the five Anuvratas. These are: Non-violence, Truthfulness, Non-stealing, Chastity and Non-possession. Most of the individuals who follow Jainism today are lay people who strive to follow the rules of Jainism in the best way they can. These include The Three Jewels:

1. Right faith;
2. Right knowledge;
3. Right conduct.

Jains worship in temples, these are often similar to Hindu temples. Temples contain images of tirthankara. A mantra is said as part of the worship in the morning and on important occasions. Worship also happens in the home and many Jain will have a shrine containing images in their home.

Major festivals

Jainism follows the Indian calendar. When transferred to the Gregorian calendar the festivals may take place in different months in different years. Many of festivals mark significant occasions in the life of Mahavira (see Table 3.18).

Table 3.18 Major Jain festivals

Month	Festival	Background information
March / April	Mahavira Jayanti	Celebrates the day of Mahavira's birth.
August / September	Daslankshana	The great festival of ten virtues.
August / September	Paryushana	Time of reflection and repentance. 8 or 10 days of fasting.
October / November	Divali	Divali is one of the most important festivals celebrating the Nirvana of Mahavira.
October / November	New Year	The day after Divali
Follows Divali	Kartak Purnima	A time of pilgrimage.

Jain symbols

There are many symbols in Jainism. The Jain emblem is made up of various symbols. The outline of the symbol is the universe inside is a Swastika and Jain Hand. There is a mantra written at the bottom PARSPAROGRAHO JIVANAM which means 'Live and Let Live'. The Swastika contains 4 dots on it and 3 dots above it. These 3 dots represent the three jewels of Jainism, (see above for an explanation of these). Above the 3 dots are a crescent moon and the dot representing the abode of the liberated souls. The Jain hand means 'Do not be afraid'. It has a wheel inside it that represents reincarnation with the word 'Ahimsa' that means 'non-violence'. There is also the Jain flag which has five different colours and a swastika in the centre. The colours of red, yellow, white, green and dark blue (or black) each represents are particular part of the Jain faith. There are also many other important symbols not mentioned here.

Dietary requirements

Jains are strict vegetarians. They believe in non-violence and causing no harm to living things and so do not kill animals (see Table 3.19).

Table 3.19 Dietary requirements

May eat	May not eat / drink	Fasting
Fruit Vegetables Grains, e.g. wheat, rice, lentils or pulses and beans Dairy produce	Meat Fish Alcohol Certain vegetables that grow underground and produce numerous sprouts, like potatoes, or fruits with many seeds, such as figs. Eggs Honey	During festivals and holy days.

Dress guidelines

There are dress guidelines for monks and nuns who wear un-stitched or minimally stitched white clothes. Some Jain monks belonging to the Digambaras (sky clad) group do not wear clothes. For lay people when visiting a temple clothing should be modest, and shoes must be removed

Jehovah's Witnesses

History and beliefs

Jehovah's Witnesses are a worldwide religious group who base their beliefs solely on the Bible. They believe in one God called Jehovah. Christ is God's son who died on a stake, not a cross. The origins of Jehovah's Witnesses can be traced to 1870, when a Bible study group was started by Charles Taze Russell, from Pittsburgh in the United States. The name of the group was changed to the Jehovah's Witnesses in 1931. Jehovah's Witnesses believe in the Bible as the word of God, and consider its books to be inspired and historically accurate. The New World translation is a translation of the scriptures from Hebrew, Aramaic and Greek into modern-day English.

The place where Jehovah's Witnesses meet to worship is called the Kingdom Hall. There are two formal parts to worship. The first is Baptism, which is an outward symbol by which individuals are welcomed into the faith and dedicate their lives to God's will. The second, Memorial, is a symbol of Christ's death, and is known as 'The Lord's Supper' or 'The Lord's Evening Meal'. Jehovah's Witnesses meet together at five weekly meetings to study the Bible and other writings. They do not attend any kind of worship or religious education that is not held by the Jehovah's Witnesses themselves.

Jehovah's Witness believe they are not allowed to receive blood into their body in any form as it violates God's laws. This means that they are not allowed to have blood transfusions, although alternatives to transfusions (e.g. synthetic blood substitutes) are permitted.

Major festivals

Jehovah's Witnesses do not celebrate any special festivals, as they do not appear to them to have any religious significance, although they respect the right of others to celebrate.

Jehovah's Witnesses symbols

Jehovah's Witnesses do not use the cross as a symbol as they believe it is a symbol of torture as Jesus died on a stake. The Mother Church of Jehovah's Witnesses, The Church of Christ Scientist uses a seal called the Cross and Crown. It is the registered trademark of the church and those wishing to use it must apply for permission to do so.

Dietary requirements

Jehovah's Witnesses try to following a healthy diet and make healthy choices in their food (see Table 3.20).

Table 3.20 Dietary requirements

May eat	May not eat	Fasting
All foods	Avoid eating the flesh of animals that have not been properly bled.	No guidelines

Dress guidelines

There are no particular dress guidelines followed by Jehovah's Witnesses other than dressing modestly.

Judaism

History and beliefs

Judaism is the oldest continuing faith in the world. Its most fundamental focus is the belief in one God. The Torah, one of the holy books of Judaism, is the revelation of God's will, and contains every aspect of life. One of the most important things to strive for is the concept of loving one's neighbour and seeking justice and compassion.

Abraham is considered to be the first Jew. He was born and brought up in Chaldees (Iraq), in a society that worshiped idols. Abraham became aware that this was not right, left his birthplace and eventually moved to a land that later became known as Israel. Abraham and his descendants were the first people to worship one God.

Many centuries later, Moses, the great prophet, led the children of Israel out of Egypt, where they had been slaves for many generations. He led them for 40 years through the desert until they arrived in the land of Israel. During this time Moses received the Ten Commandments from God on Mount Sinai. This code of laws later formed the basis of both Christianity and Islam:

1. You shall have one God.
2. You shall not make false idols.
3. You shall not take the name of the Lord in vain.
4. You shall keep the Sabbath day holy.
5. Honour your father and mother.
6. You shall not murder.
7. You shall not commit adultery.
8. You shall not steal.
9. You shall not give false testament.
10. You shall not covet your neighbour's house.

The Jewish Bible (called by Christians 'the Old Testament') is divided into three main sections. The first is called the 'Torah' and consists of the first five books of the Bible. It contains the 10 commandments and the 613 laws given by God dealing with every aspect of daily life; ethical, spiritual and practical. The Torah covers a time span from the creation of the world until the death of Moses.

The second part of the Jewish Bible is called the 'Nevi'im' (prophets), and consists of books of the greater prophets, Isaiah, Jeremiah and Ezekiel, as well as 12 lesser prophets, and the books of Joshua, Judges, Samuel and Kings. Nevi'im continues with the history of the Jews up until the Babylonian exile. Throughout the writings of the prophets is the fundamental belief that the Messiah will come heralding a time of peace and tranquillity. The Jews do not believe that the Messiah has yet come, believing that the world needs first to be a worthwhile place. The third part of the Jewish Bible is called Ketuvim (writings).

There are different ways of observing Judaism. As in other faiths, people choose their own level of practice, which can extend from the very observant to the liberal or progressive. Some Jews move from one strand to another.

Ultra-orthodox Jews believe that God personally wrote the Ten Commandments and the 613 commandments that followed. They believe that it is not up to any human to change any of these divine laws. The ultra-orthodox tend to live among themselves, have their own synagogues (place of worship) and schools and only employ each other. Many adopt a style of dress that has not changed for centuries and generally exclude the modern world from their midst. Ordination of women rabbis (teachers / preachers) is not allowed.

Traditional orthodox Jews regard themselves as representing mainstream Judaism. They also believe that the laws were made by God, but at the same time they adopt a way of life that allows them to live as committed Jews in a changing modern world. In this group, too, the ordination of women is not allowed.

The Reform or Progressive movement began in the nineteenth century in an attempt to recreate Judaism to allow its followers to conform more easily with life outside Judaism. Reform Jews believe that the Torah was inspired by God but written by human hand. Therefore the law is open to interpretation to meet the changing needs of the community. The Reform belief is that it is more important to observe the external parts of Judaism, like Shabbat, pursuit of justice and compassion, as against the laws that, for instance, disbar women from participating in certain rituals. The ordination of women is therefore accepted.

The Liberal movement began as a splinter group of the Reform movement and believes that sincerity in behaviour is more important than ritual. Women are ordained as rabbis.

The Conservative movement began at the beginning of the twentieth century and is seen as being positioned between Orthodox and Reform Judaism, believing that the laws were inspired rather than written by God.

All the different sections within Judaism have rabbis. The rabbi is very learned in Jewish law and his or her role is as spiritual leader and teacher in the community. Rabbis do not act as an intermediary between the people and God, and they do not necessarily lead the congregation in prayer.

The word 'synagogue' is Greek meaning 'house of assembly'. This is the place Jews meet to worship. It is also a focus for social events for people of all ages. In an orthodox synagogue men and women sit separately, with all the women in a gallery, or if this is not possible or on the same level behind a partition. Only men conduct services. In Reform synagogues men and women can sit together and, religiously speaking, women can do anything men can do. Keeping the head covered is a sign of respect. Men always wear some form of headgear, in the synagogue, traditionally a small skullcap called in Hebrew a kipah. In an Orthodox synagogue married women also wear a hat. Men in all synagogues wear a prayer shawl and in Reform synagogues women are encouraged to do the same. The most important part of the synagogue is the cupboard or alcove fronted by a decorative curtain and ornate doors.

It contains the Torah scrolls and is usually on the eastern wall facing Jerusalem, the city holy to the Jews. The scrolls are sacred and must not be handled casually. A pointer is used to prevent people touching them while reading them.

Saturday is the Jewish Sabbath (Shabbat). Although it comes every week it is considered to be the Day of Atonement, the holiest day of the year. Shabbat begins just before sunset on Friday and finishes just before nightfall on Saturday, with a short ceremony in the home called havdallah (separation). During Shabbat it is forbidden for Jews to engage in activities that are considered to be work or creating; using electrical appliances or driving a car are considered to be work. The Shabbat laws are kept strictly by the Orthodox but not so rigidly by Progressive Jews. In all cases the Shabbat laws are set aside if there is a question of saving life.

Certain important events are marked in a person's life. For boys, the first of these is his Brit Milah, usually taking place eight days after birth, when he is circumcised. Circumcision takes place at home and is carried out by a qualified person, in the presence of family and friends. There is no equivalent ceremony for girls, but in Orthodox synagogues prayers are said and in Progressive synagogues a 'baby-naming' ceremony takes place.

At the age of 13 a boy becomes Bar Mitzvah. He marks the occasion by reading for the first time in public, and in Hebrew, the weekly portion from the Torah scroll, usually on Shabbat. He can now form part of the quorum of ten men needed to start a service and is expected to perform certain religious duties and be aware of his religious responsibilities. In Orthodox synagogues there is now a ceremony called a Bat Chayil, which marks a girl's 12th birthday. It is not a religious ceremony and usually takes place on a Sunday. Progressive synagogues hold a service for girls in the same form as for boys

Marriage takes place under a wedding canopy called a Cupah. Divorce has always been permitted but is regarded very seriously. The bill of divorce is called a 'Get'.

A person's body is regarded as belonging to God and must be treated with respect. When someone dies the body is not left alone, a vigil is maintained until the burial. After the funeral, parents, spouses, siblings and children sit Shivah for seven days. They sit on stools in their homes and are visited by friends. Prayers are said every day.

Major festivals

The Jewish calendar starts counting from the creation of the world, and the year 2010 is the Jewish year 5770. The Jewish calendar is based on the lunar cycle. A year is usually 354 days. In a 19-year cycle an extra month is inserted seven times, each insertion forming a leap year. Because the solar and lunar years are different, no fixed dates can be given in the Gregorian calendar for Jewish festivals, although the dates in the Jewish calendar are fixed. Festivals are divided into three types: days of Awe, harvest festivals and minor festivals that are historical (see Table 3.21).

Table 3.21 Major Jewish festivals

Month	Festival	Background information
Month 1 Tishri (September / October)	Rosh Hashana	New year's day and the start of the Days of Repentance. The most serious time of the year. In the synagogue a ram's horn is blown to remind people of their sins and to think about how to get it right in the new year.
	Yom Kippur	This is the last of the ten days of repentance. It is the most solemn day in the Jewish calendar. People fast on this day and go to the synagogue to pray.
	Sukkot	This is a harvest festival. It commemorates the journey of the Jews from Egypt to Israel. Huts called sukkots are built and decorated with leaves, fruit and pictures. This is an eight day festival. People may use the huts for eating in during this time.
	Simkhat Torah	Comes straight after Sukkot. It celebrates the fact that the Torah has finished being read and it is time to begin reading it all over again. The Torah will be danced around in the synagogue.
Month 3 Kislev (November/ December)	Hannukah	Celebrates the re-dedication of the second temple in Jerusalem. An eight day festival. Every evening in the home one more candle is lit in the candelabrum known as a *chanukiah* until on the eighth day all the candles will be lit.
Month 5 Shevat (January /February)	Tu B'Shavat	The new year for trees. The end of the winter season. Jewish communities all over the world plant trees.
Month 6 Adar (February/March)	Purim	Celebrates the fact that Queen Esther saved the Jews form Haman, who tried to destroy them. Children wear fancy dress and go to the synagogue, where the book of Esther is read from the Bible. It is a happy carnival time.
Month 7 Nisan (March/April)	Pesach (Passover)	Pesach lasts for eight days. It commemorates the Jews fleeing slavery in Egypt and returning to the Promised Land. When they left Egypt there was no time to wait for the bread to rise and at Pesach no food containing yeast will be in the house. *Matzah* is eaten instead of bread. Pesach begins with a celebration meal called *seder*. The word *seder* means 'order'. A happy festival in which all are encouraged to participate.
Month 9 Sivan (May/June)	Shavuot	Also known as the Festival of Weeks as it comes seven weeks after the start of Pesach. Celebrates the Jews receiving the Torah at Mount Sinai. The synagogue is decorated with flowers and the book of Ruth is read. Lasts for two days and is the harvest festival of olives, dates, grapes and figs. Dairy foods are eaten.

Jewish symbols

The origin of the six-pointed star is clouded, and probably has no connections with King David. Although it has been found in the Ancient Synagogue of Capernaum, it was only officially adopted about 100 years ago. Today it is the central figure in the flag of Israel, and is often worn by men and women as a necklace. The seven-branched candlestick, or *menorah,* has a longer association as an official Jewish symbol than the Star of David. The seven-branched candlestick was used in front of the altar in the temple and was never to be put out. Today it is the official symbol of the state of Israel.

Figure 3.5 Star of David

Dietary requirements

There are very strict dietary laws in Judaism. The law of *kashrut* means that meat and dairy products must be stored separately and not be eaten together in the same meal. Some families have two sets of utensils for preparing meat and dairy products respectively. Families who do not use two sets of utensils will wash utensils thoroughly between using them for meat and dairy products. Workers should ensure they use separate utensils. If this is not possible, utensils should be washed between serving of the different foods. All animals eaten must be slaughtered according to Jewish laws. Food that complies with Jewish law is called *kosher,* and forbidden food is called *trayf.* All fruit and vegetables are kosher but not all animals are. In order for an animal to be kosher, it must have cloven hooves and chew the cud. Before meat is cooked it must be soaked and salted for one and a half hours to remove as much of the blood as possible (see Table 3.22).

Table 3.22 Dietary requirements

May eat	May not eat	Fasting
Eggs (with no blood spots) Milk Yogurt Cheese (not made with rennet) Chicken (kosher) Lamb (kosher) Beef (kosher) Fish (with scales, fins and backbone) Animal fats (kosher) Fruit Vegetables	Pork or pig products Shellfish Rabbit Horse	Jew fast during Yom Kippur (see festivals)

Dress guidelines

The different groups in Judaism have different guidelines on dress. Women should dress modestly. Some Jewish women cover their hair. This may be done by wearing a wig, hat or headscarf. Some jewellery worn has religious significance; other jewellery may be worn from personal choice.

Men may cover their head with a hat or they may wear a kippah (in Hebrew and yarmulke in Yiddish). This is a small skullcap worn at all times by some men and by all men in the synagogue.

A Chance to Think 3.6

Judaism

Elizabeth, a Jewish parent in your setting, has offered to come in and tell some stories to the children about Hanukah.

How would you react to this?

What value could this have to Elizabeth, the children and the staff in your setting?

Compare your answers with the sample answers in Appendix 3.

Mormons – the Church of Jesus Christ of the Latter Day Saints

History and beliefs

Mormons belong to the Church of Jesus Christ of the Latter Day Saints, which was founded by Joseph Smith, who was born in the United States in 1805. At the age of 14, Smith saw a vision of God, who told him not to join any of the churches but to be prepared for important work. When he was 18 he had another vision. This time it was of an angel called Moroni. The angel told him how to find a book written on plates of gold in a language that was not English, which told the story of the history of the Americans. When he was 22, Smith translated the book he had found. The book was called *The Book of Mormon* and was published in 1830, the year that the Church of Jesus Christ of the Latter Day saints was founded.

Joseph Smith and the church moved around America, often attracting trouble because of the views they held. Smith was imprisoned and in 1844 at the age of 38 he was killed in prison. The Mormons decided to move to Utah, where they built Salt Lake City, which is still the centre of the Mormon faith. Mormons classify themselves as Christians who believe in Jesus Christ as a prophet of God. They also believe that God sent other prophets and that Joseph Smith was a prophet of God who revealed the word of God as written in the book of Mormon. The Mormons have 13 'Articles of Faith' which they follow. The first of these is: ' We believe in God, the Eternal Father, and in His Son, Jesus Christ, and in the Holy Ghost'. Mormons also believe in Baptism, a ceremony to mark a person's entry into the Church. This takes place from the age of 8 when Mormons believe that a person reaches the age of accountability.

Mormons worship in a chapel on a Sunday which is a holy day. The chapel does not have any pictures or statues in it. The Church of Jesus Christ of the Latter Day Saints does not have priests but people who have priestly authority. These are always men. As well as chapels there is also The Mormon temple which is a building that is regarded by Mormons as the house of the Lord and is only used for the Church's holy ceremonies, education and the making of covenants, for example, Baptism. Non-Mormons are not allowed to go into a temple. Before Mormons enter the temple they dress in modest white clothing and prepare themselves both physically and spiritually.

All Mormons are encouraged to give one-tenth of their income to the Church. This is known as Tithing. Young men and women are encouraged to serve as missionaries from the age of 19. Men serve for 2 years and women for 18 months.

Major festivals

The Church of Jesus Christ of the Latter Day Saints celebrate two religious festivals from the Christian calendar, Easter and Christmas (see Table 3.23). The date of Easter changes every year and is dependent on the first fasting day of Lent. This falls on the Friday of the first full moon of the spring equinox. Christmas always falls on the same day the 25th December.

Mormons also celebrate Pioneer Day, the day that the first pioneers arrived in Salt Lake City.

Table 3.23 Major Mormon festivals

Month	Festival	Background information
March or April	Easter	Easter begins on Easter Eve Sunday. The day when Christ rose from the dead. The date of Easter is set by the date of the start of Lent.
July	Pioneer Day	Celebrated on the 24 July. Also known as Covered Wagon Days and Days of 1847. Celebrates the arrival in Salt Lake Valley in 1847, of the first pioneers of the Church of the Jesus Christ of the Latter Day Saints. In Salt Lake City in Utah it is both a state and church holiday and it is celebrated with fireworks, dances and food. Outside the USA it is celebrated by Mormons informally by meeting together.
December	Christmas	Mormons celebrate the birth of Jesus Christ on the 25th December.

Mormon symbols

Mormons use the Christian symbol of the cross.

Dietary requirements

Mormon dietary requirements are laid down in a document called the *Word of Wisdom* which came from the Doctrine and Covenants of the Church of Jesus Christ of the Latter Day Saints as given to Joseph Smith in 1833 (see Table 3.24). Many Mormons will not eat or drink anything that contains caffeine in it, as this is a stimulant. This means workers need to check lists of ingredients in food products to ensure they do not contain caffeine.

Table 3.24 Dietary requirements

May eat	May not eat / drink	Fasting
Fruit Vegetables Herbs Meat – sparingly Grain Anything that does not contain caffeine	Wine or Strong Drink (alcohol) Tobacco Hot drinks (tea and coffee) Some may avoided caffeine Drugs of abuse	Fast once a month on the first Sunday of the month. This is defined as going without two consecutive meals

Dress guidelines

Mormons are advised to dress modestly. Special clothes are worn in the temple.

Quakers – the Religious Society of Friends

History and beliefs

Quakers have their roots in Christianity although not all Quakers view themselves as Christians. Quakers were founded by George Fox, who was born in England in 1624. He believed that everyone should try to encounter God directly. Quakers believe in one God and value all people equally. They try and integrate religion into their day to day lives and try to make the world a better place. Quakers are particularly concerned with human rights, social justice and value diversity. Quakers meet together in a meeting room but do not have priests, ceremonies or rituals. At meetings for worship people sit for an hour in silence. The Quaker movement is an avowedly Pacifist organization.

Major festivals

Quakers do not celebrate any of the Christian festivals such as Easter or Christmas.

Quaker symbols

There is no one unifying symbol.

Dietary requirements

There are no specific dietary requirements. Some Quakers may avoid alcohol (see Table 3.25).

Table 3.25 Dietary requirements

May eat	May not eat / drink	Fasting
Everything	Alcohol	No guidelines

Dress guidelines

No specific guidelines but dress modestly.

Rastafarianism

History and beliefs

Rastafarianism is a fairly new religion. As well as being a religion it is also a way of life. It began in Jamaica in the 1930s and has links with both Christianity and Judaism. Marcus Garvey, who died in 1937, is the prophet of Rastafari. He was aware that the effects of slavery were still being suffered by black people. He is said to have prophesied 'Look towards Africa where you will see a black king crowned, then you will see redemption'.

In 1930 in Ethiopia, a prince called Ras Tafari was crowned the emperor of Ethiopia. 'Ras' means 'prince' and 'Tafari' means 'to be feared'. Ras Tafari took the name Haile Selassie when he became emperor. Rastafarianism has taken its name from the original name of Ras Tafari. Haile Sellassie traced his descent from King Solomon and the Queen of Sheba . At his coronation he was given the titles King of Kings, Lord of Lords, Conquering Lion of the Tribe of Judah. Rastafarians believe that Haile Sellasie was the king that Marcus Garvey was talking about. They believe this is backed up by a passage in the bible (Revelation 19.16), which says 'And on his robe and on his thigh was written the name: King of kings, and Lord of lords'. Rastafarians believe that Haile Salassie was the living God, whom they called Jah. They believe that God became man as Haile Sellasie, not as Jesus. They see Jesus as one of God's prophets, who came to live out the word of God, not as his son. Haile Sellasie visited Jamaica in 1966, where he received a great welcome. Legend has it that he said to his followers 'Warriors, priests, dreadlocks, I am he!' Haile Sellasie was thought to have dreadlocks when he was young.

Rastafarians base their beliefs on the Bible, both the Old and the New Testaments. They do not have a particular place of worship. Some Rastafarians go to the Ethiopian Orthodox church to worship. Others may meet weekly in a hall or in each other's homes to discuss the Bible. Rastafarians also meet together on special occasions. Such gathering is called a *nyahbinghi* or *binghi*. Music, drumming, chanting and singing play an important part in these gatherings.

Reggae music is a popularized form of *nyahbinghi* drumming and chanting. A *binghi* may last between three and seven days. Marijuana is smoked at these gatherings (and on a daily basis), as Rastafarians believe it is a natural herb given by God to be used to communicate with him. Rastafarians also use their own version of English. They believe that God is within them. God spoke of himself as 'I' and so the language is based on the letter 'I'. This is also to symbolize oneness with God. Vital food is 'Ital', holy is 'Ily', I an I means 'you' and me' or 'we'.

Major festivals

Rastafarians follow the Ethiopian calendar. This is made up of 13 months, 12 of 30 days and the 13th of 5 days or 6 in a leap year (see Table 3.26). The years follow a four-year cycle. Each year takes the name of an Apostle: Matthew, Mark, Luke or John. The year starts in September.

Table 3.26 Major Rastafarian festivals

Month	Festival	Background information
September	Ethiopian New Year's Day	This takes place on 11 September. Each year is named after an apostle. It may be celebrated with praying, singing, dancing and drumming.
November	Anniversary of the coronation of Haile Sellasie as emperor (1930)	This takes place on the 2 November. It is one of the holiest days in the Rastafarian year. It may be celebrated with praying, singing, dancing and drumming.
January	Ethiopian Christmas	This is celebrated on the 7 January. It does not celebrate the birth of Jesus but recognizes his life and work. A feast may be held during which prophecy and readings take place.
April	Groundation day	Takes place on the 21 April. Marks the day Haile Selassie visited Jamaica in 1966. It may be celebrated with music, chanting and prayer.
July	Birthday of Haile Selassie (1892)	This is celebrated on the 23 July. It is one of the holiest days of the Rastafarian year. Usually celebrated with *nyahbinghi* drumming, hymns and prayers.
August	Birthday of Marcus Garvey (1887)	Celebrated on 17 August. Rastafarians remember the life and work of Marcus Garvey.

Rastafarian symbols

Rastafarians may wear Ethiopian Orthodox crosses as a symbol of their Christian beliefs, and in acknowledgment of Ethiopia as their spiritual home. The lion is also an important symbol. It is considered to be a royal animal. It is mentioned in the title 'Conquering Lion of Judah', given to Haile Selassie at his coronation. Haile Selassie kept lions in his palace in Ethiopia. Rastafarians believe that Haile Selassie symbolized the bringing together of the power of animals, humans and all life on the last days.

Figure 3.6 Lion and Ethiopian cross

Dietary requirements

Some Rastafarians are vegetarians. Most Rastafarians follow an Ital, a natural and clean diet (see Table 3.27). Workers should ensure that separate utensils are used to serve food that is forbidden and food that may be eaten.

Table 3.27 Dietary requirements

May eat	May not eat	Fasting
Eggs Milk Yogurt Fruit Nuts Herbs Vegetables Chicken (unless vegetarian) Lamb (unless vegetarian) Fish (but not more than 12 inches long or unless vegetarian)	Pork or pig products Alcohol Shellfish	There are generally no periods of fasting

Dress guidelines

Rastafarian men, women and children may wear clothes in red, yellow and green. These are the colours in the Ethiopian flag. Some Rastafarians do not cut their hair. It is left to grow and coiled into dreadlocks to symbolize the lion's mane, and covered with hats or scarves. This is based on the book in the Bible called Leviticus: 'They (priests) shall not make bald patches on their heads as a sign of mourning, nor cut the edges of their beards' (Leviticus 21.5). Some jewellery is worn for religious significance, such as an Ethiopian cross; other jewellery may be worn from personal choice.

A Chance to Think 3.7

Rastafarianism

Tafari, a Rastafarian boy in your setting, keeps his locks covered with a hat. You hear a new member of staff telling him to take off his hat indoors.

What would you do in this situation?

Compare your answers to the sample answers in Appendix 3.

Scientology

History and beliefs

The Church of Scientology was founded by Lafayette Ron Hubbard who was born in Nebraska in the United States in 1911. L. Ron Hubbard served in the US navy during the Second World War and was certified dead on two occasions. He said he got his health back using the principles of 'dianetics'. He wrote a book about it in 1950, called *Dianetics – The Science of Mental Health*. This was the beginning of Scientology. In 1967 there was some debate in the United States as to whether Scientology could be classed as a religion, but it is now seen as one. The church claims that it can improve people's lives and help with their problems. L . Ron Hubbard died in 1986.

Scientologists believe that there are four parts to man:

1. The thetan; an immortal spirit, which is reincarnated;
2. The physical body; at conception a thetan enters the body;
3. The analytical mind; consciousness when a person acts normally;
4. The reactive mind; the subconscious.

The word 'thetan' comes from eighth letter of the Greek alphabet theta. Scientologists believe that man is good: Scientology can help man be closer to God; salvation can only be achieved through counselling and Scientology can help people solve their problems. One of the central parts of Scientology practice is spiritual counselling known as 'auditing'.

Major festivals

Most of the special days celebrated in Scientology celebrate aspects of L. Ron Hubbard's life (see Table 3.28).

Table 3.28 Major Scientologist festivals

Month	Festival	Background information
March	The Birthday of L. Ron Hubbard (1911)	Celebrated on 13 March.
May	Publication of Dianetics	Celebrated on 9 May. Dianetics is one of the texts written by L. Ron Hubbard central to Scientology.

Scientology symbols

Scientology has two symbols. The first one is an intertwined letter S and two triangles. The letter S represents Scientology. The three sides of the first triangle stand for knowledge, responsibility and control. The three sides of the second triangle stand for affinity, reality and communication.

The second symbol used in Scientology is an eight-pointed cross.

Dietary requirements

There are no particular dietary requirements in Scientology (see Table 3.29). But they believe that all drugs are poisons.

Table 3.29 Dietary requirements

May eat	May not eat / drink	Fasting
Everything	All drugs	Personal choice

Dress guidelines

There are not particular dress guidelines in Scientology.

Shinto

History and beliefs

Shinto has no known founder or single sacred scripture. It came out of Japanese folk religions. The word Shinto means 'way of the spirits'. It is a religion that has many traditions and rites including the belief in, and worship of, kami.

Kami are spirits which can be both good or evil. The Kami live in shrines that are considered to be sacred. A shrine can be a building but may also be a rock or mountain. Some shrines may have priests, others may not. Priests may be male or female. People may visit shrines to worship or just to try and find peace and quiet. There is not a particular day of the week reserved for worship or visiting the shrine. Individuals will go when they feel the need to, or for a particular reason, for example, to give thanks.

Rituals form an important part of Shintoism and are seen as a religious act and it is important that they are carried out in the correct way. Rituals help bring people together. Shinto believes that humans are born pure, and that impurity comes as individuals grow and develop. Impurity can be washed away through rituals that cleanse.

Shinto worship can take place at the shrine or at home and many homes will have a small shrine. There are two holy books the *Kojiki* or 'Records of Ancient Matters' and the *Nihon-gi* or 'Chronicles of Japan'. Shinto has much in common with Buddhism and Confucianism.

Major festivals

Many of the Shinto festivals mark the seasons in the calendar (see Table 3.30).

Table 3.30 Major Shinto festivals

Month	Festival	Background information
January	Oshogatsu	New Year. People visit shrines and ask the Kami for good luck in the coming year.
January	Seijin Shiki	Adults' Day. Marks the day when individuals become adults age 20.
February	Rissun (or Setsubun)	Marks the start of spring. Known as the bean-throwing festival as lucky beans are thrown into the congregation in shrines.
November	Niinamesai	Originally a harvest festival now also marks labourthanks giving day.
November	Shichigosan (7–5–3 festival)	Parents take boys of 3 and 5 years old and girls of 3 and 7 to shrines to give thanks to the gods for a healthy life so far and pray for a safe and successful future.
Dependant on local shrines	Rei-sai	Annual Festival celebrating the day that is important to a shrine.

Shinto symbols

White is a symbol of purity in Shinto.

Dietary requirements

Many of the dietary requirements of Shinto are based on the dietary customs of Japan (see Table 3.31). Rice is one of the staple foods and is eaten every day.

Table 3.31 Dietary requirements

May eat	May not eat / drink	Fasting
Rice Sake Seaweed Fruit Vegetables Fish	Meat	No particular guidelines on fasting

Dress guidelines

Priests wear special clothes that are guided by the seasons and festivals. Individuals attending religious ceremonies may also wear a special garment called a Jōe or 'pure cloth'.

Sikhism

History and beliefs

People following the Sikh religion believe in one God. The founder of the religion was Guru Nanak. Guru Nanak was born in 1469 in a small village called Talvandi, which is now in Pakistan. He married and had two sons. He gave up married life to try and find God's way. When he was 50 years old he built a town called Katarpur. Many people came to see him and listen to his teachings. These people became his followers and were called Sikhs.

One of the teachings of Guru Nanak was about how to find salvation. He taught that salvation can only be reached by meditating on the name (*nam*) and the word (*sabad*) of God. In order to do this, people need teachers (*gurus*) to help them. When they think about the name and the word of God they will have harmony (*haukam*). When Guru Nanak died he chose another guru to carry on his work. All gurus chose the people who were to continue their work. Some chose their sons and others chose their followers as the next guru.

There were ten gurus who all made a contribution to the Sikh faith and helped it evolve to how it is today:

Guru Nanak, who founded the Sikh faith and wrote hymns;
Guru Anghad, who built temples and wrote down Guru Nanak's hymns;
Guru Amar Das, who introduced religious ceremonies and communal meals;
Guru Ram Das, who founded the town of Amritsar, a holy place;
Guru Arjan, who built the golden temple at Amritsar, put together all the hymns of the gurus in one book, called the Adi Granth, and who was put to death as a martyr;
Guru Hargobind, who developed guidelines of living;
Guru Har Rai, who started hospitals;
Guru Har Krishna, the youngest guru, who died when he was eight years old;

Guru Tegh Bahadur, who preached that everyone should be able to worship whom he or
she wants to, and was put to death because of this;
Guru Gobind Singh, the last human guru.

Guru Gobind Singh did not chose a human guru to follow him. He says that
the scriptures were more important than the people who interpreted them. He
felt that the Sikh faith had grown and developed, and did not need another
person to take it forward. He made the Guru Granth Sahib the last guru. The
Guru Granth Sahib is the writings of the Sikh faith. They are written in the
script called Gurumukhi, a script started by Guru Anghad, the second guru.
The Guru Granth Sahib has 1430 pages contains writing on how to live life.

Guru Gobind Singh also formed the Khalsa. This is a form of Sikhism that
follows the guidelines laid down by Guru Gobind Singh. The word 'Khalsa'
means 'God's own'. There are five symbols traditionally worn by the Khalsa,
called the five Ks:

1. Kesh: uncut hair. Sikhs do not cut their hair.
2. Kanga: combs to hold the hair in place.
3. Kirpan: dagger. This is a sign of defending the faith, and is not used as a weapon.
4. Kara: steel bangle, a sign of eternity.
5. Kaccha: short trousers, a sign of action.

Men may also wear turbans like Guru Gobind Singh. This is to keep their hair
clean and in place. However some Sikhs cut their hair and do not wear a
turban.

Sikhs believe that there are five prayers that should be said every day,
three in the morning and two at night. They may be said at home or in the
'gurudwara', the place where Sikhs meet together. The word 'gurudwara' means
'the place of the gurus'. The gurudwara is an important place used for worship
and for community activities. There are no statues or pictures of God in it.
When people enter the gurudwara they take off their shoes and cover their
heads. The Guru Granth Sahib sits on a cushion with a canopy over it. It is
treated like a person. It has a special resting place where it is taken each night,
and it is returned to the cushion in the morning. Women and men sit separately during services. Music is an important part of the service. Everyone
going to the gurudwara will be given special food to eat, called karah. After
each service there will be a meal to which everyone is invited. The meal will be
prepared by women and men, who have equal status in Sikhism.

In Sikhism there are important events that take place during life. The first
is the naming ceremony, were a new baby is taken to the gurudwara to be
named. The second is the initiation ceremony. This marks the time when

children become adults and join the Khalsa. This is where they will formally take the Sikh family name. This was the name chosen by Guru Gobind Singh to show that all Sikhs belong to the same family. Boys are called Singh, which means 'lion' and girls are called Kaur, which means 'princess'. Marriage is the third important ceremony in a person's life. The last ceremony is cremation, which happens soon after the person's death. This is the ceremony where he or she goes to meet God.

The holiest place in the Sikh religion is the Golden Temple at Amritsar in the Punjab, which was built by Guru Arjan, the fifth Guru. Some Sikhs will visit the Golden Temple as a form of pilgrimage.

Major festivals

The Sikhs use the same lunar calendar as the Hindus. Because the calendar is dictated by the movements of the moon, the festivals fall on different dates each year. All festivals centre on the events that happened in the life of the gurus (see Table 3.32). The Sikh calendar starts in the spring.

Table 3.32 Major Sikh festivals

Month	Festival	Background information
April / May	Baisakhi	Celebrates the founding of the Khalsa by Guru Gobind Singh, and the new year. People may go to the gurudwara. Verses from the holy book are recited for 48 hours before the festival starts. This is seen as the first day of the Sikh year.
May / June	Martyrdom of Guru Arjan	Guru Arjan was the guru who put together the Sikh holy book, the Guru Granth Sahib. He built the golden temple of Amritsar, He was tortured and put to death by the Mogul emperor. This festival remembers him.
October / November	Birthday of Guru Nanak	Guru Nanak founded the Sikh religion. This is the most important festival of the Sikh year. The Guru Granth Sahib is read from start to finish. This is called Akhand Path, and starts 48 hours before the festival, so that it finishes on the morning of the festival. People may spend the whole day in the gurudwara singing and listening to sermons. Food will be provided during the day.
December / January	Martyrdom of Guru Tegh Bahadur	This festival remembers Guru Tegh Bahadur, who was put to death by the Mogul emperor. This was because he preached that people should be able to choose the faith they wanted to follow and he would not change his faith to Islam. Special hymns are sung in the gurudwara.
January / February	Birthday of Guru Gobind Singh	Celebrates the birth if the last human guru and all his achievements. People go to the gurudwara, where verses are read from the holy book and hymns sung. Food is provided.

Sikh symbols

The five Ks are the main symbol of the Sikh faith. There is also a special emblem called the Khanda. This emblem is made up of a circle, a double-edged sword and two scimitar swords. The circle symbolizes eternity; the universe has no beginning or end. The edges of the double-edged sword in the centre symbolize protection and punishment.

Figure 3.7 The Khanda

Dietary requirements

Many Sikhs are vegetarians (see Table 3.33). The cow is regarded as a holy animal and Sikhs do not eat beef or any meat products from the cow. Eggs are seen as a source of life and generally not eaten. Workers should ensure that vegetarian and non-vegetarian foods do not come into contact with each other. Separate utensils should be used to serve the different foods. If this is not possible, utensils should be washed between serving of the different foods.

Table 3.33 Dietary requirements

May eat	May not eat	Fasting
Milk Yogurt Cheese Chicken (unless vegetarian) Fruit Vegetables	Beef or any meat products from the cow Eggs Fish Animal fats Coffee Tea Alcohol	Some Sikhs may fast or restrict themselves to certain foods.

Dress guidelines

Women should cover their legs, breasts and upper arms. Some women wear a shalwar kameez, and some cover their hair with a chuni or dupatta. Some Sikh women wear a sari, usually over a blouse and underskirt. Married women may wear wedding bangles, which are generally not removed. Young girls may also wear bangles and other jewellery. Women may also have a bindi, a dot in their forehead which is considered fashionable. Other jewellery may be worn from personal choice. Men should be covered from the waist to the knees. Some men may wear kameez and pyjama. Many Sikh men wear a turban. Young boys may wear a hair covering which should not be removed. Some men also wear the five Ks.

A Chance to Think 3.8

Sikhism

Rajinder is a father of two children in your setting. He wears the five Ks'. You hear some of the other parents talking about this and saying that he must be looking for violence because he wears a dagger.

What would you do in this situation?

Compare your answers with the sample answers in Appendix 3.

Taoism

History and beliefs

Taoism originated in China and it describes all religions and movements that seek access to the Tao also known as 'the way'. It was first recognized as a religion in the third and fourth centuries. The central belief of Taoism is that the Tao is the unchanging principle behind the universe and life is to be lived in accordance with the Tao 'which never acts, yet nothing is left undone'.

Taoists live lives of balance and harmony. The Yin Yang is the principle of natural and complementary forces, patterns and things that depend on one another which do not make sense on their own. They are opposites that fit together and work together, for example, male and female, light and dark. The Tao is a system of guidance and there are rules concerning ethics and morals which guide the way to live. Meditation is an important part of Taoism.

There are two key texts: the Tao Te Ching and the Chung Tzu. The Tao Te Ching is said to be written by Lao Tzu in the sixth century. Taoism does not have a God that is worshiped but it does have many gods, borrowed from other cultures and Lao Tzu is viewed as the first god of Taoism. It has temples, monasteries and priests and many rituals that are carried out by the priests. These may involve rituals to regulate the chi or the yin and yang or may involve prayers and meditation.

The human body is seen as an energy system which consists of patterned flows of chi, also known as vital energy, and blood. Taoist practise breathing exercises, massage, martial arts, yoga and meditation all of which are designed to transform them both mentally and physically and so bring them into closer harmony with the Tao. Tai Chi has its roots in exercises performed by Taoists.

Major festivals

Taoism follows a lunar calendar which means that some dates are not set but vary from year to year. There are many festivals celebrated each month (see Table 3.34).

Table 3.34 Major Taoist festivals

Month	Festival	Background information
1st luna Month	Chinese New Year	Marks the first day of the new year.
1st luna Month	Lanten Festival and Birthday of Tianguan	Marks the end of the new year celebrations.
5th luna month	Dragon boat festival	Taoist holiday.
7th luna month	Ghost festival	Taoist holiday and a time for honouring the dead.
8th luna month	Mid Autumn festival	Second most important celebration after Chinese new year.

Taoist symbols

The Ying and Yang symbol is very important in Taoism.

Figure 3.8 Ying and yang symbol

Dietary requirements

Taoists may eat a vegetarian diet before festivals (see Table 3.35).

Table 3.35 Dietary requirements

May eat	May not eat / drink	Fasting
Most things	Alcohol Meat Beans Grains	No guidelines

Dress guidelines

There are no specific dress guidelines.

Unification Church

History and beliefs

The Unification Church was founded by Sun Myung Moon in 1954. Its followers are sometimes known as Moonies but members of the religion refer to themselves as Unificationists.

Moon was born in 1920 in what is now North Korea and was brought up in the Presbyterian Church. At the age of 16 Sun Myung Moon had a vision of Jesus Christ who told him to complete the work he had begun. He spent nine years studying the Bible and becoming an engineer. During this time he believed he received further visions of Jesus, God and other prophets, who, he said told him about the teachings of the Unification Church. These teachings were later written down by one of his followers in a book called *The Divine Principle*.

Unificationists believe that they are to build a healthy and moral society by having God-centred families. They believe that because the first man created by God, Adam, sinned against God, this affected the rest of humanity. God then sent Jesus, who was killed before he could finish his work. So the world is still waiting to be saved by a new messiah. In 1992 Sun Myung Moon announced that he is the Messiah, or the second coming of Jesus.

Marriage is important in the Unification Church. It is the way in which God-centred families will be produced. Unificationists also believe that people can only enter heaven in families. Marriages are arranged for people by the church. Unificationists usually live together in large communities, spending their time involved in praying, worshiping, and recruiting new members. Worship takes place on a Sunday, with men and women sitting separately.

Major festivals

The Unification Church follows both a lunar and solar calendar. Dates of festivals and celebrations change yearly. There are many days of celebration (see Table 3.36). The major ones are listed.

Table 3.36 Major Unification Church festivals

Month	Festival	Background information
Established 1 January 1968 (Solar calendar)	True God's day	The most important holiday.
Established 1 March 1960 (lunar calendar)	True Parents day	The day celebrates the True parents.
Established 1 May 1963 (lunar calendar)	True day of All Things	The day when the love of God is received through human beings.
Established 1 October 1960 (lunar calendar)	True Children's day	The day a covenant is made with God.

Unification Church symbols

Sun Myung Moon designed a symbol for the Unification Church. It is based on two circles, a square and the number 12 which is considered to be an important number. The inner circle represents God, truth, life and light and the outer circle represents the harmony of giving and receiving .

Dietary requirements

Table 3.37 Dietary requirements

May eat	May not eat / drink	Fasting
Everything	Alcohol Tobacco	No guidelines

Dress guidelines

Unificationists dress modestly.

Zoroastrianism

History and beliefs

Zoroastrianism is one of the world's oldest religions. It was formed by the prophet Zarathustra, also known as Zoroaster, who lived in north-east Iran.

Zarathustra believed that God had taught him personally through a series of visions which he received at the age of 30.

Zoroastrians believe in one God, Ahura Mazda, and in two opposing forces. Ahura Mazda, the creator of life and goodness, is helped by Ahuras who are good spirits or angels and Angra Mainyu, who is evil and destructive, is helped by Daevas who are demonic spirits. This is known as Cosmic dualism or the battle between good and evil.

Individuals have to make choices between the two opposing forces. They believe that everything God created is pure and should be treated with love and respect, and that their daily life should be guided by the maxim, 'Good Thoughts, Good Words and Good Deeds'. Zarathustra's teachings are written in 17 hymns which are known as the 'Gathas'. These are in the Yasna part of the sacred Avesta scripture the holy book followed by Zoroastrianism.

Worship is held in a temple known as a Fire Temple or Agiary. Zoroastrians believe that all the elements are pure and that fire is the supreme symbol of purity and represents god's light or wisdom. A fire is always burning in the temple. Fire is always part of their ceremonies and rituals. Zoroastrians pray several times a day. Some individuals will wear a cord knotted three times called a Kusti. This is to remind them of the maxim, 'Good Words, Good Thoughts, Good Deeds'. The kusti is wrapped around the outside of a sudreh, a long, clean, white cotton shirt. At 7 years of age a child will undergo an initiation ceremony, performed by a priest, called the Navjote or Sedreh-Pushi where they are given their suhreh and kusti.

Major festivals

The calendar is divided into 12 months with each month named after Ahura Mazda (god) or Amesha Spentas (the holy immortals) or the Yazatas (venerable ones). Zoroastrians follow three different calendars: the Fasli, Shahanshahi and Qadimi calendars. There are many holy days and festivals and the dates will vary depending on which calendar is being used (see Table 3.38). There are also seven obligatory feasts throughout the year.

Table 3.38 Major Zoroastrian festivals

Month	Festival	Background information
March (*Fasli*) July (*Qadimi*) August (*Shahanshahi*)	*Jamshidi Noruz*	New Year.
March (*Fasli*) July (*Qadimi*) August (*Shahanshahi*)	*Khordad Sal*	Birthday of Zoroastra.

Zoroastrian symbols

A winged symbol known as the Faravahar is associated with Zoroastrianism. It shows a man emerging from a disk flanked by wings spread wide.

Dietary requirements

No particular dietary requirements (see Table 3.39). Food is considered sacred and as coming from god. Some individuals may follow a semi-vegetarian diet through choice with no beef, pork or poultry.

Table 3.39 Dietary requirements

May eat	May not eat / drink	Fasting
Everything – no dietary restrictions		May abstain from meat on particular days of the year

Dress guidelines

There are no particular dress guidelines. Priests wear white and many individuals wear traditional dress for ceremonies and festivals. Some individuals cover their head while praying.

References and useful resources

Allan, J., Butterworth, J. and Langley, M. (1987). *A Book of Beliefs: Religions, New Faiths, the Paranormal*. Lion Publishing.

Bach, M. (1977). *Major Religions of the World*. Abbingdon Publishers

Bancroft, A. (1985). *New Religions World*. Macdonald.

Bowker, J. (1997). *World Religions The Great Faiths Explored and Explained*. Dorling Kindersley.

Gabriel, T. and Geaves, R. (2007). *Isms – Understanding Religions*. Universe Publishing.

Hinnells, J. R. (2000). *Handbook of Living Religions*. Penguin.

Publications for children

Ajmera, M., Nakassis, M. and Pon, C. (2009). *Faith*. Charlesbridge.

Damon, E. (2000). *All Kinds of Beliefs*. Tango Books.

Ganeri, A. (2005). *The First Book of Festivals*. Evans Publishing Group.

Huggins-Cooper, L. (2004). *Festivals*. Hodder Wayland.

Kindersley, B. and Kindersley, A. (1997). *Children Just Like Me: Celebration*. Dorling Kindersley.

Wilkinson, P. (2008). *Encyclopaedia of Religion*. Dorling Kindersley.

Baha'i

Hatcher,W. (2003). *The Baha'i Faith: The Emerging Global Religion*. Baha'i Publishing.

Vickers. P. (1992). *The Baha'i Faith World Order of Baha'u'llah (1938) Shoghi Effendi*. Baha'i Publishing Trust.

Publications for children

Clarke-Hababi, S. (2007). *The Baha'i Children's Workbook*. Lightning Source.

Buddhism

The Tripitak

Eckel, M, D. (2003). *Understanding Buddhism*. Duncan Baird Publishers.

Publications for children

Samrasekara, D. and Samrasekara, U. (1986). *I Am a Buddhist*. Franklin Watts.

Wallace, H. (2006). *This Is My Faith: Buddhism*. Barron's Educational Series.

Christianity

The Bible

Hale, D. R. (2004). *Understanding Christianity*. Duncan Baird Publishers.

Publications for children

Killingray, M. and Killingray, J. (1986). *I Am an Anglican*. Franklin Watts.

Pettenuzzo, B. and Braham, M. (1985). *I Am a Roman Catholic*. Franklin Watts.

Roussou, M. and Papamicheal, P. (1985). *I Am a Greek Orthodox*. Franklin Watts.

Wallace, H. (2006). *This is My Faith Christianity*. Barron's Educational Series.

Nason. R. (2004). *Visiting a Church*. Evans Publishing Group.

Christian Science

The Christian Science Monitor

Baker Eddy, M. (n.d). *Science and Health with the Key to the Scriptures*. Christian Science Publishing Society.

Confucianism

Oldstone-Moore, J. (2003). *Understanding Confucianism*. Duncan Baird Publishers.

Rainey, L. D. (2010). *Confucius and Confucianism*. Blackwell.

Publications for children

Freedman, R. (2002). *Confucius*. Scholastic Press.

Hare Krishna

Bhaktivedanta Swami Prabhupada, A. C. (1983). *Chant and Be Happy: The Story of the Hare Krishna Mantrat*. Hare Bhaktivedanta Book Trust.

Hinduism

The Vedas

Narayanan, V. (2004). *Understanding Hinduism*. Duncan Baird Publishers.

Publications for children

Aggarwal, M. and Goswami, G. D. (1986). *I Am a Hindu*. Franklin Watts.
Deshpande, C. (1985). *Diwali*. A&C Black.
Ganeri, A. and Wallace, H. (2006). *This Is My Faith: Hinduism*. Barron's Educational Series.
Mead, J. and Nason. R. (2005). *Visiting a Mandir*. Evans Publishing Group.

Islam

The Qu'ran

Gordon, M. S. (2002). *Understanding Islam*. Duncan Baird Publishers.

Publications for children

Ahsan, M. M. (1987). *Muslim Festivals*. Wayland.
Nason, R. (2006). *Visiting a Mosque*. Evans Publishing Group.
Wallace, H. (2006). *This Is My Faith: Islam*. Barron's Educational Series.
Wood, J. (1988). *Our Culture: Muslim*. Franklin Watts.

Jainism

Jacobi, H. (2009). *Jaina Sutras part 1 and part 2*. Kindle Book.

Jehovah's Witnesses

Watch Tower Society (1984). *Awake*.
New World Translation of the Bible.

Judaism

The Hebrew Bible

Ehrlich, C. S. (2004). *Understanding Judaism*. Duncan Baird Publishers.

Publications for children

Wallace, H. (2006). *This Is My Faith: Judaism*. Barron's Educational Series.

Nason. R. (2007). *The Jewish Faith*. White Thomson Publishing Ltd.

Nason. R. (2005). *Visiting a Synagogue*. Evans Publishing Group.

Mormons

Church of Jesus Christ of the Latter Day Saints. (1981) (editor). Smith J. Jr (translator). *The Book of Mormon*. (first published 1830).

Publications for children

Johnson, D. (n. d.). *Book of Mormon Little Books*. Acacia Publishing.

Quakers – the Religious Society of Friends

Ashworth, T. and Wildwood, A. (2009). *Rooted in Christianity, Open to New Light: Quaker Spiritual Diversity*. Pronoun Press.

Publications for children

Hennessy, B. G. (2005). *Because of You, A Book of Kindness*. Candlewick.

Lindahl, K. (2005). *How Does God Listen?* Skylight Paths.

Rastafarianism

Rastafarian Advisory Service (1988). *Focus on Rastafari; A Report*.

Publications for children

Gaynor, P. and Obadiah, (1985). *I Am a Rastafarian*. Franklin Watts.

Yinka (n.d.). *Marcellus*. Akira Press.

Scientology

Hubbard, R. L. (2002). *Dianetics*. Bridge Publications.

Shinto

Scott Littleton, C. (2002). *Understanding Shinto*. Duncan Baird Publishers.

Publications for children

Nomura, N. S. (1996). *I Am Shinto*. PowerKids Press.

Sikhism

The Guru Granth Sahib

Publications for children

Kaur-Singh, K. and Nason. R. (2005). *Visiting a Gurdwara*. Evans Publishing Group.

Kaur-Singh, K. (2006). *My Sikh Faith*. Evans Publishing Group.

Taoism

Oldstone-Moore, J. (2003). *Understanding Taoism*. Duncan Baird Publishers.

Publications for children

Hartz, P. (2004). *Taoism (World Religions)*. Facts on File.

Unification Church

Rev. Sun Myung Moon. (1973 translation). *The Divine Principle*. Unification Thought Institute.

Zoroastrianism

Hope Molton, J. (2005). *Treasure of the Magi: A Study of Modern Zoroastrianism*. Oxford University Press.

Useful websites

www.bbc.co.uk/religion – information on a variety of religions

www.childseyemedia.com – Festivals 1 and Festivals 2 DVDs and Festival Calendar.

www.festivalshop.co.uk – for books, artifacts, posters.

www.interfaithcalendar.org – gives dates of religious festivals.

www.shapworkingparty.org.uk – information on religions.

www.thesacredsite.com – information on religions.

The Role of Play 4

We have seen in the previous chapters that there are many things that need to be considered when we are looking at how young children grow and develop in all areas; socially, physically, intellectually, emotionally and in their communication. Two of the most important influences of a child's development are the play and activities with which they are involved. Play is something that children take part in everyday, whether it is on their own, or with other children, or adults. Understanding the importance of play has a major impact on how, and what, play experiences practitioners should provide for children.

Play is considered so important that it is included in the UN Convention on the Rights of the Child. Article 31 says, 'Every child is entitled to rest and play and have the opportunity to have the chance to join in a wide range of activities'. Play is also central to the Early Years Foundation Stage (EYFS) that received legal status with the Childcare Act 2006. The EYFS practice guidance says: 'Play underpins the delivery of the EYFS. Children must have the opportunity to play indoors and outdoors . . . 'Play underpins all development and learning for young children. Most children play spontaneously, although some may need adult support, and it is through play that they develop intellectually, creatively, physically, socially and emotionally . . .' the EYFS requires providers to ensure a balance of child-initiated and adult-led play based activities. Providers should use their judgement and their knowledge of the children in their care in deciding what the balance should be'.

It goes on to give an explanation of what is meant by child-initiated activities. It says,

> When a child engages in a self-chosen pursuit, this is child-initiated activity. For example, a child might elect to play with a fire engine – fitting the driver behind the steering wheel, extracting the driver, replacing the driver, throwing the

driver back into a box and introducing a different driver. Another instance of a child-initiated choice may be were a child takes ownership of an activity and 'subverts' it to a different purpose than intended. For example, a child might prefer to pour water into a hole to make a puddle rather than watering the plants as the adult had intended. Other child-initiated activities may be instigated when the child brings something to the setting – such as an experience of having been on a bus or visiting hospital. This might lead to the provision of resources, stories and pictures to support this interest. Whatever children bring is an indication of their current interest and should be supported.

The EYFS also defines adult-led activities saying:

> Small group times are a good example of an adult-led activity – the adult has selected the time to encourage a particular aspect of learning, or discussing a particular topic. The adult may introduce a particular material, skill or idea. Often when an adult initiates an activity, for example demonstrates the skill of weaving, the child's need for adult involvement will decrease over time as they master the skill.

This chapter examines the role of play in more detail. It looks at how and why children play, and what they learn from it. It also examines the role of the adult in children's play, including how to observe, plan, provide and evaluate children's play within an anti-discriminatory framework. This chapter does not examine the different theories of play, owing to lack of space, but a list of useful resources is given at the end of the chapter for practitioners who want further information.

In Chapter 1 we saw how research shows us that children as young as 2 can tell the difference between skin colours. We also saw that by the age of 3 children are playing with what adults consider to be gender-appropriate toys. This puts paid to the idea that young children do not notice things such as colour or gender differences, and are not taking in the images they see around them. These research findings are useful information for practitioners, as they show that what we do and say in front of children, and the activities we provide to facilitate play need to be thought about and provided within an anti-discriminatory framework. The Charter for Children's Play was originally published in 1992. It has been continually revised as there have been changes in legislation and practice. It says:

> Playing is integral to children's enjoyment of their lives, their health and their development. Children and young people – disabled and non-disabled – whatever their age, culture, ethnicity or social or economic background need and want to

play, indoors and outdoors, in whatever way they can. Through playing children are creating their own culture, developing their abilities, exploring their creativity and learning about themselves, other people and the world around them.

As long as there have been children in the world there have been things for them to play with. The importance of children's play has not always been as strongly recognized as it is today. Play is now regarded as an important part of a child's life, and in order to help facilitate children's play, parents and practitioners need to provide children with environments, experiences, toys and activities to enable children's play to be rich and varied. Mia Kellner-Pringle said, 'Play is an intensely absorbing experience and is even more important to children than work is to an adult'. Play is a child's work. It is by playing that children learn about themselves and the world around them. Children need to be provided with a variety of play experiences that they can take part in on their own, with other children and with adults. They also need to be given the chance to play in different environments, both indoors and outdoors, with and without equipment.

A Chance to Think 4.1

Play Experiences
Try to remember some of the play experiences you have observed the children in your setting taking part in over the past few days. Pick two different experiences and try to describe them. The following prompts may help you.
  When did it take place?
  Where did it take place?
  How many children were involved?
  What where they doing?
  Why were they doing it?

It can be seen by looking at just two different play experiences that play can take place in a variety of ways and can be very different depending on who is playing, what they are playing with, why they are playing, where they are playing and how they are playing. The word 'play' is used by many people in many different contexts. Some adults may say to children, 'You can play when you have finished your tea'. Some adults may even say to practitioners who work with children, 'There's nothing to your job; all you do is play with children all day'. Practitioners can get quite frustrated that some people still think like this and that is why a good understanding of the role of play, the role of the adult in play, and the importance of play is necessary for practitioners. This knowledge enables practitioners to be confident in providing play experiences for children within an anti-discriminatory framework, so that both children and adults benefit from it. Awareness of, and confidence about providing play in within an anti-discriminatory framework will also mean that practitioners can confidently explain these principles to parents and others, including students in the setting. It is important that information is passed on and shared so that everyone involved with children is trying to work with the same principles in mind, bringing harmony not discord.

The Concise Oxford Dictionary defines 'play' as follows: 'occupy or amuse oneself pleasantly with some recreation, games, exercise etc'. Childcare practitioners know there is more to children's play than this; that play helps and supports children's learning and development.

The Charter for Children's Play says: 'Play is the fundamental way that children enjoy their childhood, It is essential to their quality of life as children.'

Social skills

Children learn many social skills through their play experiences. They learn who they are and how they fit into the world. Children learn very quickly that the world can be an unfair place for some individuals and groups of people. When you are providing play within an anti-discriminatory framework it is important to provide positive images of individuals and groups in everyday situations, not just individuals and groups that are represented in your setting. We live in a world made up of many different groups of people, interacting together to make up the social environment. Children get messages from many places, including television, books, play equipment, pictures and from the things people say. Some of these messages may be discriminatory and practitioners must address these issues in the setting, otherwise they are colluding with them. No setting will have all groups that make up the society in which we live attending or working in it. A setting that has no Chinese children attending, for example, should still work towards providing positive images of, and attitudes towards, Chinese people, culture and language, so that everyone in the setting will recognize, value and respect them.

Physical skills

Children learn physical skills, such as moving about and manipulating objects. Children learn to move, crawl, walk, run and jump, and most children have total control over their physical skills. Some children may not have as much control over their physical skills as others, for example, some children with cerebral palsy may be floppy, have poor balance and not be able to control all of their movements. This does not mean that a child with cerebral palsy is not able to participate in play. Indeed it is vitally important she or he is able to participate fully, along with the other children in the setting, in the whole range of play activities. Being aware of individual children's physical skills and providing appropriate play may have implications for practitioners, such as providing physical help or support for children so they are able to be fully involved in play activities. The role of the adult in play is important. All children are individuals and will have different needs and experiences with regard to physical play, be it large or small physical play. Some children may need particular aids or equipment to help them access play that helps support the development of physical skills, such as a frame to help them stand at the water tray or the provision of left-handed scissors if they are left-handed to help them develop their cutting skills. Practitioners need to be able to play and provide play activities that meet the needs of all the children in the setting which extend their experiences and physical skills.

Developing physical skills

Intellectual skills

Through play children learn intellectual and cognitive skills. They learn how to reason, solve problems, think and concentrate. Practitioners need to provide play experiences that enhance all children's intellectual abilities. We have seen that boys and girls are different and may learn and play in different ways but both need to have equal access to activities and resources. The way a child learns may be influenced by their learning style. There are three main learning styles – Visual, Auditory and **Kinaesthetic** – and children (and adults) may have a preference for one or more of them, and they may change with different activities and over time. Visual learners learn through seeing; auditory learners learn though listening and **kinaesthetic** learners learn through moving and doing. Practitioners need to ensure that their setting provides for all three learning styles. It is also important to remember the importance of food and drink in all areas of development, including intellec-tual development. Children who have a balanced diet, including regular drinks of water, and have a healthy breakfast concentrate better, which leads to improved learning and behaviour. There may be many different reasons, for example, lack of knowledge about diet, families on a low income or families in a hurry to get to the setting, that may mean some of the children attending settings may not be eating a well-balanced diet or having breakfast before they arrive at the setting. This in turn may affect their ability to concentrate and so affect their learning.

A Chance to Think 4.4

Gender

You are covering for a colleague in a room you do not usually work in. All the toys are put out in the afternoon for free play. There is a selection of toys, including the home corner, book corners, cars and a garage, pencils, paper and stencils, water play with items that sink and float, wooden construction, threading, jigsaws and a lotto game. During the time you are in the room you notice that only the boys are playing in the water tray. They are playing constructively. On several occasions two girls try and join in but are unable to. A member of staff tells them not to disturb the boys, as they are playing nicely and they can have a turn later. By the end of the session the two girls have not had a turn. You notice the same thing happens the next day.

Do you think that all the children have equal access to the water tray?

What can you do to ensure that the girls get a turn in the water tray?

Compare your answers with the sample answers in Appendix 4.

Communication skills

Another main area of development learnt and practised through play is communication. Children communicate in a variety of ways including through crying, vocalizing, gestures, body language, speech, signs and symbol language, pictures and written words and tone of voice. Play helps children to learn to communicate with peers, children older and younger than themselves and adults. It can help children to learn language skills and new vocabulary, and express themselves through language and other ways of communicating, including using language and ways of communicating that may not be used at home. This is true of all children, whatever language or communication system they use, whether it is Urdu, English, Turkish, Arabic, Makaton or with communication passports. Children can be introduced to, and helped to value and respect, all languages and communication systems through play. For example, through items in the home corner, books, music and so on. It is important that practitioners recognize that all languages and communication systems are equally important and ensure that children, parents or practitioners who have English as an additional language are not made to feel inadequate, but are respected for the skills they have in communicating, including sign or symbol languages such as Bliss symbols. Language and communication will be discussed further in Chapter 5.

A Chance to Think 4.5

Communication

All of the practitioners in your setting have English as a first language as do most of the children. You feel more needs to be done by the setting to provide positive models of languages other than English, including sign and symbol languages such as Makaton and Bliss symbols.

Where can you find out about sign and symbol languages if you don't already know about them?

What is your setting doing already? Try and evaluate how effective this is.

Now try to provide suggestions as to how the setting can improve its provision in this area.

Compare your answers with the sample answers in Appendix 4.

Emotional skills

Play provides one of the safest ways for children to learn about emotions, both their own and other people's. Practitioners need to provide experiences to stimulate this, and a safe and secure environment in which to do it. In order for children to do this they need to trust the practitioner and have an attachment to them. That is why the key person role is so important. Through play children can role-play different situations, such as being different people and experiencing the emotions generated by the situations, for example, going to the dentist.

Children feel a vast range of emotions and practitioners need to acknowledge this and help children to recognize, name and come to terms with different emotions. If children are feeling angry or frustrated they can release their emotions in a secure way by pounding on malleable objects, such as clay or dough, by kicking a ball outside or by talking with their key person. All children feel emotions and practitioners should provide an environment where children are able to express their feelings and emotions in a safe, secure and non-judgmental way. For example, if one child is upset by the way he has been treated he should be allowed to vocalize that and express it. This, it is to be hoped, will mean that all those involved in the situation can try to examine why the child is upset, what, or who, has upset him and how it can be put right. Sometimes the play in which children are involved, or people's response to it, may trigger an emotional reaction. Practitioners should respond to this in a way that will help the child deal with it in a constructive way. For example, if a boy falls off a bike and is hurt, he may cry. This is a natural reaction, and if every time this happens he is told, 'boys don't cry' he may come to think that the reaction he has when hurting himself is wrong and unacceptable. There are times when it is all right for people to cry, no matter who they are.

Some children may act out, through play, emotions they have seen at home or in other settings, such as anger or violence. Practitioners need to be aware that some children may live in home situations where emotions may be expressed in a way that is not acceptable in a setting, for example, though violence, and they will express their emotions in this way as this is all they know. This can be challenging for practitioners but it is essential that they work with children to help them to express emotions in a safe way that does not harm others. These issues will be discussed further in Chapter 5.

A Chance to Think 4.6

Feelings

A parent comes to you to bring to your attention the following incident. Her child Miriam was upset at home the previous evening as her friend Jane had invited children to her house for tea, but Jane had said to Miriam that she was not invited as she would have been the only brown girl there.

What are the issues for Miriam and her parent?

What would you do and how would you support Miriam and her parent ?

Compare your answers with the sample answers in Appendix 4.

Play and planning

It is important that anti-discriminatory practices are incorporated into play in an everyday way. They are not something that should be tagged on at the end, or something that should be seen as an additional extra or something exotic. Every setting needs to discuss how good practice can be incorporated into play, so that all practitioners in the setting have a common understanding of why incorporating anti-discriminatory practice into play and planning is necessary.

Practitioners also need to examine their own attitudes towards anti-discriminatory play. Once a setting is committed to working in this way it should become an everyday occurrence and be integrated into the everyday life of the setting. Providing anti-discriminatory play only for special occasions, such as when an inspection is happening, or for particular festivals is what Louise Derman Sparks in her book 'Anti Bias Curriculum', calls a 'tourist approach'. This is about visiting different cultures or groups, but not including them into the mainstream of the setting. It keeps particular cultures, groups or individuals to one side and makes them exotic or different.

In some settings there are lots of posters displayed of children from different races and cultures, as a very visible sign that the setting is aware of differences, but this is all that is done. This is often called 'tokenism', because only a token gesture is being made to include some different ways of life. Like the tourist approach, it does not include all groups equally in the life of the setting. Everybody, all individuals and groups, needs to feel included in the setting and part of the whole setting. This can only be done by planning play and evaluating it.

A Chance to Think 4.7

Evaluation

You have been asked to evaluate the planning and play experiences taking place in your setting and make some recommendations for the way forward. Think about the approaches to play that may be taken by different practitioners in your setting using the information in this chapter to help you.

How would you describe the planning and play that takes place in your setting?

Do you think this approach is acceptable?

Does it provide a positive experience of play for all children?

What, if any, recommendations would you make for the way forward?

Having appropriate resources in a setting is only a small part of working in an anti-discriminatory environment. Indeed, just having resources that reflect positive images is in itself not enough. Resources may be used in a negative and stereotypical way that can be damaging to children if practitioners have been instructed to use them, but they are not clear why, as they have not been given any training or been given the change to reflect on their own attitudes towards issues. For example, if practitioners make negative comments when putting out the resources, or they do not play with them these, attitudes will be picked up by the children.

We have seen throughout this book that adults' attitudes towards anti-discriminatory practice are important. This is particularly true in the areas of planning and play, for we have seen that play can have a major impact on all areas of a child's development. The attitude a practitioner has towards planning and play can have a positive or negative effect on children. Indeed, as we have just seen, play, and play resources and equipment, can be used in a discriminatory way to exclude or to give negative messages about groups or individuals. For example, if all the images of elderly people show them to be ill or infirm, children may begin to think that when they become elderly they will also be ill. We saw in Chapter 1 that it is possible for children to have racist attitudes; it is also possible for them to be ageist, and practitioners need to be aware of the messages they are giving to children about elderly people. It is important that children see positive images of elderly people doing ordinary everyday things, such as using the computer, going shopping and enjoying themselves.

The role of the adult in planning and play is sometimes not easy, as it means that practitioners have to examine their own attitudes towards individuals and groups that go to make up society. Sometimes it can be hard for practitioners to know what to do or say. It can be quite frightening. Sometimes practitioners may feel it is easier not to do anything than to do something and possibly upset someone. However, it is important to pick up on, and in a sensitive way challenge or question, what has been written, seen or said – for example, other practitioners taking about the difficulties of planning for and including a child with a hearing impairment in play, or children talking about girls who cannot be doctors; they have to be nurses. It is also important for practitioners to recognize and acknowledge that no one person knows everything, and sometimes, even with planning, evaluation and reflection, mistakes are made. It is important that the fear of making mistakes does not stop practitioners trying to do the right thing as they see it.

Not everyone has experience of working with all the different groups in society, and as we saw in earlier chapters, there are as many differences within groups as there are between groups. One way of trying to ensure that as few mistakes are made as possible in the setting with planning and play provision is to talk to other people. This may includes talking to parents, colleagues, students, going to visit other settings to find out what they are doing or contacting organizations that may be able to help. Once practitioners have an understanding about what it means to plan and provide for anti-discriminatory play they will be able to discuss, plan and evaluate how effective it is.

Planning is very important and will take place in different ways and use different formats in different settings. Planning should start with what practitioners know about a child and what that child can do. Every child can do something and it is important to start with this knowledge and find out what they are interested in. Planning should start with the child and take into account the individual needs of children as well as the needs of the group. Practitioners are able to find out about children through observation and assessment. The EYFS has within it much useful information within it. One of the commitments in the Enabling Environments Theme, which all settings are required to deliver is about observation, planning and assessment. It says:

> 3.1 – Observation, Assessment and Planning Babies and young children are **individuals first, each with a unique profile of abilities**. Schedules and routines should flow with the child's needs. All planning starts with observing children in order to understand and consider their current interests, development and learning.

Observation is the first part of the planning cycle.

Observation is about observing children. This can be through watching them and listening to what they are saying, and assessment is when we analyse observations to find out what they tell us. This may be where a child is in their development, what they can do, what they like and many other things. It vital

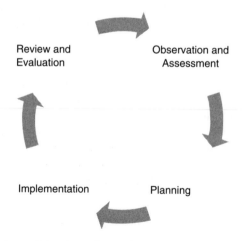

Review and
Evaluation

Observation and
Assessment

Implementation

Planning

Figure 4.1 Observation and Planning cycle

to remember that observations can, and are, influenced by the perceptions that practitioners have. All practitioners have perceptions and are influenced by them. They need to be aware of this and check them out with others.

Planning should start with the child. All children should be able to experience play at first hand. They should be fully involved in play and the planning of it. Spontaneous play is important, but in order for spontaneous play to take place, sometimes the practitioner will have to set the scene or provide the resources for it. Play needs to be planned, provided and evaluated by practitioners so they can see what has happened, what children have gained from it, and what needs to happen next. Practitioners also need to evaluate their role in planning and play. Planning is important for all settings and for all children. The EYFS which starts from birth to the end of the academic year in which a child reaches the age of 5, has in it the learning and development requirements for children of this age. The statutory guidance says:

> This section sets out the learning and development requirements that all early years providers must by law deliver, regardless or type, size or funding of the setting . . . children are competent learners from birth and develop and learn in a variety of ways; All practitioners should, therefore, look carefully at the children in their care, consider their needs, their interests, and their stages of development and use all of this information to help plan a challenging and enjoyable experience across all areas of learning and development.

It goes on to give the early learning goals, which are the knowledge, skills and understanding that young children should have acquired by the end of the academic year in which they reach the age of 5. The statutory framework clarifies this by saying:

> The statutory early learning goals establish expectations for most children to reach by the end of the EYFS. They provide the basis for planning throughout the EYFS, so laying secure foundations from birth for future learning. By the end of the EYFS, some children will have exceeded the goals. Other children, depending on their individual needs, will be working towards all or some of the goals – particularly younger children, some children with learning difficulties and disabilities and some learning English as an additional language.

The six areas covered by the early learning goals are:

- Personal, Social and Emotional Development;
- Communication, Language and Literacy;
- Problem Solving, Reasoning and Numeracy;

- Knowledge and Understanding of the World;
- Physical Development;
- Creative Development.

The EYFS goes on to say:

> None of these Areas of Leaning and Development can be delivered in isolation from the others. They are all equally important and depend on each other to support a rounded approach to child development. All the areas must be delivered thorough planned, purposeful play, with a balance of adult-led and child-initiated activities.

The early learning goals are not a curriculum in themselves but goals for children to work towards. How practitioners and settings plan for these will depend on the philosophy of the setting they work within and the age of the children in the setting – for example, a Montessori setting may plan and work in a different way from a reception class, a Steiner setting or a childminder.

The welfare requirements in the EYFS, which are also a statutory requirement, also refer to planning in the requirement of organization which says, 'providers must plan and organise their systems to ensure that every child receives an enjoyable and challenging learning and development experience that is tailored to meet their individual needs'. It then lists the specific legal requirements that settings must comply with. These are:

> Providers must have effective systems to ensure that the individual needs of all children are met. Each child must be assigned a key person. In childminding settings, the childminder is the key person.

> Providers must promote equality of opportunity and anti-discriminatory practice and must ensure that every child is included and not disadvantaged because of ethnicity, culture or religion, home language, family background, learning difficulties or disabilities, gender or ability. Providers must ensure that there is a balance of adult-led and freely chosen or child-initiated activities, delivered through indoor and outdoor play.

> Providers must undertake sensitive observational assessments in order to plan and meet young children's individual needs.

> Providers must plan and provide experiences which are appropriate to each child's stage of development as they progress towards the early learning goals.

It can be seen that anti-discriminatory practice and meeting the needs of individual children is a very clear requirement of the EYFS and a central part of it. When planning for children it is important to take into account their age and individual needs.

Careful planning is vital if anti-discriminatory practice is to become a reality in settings. Planning needs to take place at various levels, including long-term, medium-term and short-term planning. Long-term planning may take the form of a business or development plan and needs to take into account the philosophy of the setting; the development of policies and procedures; the implementation of anti-discriminatory practice; patterns of attendance; links with inspection reports; any self-evaluation reports; working with parents; curriculum development and learning objectives; staffing; resources; and any other issues that are indicated by the particular setting. Long-term planning should be followed by medium-term planning. These may be plans for a period of time between 2–8 weeks. This may include planning around themes or objectives; activity planning; planning of resources; planning of staff deployment; planning for observation and assessment and any other issues for a particular setting. Finally there is short-term planning, in the form of a more detailed working document. This may cover specific learning intentions / objectives; activities; resources; adults' role; grouping of children; differentiation for individual children; teaching and learning strategies and any other information that is helpful to practitioners. When planning, workers need to be aware of the requirements to plan for all elements of learning, including knowledge and understanding, skills and attitudes. Throughout this book we have seen how important attitudes are, and how quickly they develop. Practitioners need to be aware of this and incorporate this knowledge into their planning. For example, when considering the creative development area of learning some of the attitudes practitioners may want to encourage and support are self-motivation;, excitement, enthusiasm, experimentation, curiosity, persistence and concentration, willingness to co-operate, critical reflection of one's own and other people's work, non-judgmental; openness to new experiences; confidence and imagination . Planning needs to be based on a thorough knowledge of child development and individual children's needs. All planning documents should be written in a way that makes them accessible and easily understood by others. Planning documents need to be working documents that are helpful to the practitioners and children in the setting. Although we have just seen that planning is a necessary part of working with children and young people, practitioners should remember that not everything can be planned, and not all learning can be planned. Children also learn through unplanned experiences and from the hidden curriculum.

A Chance to Think 4.8

Observation, Assessment and Planning

Find all the relevant documents in your setting and examine them.

Do they meet the needs of the setting and the needs of the individual children?

Is it helpful to you?

If someone else had to read and use your documentation would they be able to understand it and follow it?

Children of different ages have different needs. Some settings may work with children of different ages. For example, childminders may have a 3-month-old baby and an 8-year-old. Other settings may have children from birth–5 in family groups and another setting may have children from 3–5 in age based rooms. Each setting needs to find a way of planning that meets its needs and the needs of the children attending it.

Planning for children under 3

Children under 3 have their own particular needs and requirements as individuals and as a group that need to be planned and catered for. Children under 3: Are forming attachments and developing relationships; Are still very dependent on adults to provide for their needs; Are growing and developing very rapidly in all areas of development; Are learning through all experiences and routines, not just those that are those that practitioners have planned for them; Are learning about who they are, how they fit in and what they can do; need to be able to do things again and again; need to be able to explore in safety; need to have fun; need to be able to move all parts of their body; need adults who support them and provide for their needs. We have seen how quickly young children develop attitudes and practitioners need to remember this in their planning. Children under 3, like all children, need to feel valued and respected. They need to have a planned routine that makes them feel secure in themselves and in those caring for them.

Jennie Lindon in her book 'Helping Babies and Toddlers to Learn' says,

> Good forward planning can support the learning of very young children so long as any tentative plans are grounded in a knowledge of young children, attention to their skills and positive attitudes within the early years team . . .
> Useful plans remain flexible and there should never be a sense of "but it's

on the schedule, we have to do it." If toddlers have become interested in another activity or use of the materials, they will learn through following this sense of exploration.

As with all age groups, practitioners need to plan routines, the environment and play and other experiences so that they meet individual needs, group needs and provide anti-discriminatory practice. All the activities discussed later in this chapter can be adapted so that children may take part in them. This may be done by being aware of child development; being aware of children's individual needs; planning effectively for this age range; doing activities on the floor; using larger equipment so that children are able to hold or see it; using different equipment as needed – for example, board, books instead of paper books; having a larger adult:child ratio; planning for different time scales for activities when required; providing protective clothing and covers so it does not matter about the mess; ensuring it is the process and not the end product that is important; ensuring that practitioners are aware of children's individual needs and likes and dislikes; allowing and supporting children to explore and discover; repeating activities and giving children time and space to do things.

It is particularly important that young babies are given the chance to move around and move all parts of their body. There are many pieces of equipment available for young babies that can be useful if used carefully, such as bouncy chairs, high chairs, car seats and so on, but that can also inhibit movement if not used carefully. Babies and young children need to be able to move all parts of their body in order to grow and develop in all areas. Movement links to learning, the development of the brain, social skills, co-ordination and much more. There are of course particular resources that children of this age need that may be different from the requirements of older children – for example, pull / push toys, posting boxes, a ball pool, mirrors, rattles, mobiles, soft toys, treasure baskets, heuristic play, sensory toys, rolling toys, ride on toys, comfort objects and shape sorters are but some examples. It is important to evaluate all of these within an anti-discriminatory framework. The choosing and using of resources will be discussed later in this chapter.

When planning for the under 3s the four themes and the principles of the EYFS need to be taken into account and planned for. The Areas of Learning and Development in the EYFS now start from birth, but it important to remember that babies and young children do not learn in 'areas' but from 'experiences' and practitioners need to plan for an environment and experiences that meet children's needs.

A Chance to Think 4.9

Planning for Babies

Think about a baby in your setting.

What could they do when they first arrived in your setting? How do you know that?

Write down a list of all the things that they can do now.

What has happened to help the baby learn new skills and grow and develop? How do you know this?

Write down what you need to do in order to help the baby move forward in their development and say how you will work with parents to try and do this.

Planning for 3- to 5-year olds

There are many different ways of planning for children and many planning documents in existence for long-term, medium-term and short-term planning. These include topic or theme planning, activity plans, weekly plans, individual children's plans and many more. As with planning for the under 3s the themes, principles and areas of learning and development need to be planned for. Another area that needs to be considered is how the routine and the 'routine' parts of day need to be planned for and linked to the Early Years Foundation Stage. These include welcoming children to the setting in the morning and saying goodbye at the end of the day; mealtimes; hygiene routines; dressing; the pattern of the day and many other parts of the day.

A Chance to Think 4.10

Mealtimes

Think about the mealtimes or snack times in your setting and how they are carried out. Evaluate how well you think they meet the needs of the children.

Write down how mealtimes link to the themes in the EYFS.

Compare your answers to the sample answers in Appendix 4.

Whichever type of planning documentation is used, practitioners need to ensure they show: how they provide for differentiation and take into account individual children's needs; how the indoor and outdoor environment will be set out; a balance between child-initiated / adult-led activities; what resources are to be used and how; how staff are to be deployed; what the learning outcomes are for activities and how they will be evaluated.

Some settings find it useful to have a long-term plan around a theme with short-term plans to provide further detail. This allows the whole room, or if appropriate, the whole setting, to concentrate on one theme, ensuring continuity between practitioners. It should be flexible enough to take into account the needs of individual children in the setting. It ensures that anti-discriminatory practice is incorporated into the theme from the start, and extends all children's learning in a planned and positive way.

A Chance to Think 4.11

Planning around a theme

We have seen the six areas covered by the early learning goals are: 1) Personal, Social and Emotional Development; 2) Communication, Language and Literacy; 3) Problem Solving, Reasoning and Numeracy; 4) Knowledge and Understanding of the World; 5) Physical Development; 6) Creative Development.

Using these areas, plan two activities for each area around the theme of food. You may wish to look at the theme of Toys in Figure 4.2 for guidance.

Compare your answers to the sample answers in Appendix 4.

This is not the only way of planning. As we saw earlier there are many other ways with which practitioners will be familiar. Try and think about the different ways of planning, what their good and bad points are and which ones would be most suitable for your setting.

Planning is good practice and helps practitioners to provide a balanced high quality play that incorporates anti-discriminatory practice as a central focus to meet children's individual needs. Play is essential for all children and as we have seen a requirement of legislation in the UN Convention on the Rights of the Child and in the Childcare Act 2006.

Children and young people age 5–16

In Chapter 1 we discussed the national curriculum and the key stages in it. It is easy to think that as children grow older they do not need to play, or they 'grow out of play'. As children grow older the nature of and how they play will change, but play is still a vitally important part of a child's life at any age. Older children still need to be able to play for all the same reasons that younger children play, and play needs to take place both indoors and outside. Anti-discriminatory practice needs to be incorporated into this, as with any other stage of a child's life. All areas of play need to be provided for and children and young people need the opportunity to play on their own and with others.

Topic Planning – Toys and Games

Personal, Social and Emotional Development

1. Talk about children's favourite toys and how it makes them feel
2. Play games that encourage sharing toys
3. Go on a trip to a toy museum
4. Invite people in to talk about the toys they like and to play games.
5. Making choices about what to play with
6. Set up a toy shop and take encourage children to take on different roles.

Knowledge and Understanding of the World

1. Design a toy, talk about how it can be made and what tools and materials are needed.
2. Talk about toys now and then. Find pictures of toys from different eras. Talk to parents about what they liked to ploy with as a child.
3. Talk about toys and games played in different countries and where possible try them.

Communication, Language and Literacy

1. Introduce vocabulary around toys and talk about the role of toys. Are toys and games known by different names?
2. Read and look at books about toys e.g. Ruby the parcel bear.
3. Make a book about the visit to the toy museum
4. Look for and talk about pictures and writing on toys and games, what do they tell us?
5. Make instructions for games and signs for the toy shop

Physical Development

1. Use tools to make the toy they have designed.
2. Use toys and play games outside e.g hopscotch, skipping games, obstacle course
3. Encourage children to put games pieces together

Problem Solving, Reasoning and Numeracy

1. Play negash, dominoes, talk about numbers, and use language such as more than, less than, how many is that?
2. Make a Dreidel and use it to play games with
3. Draw out a hopscotch game, what shapes and numbers do you see?
4. Make a time line of toys and games.
5. Make signs and money for the toy shop

Creative Development

1. Make a toy using a variety of materials. Display them.
2. Move like toys to music about toys e.g. Coppalia, Serenade to the Doll
3. Sing songs about toys e.g. jack in a Box
4. Play in the toy shop.
5. Act out stories about toys.

Figure 4.2 Planning on the theme of Toys

We have seen what play is, why children play, what they learn from play and have touched on the role of the adult in play. We will now look in more detail at the role of the adult, the environment, resources, and at some very practical examples of anti-discriminatory play activities that can be used and adapted for children and young people. It is not possible to mention every single idea, but the following sections give some ideas for different areas. Some of the suggestions may be adapted, depending on the age, abilities and particular needs of the children involved in them.

The role of the adult

The practitioner has many things to think about when working with children. Practitioners need to provide a choice of anti-discriminatory planned, child-initiated and adult-led activities in a safe, stimulating and secure environment. Practitioners should check resources for safety and evaluate them before the children use them to ensure they fulfil the requirements of anti-discriminatory practice.

Equipment, resources and activities should be displayed attractively so that they look inviting to play with. Children like to choose and put out toys and practitioners should encourage them to do this, as it helps develop a child's independence and self-esteem. There needs to be a choice of activities that support all areas of learning laid out in an environment that enables all children to have access to them. Some may be on tables and some may be on the floor. Whatever the layout, practitioners need to ensure that all children are able to move around the environment easily. Sometimes the environment or the equipment will need to be adapted or used on a one-to-one basis with children, depending on their age, individual needs and abilities. Practitioners also need to be aware of the requirements of children's dress, when to provide protective clothing, and how and when it may not be appropriate to adjust or remove children's clothing because of religious or cultural requirements.

One of the most important aspects of the practitioners role in children's play is his or her attitude towards it. Practitioners should encourage children in their play and be positive about their achievements. Children should be provided with both familiar and new experiences in play that stimulate them, so that they learn through play and have fun at the same time. If workers have a negative or discriminatory attitude towards play or particular types of play, this will be picked up by the children. We saw in Chapter 1 that young children pick up behaviour and attitudes from people and the environment in which they live. The same applies to play. If children are told that certain toys are boys' or girls' toys they will accept this and it will influence the attitudes they have towards them and if and how they play with them. It is therefore important for practitioners to try and present a positive attitude. Practitioners should provide children with experiences that help them to counteract stereotypes both in the resources they provide and in the way they help children to become individuals who are proud to be who they are and feel a valued member of the setting.

Another important role practitioners have in children's play is supervision, direction and involvement. The level of supervision that is required will vary according to the type of play, how familiar the children are with the resources, and the children themselves who are involved in it. Practitioners will need to make continual judgements about what is appropriate for different situations. Some activities require one-to-one supervision or adult involvement. Other activities require the practitioner to 'keep an eye on them' from a short distance away, with no direct involvement in them. Because of the different levels of supervision or involvement needed, it is important for practitioners to know all the children in their care well and know what their needs are. This will guide practitioners as to when, how and what is appropriate and necessary on each occasion. One day it may be appropriate to sit on the floor and be involved in children's play. Another day it may not be appropriate. Sometimes it is necessary to intervene carefully and sensitively in children's play. This may be at a child's request; in order to extend play, or to introduce a new concept; if play or language is becoming discriminatory and children are being upset; or if play is becoming dangerous. Practitioners should not interfere in children's play but intervene appropriately.

Practitioners need to have a thorough knowledge and understanding of child development and how children grow and develop at their own individual rate within this framework. The Early Years Foundation Stage has a commitment on child development. It starts by saying: 'Babies and young children develop in individual ways and at varying rates. Every area of development – physical, cognitive, linguistic, spiritual, social emotional, is equally important.' Practitioners need to know and respect every individual they care for and provide for their needs. This includes knowing the children's likes and dislikes, as well as being aware of, and providing for, the resources they need to help them to grow and develop as secure individuals possessing a strong sense of self, identity and self-esteem. Resources will be discussed later in this chapter and the development of identity and self-esteem in Chapter 5. We saw earlier the importance of observation skills linked into the planning cycle. In order to provide for individuals and groups of children, practitioners need to develop good observational skills, which are then used to observe and evaluate practice. By observing children, practitioners can gain a greater understanding of them. They can find out a great deal about the skills, knowledge, understanding and attitudes that children possess, as well as the strengths and needs a child may have. This information can then be used to help practitioners plan their provision and also share and exchange information with the parents of the child. In addition it can be used to help the development of the team and the setting.

Before undertaking observations, practitioners need to ensure they have thought about and planned for the purpose of the observation. Practitioners need to have thought about confidentiality, what this means, how to maintain it, when issues cannot be kept confidential and they must have spoken to parents about observations and obtained permission for them and ensure that parents are clear about how observations will be used in the setting, the resources needed, the context of the observation and its aims and objectives, the type of observation needed, the rights of the child and parents, their own role in observing and what will be done with the observation. Practitioners need to be aware of the role they play in observing and the bias they bring to it. As we have seen, all practitioners bring a part of themselves to their practice. The same is true for observation skills. Just by observing a child, practitioners are choosing what to, and what not to, observe. These choices can influence the picture of a child that comes from the observations. They may be a participant observer or non-participant observer. Just by being present, a practitioner may alter a child's behaviour, and they need to be aware of that. We have seen how children's behaviour and attitudes may be influenced by, for example, culture, gender and the environment in which they live. All children are different, and practitioners need to be aware of a child's background and take this information on board when observing. Practitioners may subconsciously 'set children up to fail' by their own lack of understanding about observations and how to undertake them. Observation styles and recording can take many different forms, including free description, structured description, pre-coded categories, longitudinal studies, target child, sociograms and tracking. Practitioners need to ensure they are clear when making observations, how to make an assessment from them and how to use this information. Practitioners need to keep records in their setting as required by the EYFS. Practitioners also need to be aware of the requirements of the Data Protection Act 1998 and the Freedom of Information Act 2000 when keeping records. Chapter 1 illustrates some of the issues practitioners need to be aware of when working with parents within an anti-discriminatory framework. When keeping records it is important that practitioners share information with parents and are aware of the difference between fact and opinion, and how they are recorded. As with all areas of work record-keeping needs to be discussed and understood by the whole team.

Teamwork and its importance was discussed in Chapter 1.

One of the most important things that practitioners need to be aware of at all times, and in all areas of their work, is that they are seen as role models and representatives of the setting in which they work. Everyone they come into contact with – children, parents, other professionals and individuals who visit the setting – will see them in that light. They will either consciously or subconsciously make judgements about the way practitioners present themselves, what they do, or do not do, and what they say, or do not say. We saw earlier in this chapter that individuals develop attitudes and opinions from the things they see, or do not see, in their environment. Practitioners are part of that environment and so need constantly to be aware of the role and the impact they have in people's lives.

Resources

The resources and equipment used in the setting are very important for many reasons. They can have a powerful effect on children. They provide a starting point for play, as well as extending it. How resources and equipment are presented to children will influence how it is used. The images in it will be absorbed by children, and because they are presented by adults whom children trust, children will take these images, and the messages they contain, on board. This is why it is extremely important for practitioners to evaluate all resources before children have access to them, including resources and equipment that have been bought, borrowed or made. All children should have access to the resources that are available in the setting.

All equipment and resources in the setting need to be evaluated to see what kind of messages they give to people who use them. Resources containing visual images, such as books, jigsaws, and posters, should contain positive images of the individuals and groups that make up society. Images should be realistic, and not exotic or caricatured. They should not marginalize people, (e.g. jigsaws containing pictures of people in wheelchairs but in the background). The images should not stereotype individuals, (e.g. women always doing the cleaning). Pictures of families should show the different types of families that are represented in society. Not all families are made up of a mother, father and two children. Some families have one parent; some have step-parents or extended families. Some children live in gay and lesbian families and some children live with foster parents or in residential settings away from their birth families. It is important that whatever background children come from, or whatever individual characteristics children have, they see positive images of themselves and their family in the equipment and resources in the setting. Children also pick up messages from what they do not see and practitioners need to be aware of this. Parents, carers, television and other media may give children negative messages about some individuals and groups in society, and practitioners need to address this. We live in a diverse world. The equipment and resources that are used with children need to reflect this. They should help everybody to value and respect diversity.

Resources

Sometimes it is difficult or expensive to get good-quality resources and equipment that have positive images of different groups in society. Recently a practitioner was looking for good-quality books featuring families and children of mixed heritage. It was possible to find some, but not many compared with the total number of books published and it took time and going to a specialist early years book seller to find them. This, though, should not be seen as an excuse for not having any resources. There are many ways to get equipment and resources. Parents can be a good source of resources, and asking them to be involved in helping the setting promotes partnership working and good practice. By working together, children and parents know that they have a valuable contribution to make to the setting. It is also something that parents can do that does not cost any money but has a big impact on their child's life and the setting. Parents may be able to write captions for displays in languages other than English. They may be able to lend the setting equipment from their home or provide suggestions for cooking or menus. Local markets can often be a good place to buy resources that are cheaper and more authentic than those in catalogues. Visiting local markets also makes a good outing for the children, who get to see the variety of goods for sale, and can also help to choose what to buy (e.g. fruit and vegetables such as yams, mangoes and lychees for lunch; hair extension for a hairdressing corner; or materials for the tables or displays). It also is possible for practitioners and children to make resources. Photos of children, or that children have taken, are useful and very versatile. They are specific to the children and the setting and can be used to create, for example, a photo book about an outing, an 'All About Me' book or a time line. Children can see images of themselves involved in something positive and will enjoy the process of making it together. Remember that it is essential to get permission from parents to take and use photos of children.

Observation and planning can help practitioners to decide when and which resources to use. All resources should meet the needs of individual and groups of children. A child with a disability may also need some particular toys and resources to enable them to play and participate in activities. The fact sheet 'Choosing Children's Play Equipment' published by the Disabled Living Foundation says,

> because there are so many toys available in high street shops and specialist catalogues, parents need to take care when choosing to ensure they are not wasting their money . . . Remember that children need access to fun toys as well as therapeutic and educational toys. However, parents can be creative in their use of household objects and scrap materials, as well as with brought toys, so that as many stimulating and fun activities can be achieved from each toy by using them in ways other than the purpose for which they were designed.

While having a variety of resources in the setting that promotes positive images is important, it is equally important for practitioners to continually evaluate these resources. Teams need to consider how they choose and use resources. Having resources that are anti-discriminatory does not make a setting, or the practitioners in it, work in an anti-discriminatory way. Indeed, as stated earlier, it is possible to use resources in a negative, discriminatory or stereotypical way – for example, by using resources only at a particular time of year for example, putting woks and chopsticks in the home corner only at Chinese New Year, or if practitioners make discriminatory comments when putting out resources or do not sit down and use them actively with the children. All these actions give children messages that the resources, and those individuals reflected in them, are not valued and respected by the individuals using them. As we have seen all the way through this book, it is the attitudes that practitioners have and the way these come out in their behaviour and language which is important. Practitioners need to be constantly evaluating their own attitudes and ways of working, as well as providing resources and using them effectively.

> ## A Chance to Think 4.12
>
> ### Resources
> Look at some of the equipment and resources that are used regularly with the children in your setting. Think about the images they contain, how they are used, who uses them and the messages they are giving to the children.
>   Is there any equipment, or way in which the equipment is being used, of which you feel particularly proud? Why is this?
>   Is there any equipment, or way in which the equipment is being used, about which you feel uneasy? Why is this?
>   Can you think of what you can do to celebrate and build on the positive, and anything you can do that will stop you feeling uneasy?

The environment

The environment plays a huge part in how children feel and act in a setting. The EYFS has a theme called 'Enabling Environments' and the principle that underpins this theme says: 'the environment plays a key role in supporting and extending children's development and learning'. It also has a welfare requirement in the statutory framework titled 'Suitable Premises, Environment and Equipment'.

When thinking about the environment it is important to remember that it is much more than just the physical environment, although this is very important and has a big impact on all other aspects of the environment. The emotional, social, communication and intellectual environments are equally important and all overlap and interlink with each other.

The physical environment includes both the indoor and outdoor surroundings. Practitioners need to evaluate how accessible their environment is to both children and adults. Can people get into the setting and can they move around within it easily and are children able to play outside every day? How does the layout of the environment affect and influence who comes into it? How it is used and what happens in it? The emotional and social environment relates to how people feel and interact in the setting. Do they feel welcome, valued and respected? Do they feel 'at home' in the setting and feel part of the whole of the setting and not just there on sufferance? Are children and adults encouraged to express how they feel in and about the setting? Does the setting promote and provide for developing a positive sense of self? Does the physical layout of the setting allow for people to be on their own when they need to, and in pairs or in small and larger groups? Does the environment allow for different types and styles of communication? Is the notice board accessible and up to date? Can people hear each other or is there lots of background noise, for example, from radios that distract people? Is there a place to go for private or confidential communications? Are practitioners tuned into children and parents and helping to engage in and facilitate communication? Is the environment set up to cater for different learning styles as mentioned earlier? Do practitioners welcome and respond to questions from both children and adults and promote questing, thoughtful, reflective and inquisitive attitudes in children and adults? Do practitioners think about their own learning and intellectual styles?

Art

Art in one form or another takes place in most settings on most days. The Concise Oxford Dictionary defines 'art' as 'creative activity, especially painting and drawing resulting in visual representation'. 'What is art to one person is not art to another person.' It is a very individual concept and everyone knows what they like and do not like and it can evoke strong feelings in people. This is as true for children as it is of adults.

How can anti-discriminatory practice be incorporated into art? When thinking about painting we need to acknowledge that there are many different forms and styles of painting. Most settings have an easel that is set up for the children to use. It is important that children are able to reach the easel and use it. Some children may need physical help to stand at an easel. Some children may not be able to use an easel at all. If this is so, they should still have access to painting. It may be easier for them to paint at a table, on the floor or on an adapted easel.

Thought needs to be given to the colours of the paint, pencils and crayons provided. It is important to provide skin-coloured paints, crayons and pencils in all the different skin tones, so that children can produce representations of themselves or others. These should be available all the time, not just on special occasions or for particular activities. Most catalogues now sell skin-tone crayons, pencils and ready mixed skin-tone paints, but if settings cannot afford these or are having difficulty getting hold of them, they should mix up their own paints. This is a good activity to do with children, as it gives them chance to talk in a positive way about their skin colour and that of their friends and other people. Children like drawing pictures of themselves and other people. They are aware of differences in skin colour and it is the responsibility of practitioners to ensure that an environment is created where children value both themselves and others. It is only by talking about skin colour differences and addressing the issue that this can be done.

Painting does not just have to take place with brushes. There are many other methods of painting including bubble painting, string painting, foot painting, finger painting , fruit and vegetable painting, roller painting and bike painting to name but a few. These various forms develop different skills and different results. All children can have a go at them and they can produce beautiful results, although it is important to remember the process of creating art is as valuable as the finished product. When you are painting or printing with fruit and vegetables, try to use things like pineapples and plantains as well as apples and potatoes. Teams need to talk about how and why they use food for activities as some practitioners and parents may not feel comfortable using food in this way. Bike painting takes place outdoors, which may be a new experience for some children. Cover the floor with paper, put down the paint and let children ride through it creating an abstract design. Children in buggies or wheelchairs can also take part in this with practitioners making sure they wash the wheels when they have finished. Children's efforts should be noticed and acknowledged. Not all children will be producing the same thing; each one will produce a unique piece of art work. Ten children producing ten identical pieces of work is not art.

Art is an individual experience. If a child thinks something is beautiful, then it is beautiful to him or her. Art is also about appreciating the creations of others. Children should be given the opportunity to see art created by others, perhaps by a visit to an art gallery, or by watching a parent or other adult doing an art activity. It is also important to display both the children's and other people's art attractively. Posters of original paintings can now be brought quite cheaply. Again, there should be a variety of these by different artists from different cultures and backgrounds (e.g. African art, Indian art, modern art etc.). Children should be encouraged to talk about these. How do they make them feel? Which ones do they like? Do they have pictures at home? If so, what sort?

Communication, language and literacy

Communication, language and literacy can often be difficult to separate from other activities, as communication and language are such a central part of most activities. It is important, though, to think about them separately, so as to ensure that practitioners are meeting the needs of children and families in the setting, as well as providing positive examples of communication, language and literacy styles. Language development is discussed in greater detail in Chapter 5. One of the first areas of mind when thinking about communication is how effective children are at communicating in a variety of ways, including body language, tone of voice, signs and gestures and spoken language. Practitioners need to be able to communicate effectively with children who may not use a spoken language or who have started using words yet. Games that enhance mutual communication including finger rhymes such as 'round and round the garden' are effective, as are song boxes which are discussed further in the section on dance and music.

Another activity that promotes communication, language and literacy is the book corner. Practitioners should provide a variety of books for children; story books with stories from a variety of countries and cultures; different themes, non-fiction and interest books; picture books in a variety of illustrative styles; books in a variety of different languages including dual language books, and books with sign and symbol languages and Braille. Practitioners must check books before using them with the children so as to evaluate whether they are suitable. The sort of things they should be looking for are the suitability for the age range of the children, the language used in it, the images the books contain, and whether the images are, or are not, stereotypical, tokenistic or caricatured. Children need to see positive images of individuals and groups of people. Books should not present people or situations as exotic. Children need images to which they can relate and that are part of their everyday experiences, as well as books that will introduce them to new ideas in a way that values the diversity of the world. All children need to see themselves reflected in the books in the setting, so that they feel valued as individuals. For example, a child who wears glasses needs to see children who are the main character in books wearing glasses. Children also need to be introduced to new concepts, images and ways of doing things that may be unfamiliar to them as well. There are a variety of places to get books from, including book clubs, shops and libraries. Children often like to bring in their own books to read in the setting and it is equally important for practitioners to check these before reading them to the children. Another way of getting books into the setting that reflects all the children in the setting is to make books with the children. These can feature illustrations done by the children or photos of the children, or taken by the children (with parental permission). Parents might also be able to provide books, illustrations, or text written in languages other than English. This makes the books very specific to the setting and helps children to be involved in making books and becoming an author. Another idea to help all children develop communication, language and literacy skills is to make a story sack. Parents can help to make these. Choose a story that the children like as a starting point. Find, or make, a bag to put everything in. In the story sack should be everything relating to the story you have chosen; a book of the story, if possible in more than one language, props, a fact book relating to the story, a game, if possible a tape of the story, a poem related to it and any other items you feel you would like to include. A story sack benefits all children as it can be used on a one-on-one basis and with small and large groups. Parents can be involved in making it and can take it home to use with their children. It is also possible to play stories on a tape, CD or player. These can be put in the book corner so that children can listen to stories on their own, learning to turn pages on their own when the story tells them to. Children can then listen to parts of the story again and again and take their time over it.

Another way to develop language and listening skills is to play sound lotto games. The soundtracks lotto from UNICEF has many positive sounds and images from a variety of countries and cultures on it. Music CDs in a variety of languages are also a good way of introducing children to a variety of languages. This will be discussed further in the section on dance and music. Picture cards can also be used to promote language skills. These are cards with either just a picture on them or a picture and caption on them saying what the picture is. There may be several cards in a series, which need to be put together in the right order to tell a story. These can be brought from most catalogues but it is very easy to make them with the children with photos or pictures cut

Children looking at books

from magazines. This has several advantages; it is cheaper than buying them, practitioners can ensure the images are positive, they are specific to the setting and parents can be involved in providing images and helping write captions. All labelling, wherever it is in the setting, should be clear and in a variety of languages; on children's paintings, the notice boards for parents and on displays. If children's coat pegs are labelled with their names, then for those children whose home language does not use the Latin script, it is possible to write their names in both English and their home script, thus encouraging children to recognize their names in both scripts and showing that both are valued. This can also be done for any work they produce, such as paintings, if the setting has labels printed off with children's names on in one or two languages. This supports all children as they can then take a label with their name on and put it on their own work.

Construction

Construction toys are available in most settings from traditional wooden blocks to kits such as Duplo, stickle bricks and many others. There are many wonderful things that can be done with construction kits, and it is important that all children have access to them. Some people may think of them as boys' toys. We know this is not true: girls have as much enjoyment and learn a great deal from construction toys just as boys do.

As already discussed, the role of the adult in setting out construction toys, whether on the floor, or on a table, and how they supervise and join in this play is important in ensuring that all children have access to this type of play. Some children may need help in manipulating, or putting together, some construction toys. In addition it might help if practitioners describe the equipment, as all children learn from hearing about things. This can be particularly true for children with a visual impairment, who might also need time to explore the equipment. It is possible to get construction toys with very large pieces, which may be more appropriate for some children. They are fun, as all children can see progress being made very quickly and almost life-size models can be created.

There are many exciting things that can be put out with construction toys. Farm animals, wild animals, sand and water can make landscapes, countries, seas and boats, diggers and dumpers to make a building site. Pens and paper can be put out with construction toys so that children can plan and design what they are going to make. Pictures can also be put out to give children inspiration: for example, pictures of different styles of homes; caravans, house-boats, houses, high-rise flats. Play people, dolls or Duplo world people can be put in the homes or other buildings children make to add realism.

Cooking

The only chance some children get to experience cookery activities is in a child care setting. When cooking activities take place it is important to ensure that both boys and girls participate in all aspects of them, including the preparation of ingredients, the actual cooking and the clearing away. The ingredients used must be appropriate for the children taking part in the activity. For example, a Hindu child may not be allowed to use ingredients that have beef products in them, because the Hindu religion considers the cow to be a holy animal and it is not eaten.

Children can be introduced to ingredients and food that they have not experienced before. For example, fresh fruit salad could use mangoes, pineapples and lychees as well as oranges, bananas and apples. Sandwiches could be made using French bread, wraps, pitta bread, and chiabatta as well as sliced bread. Shopping in the market or in a supermarket can be an activity in which the children are involved in choosing ingredients. Practitioners can also point out the different languages and scripts used on some packaging and talk about from where things originate. Some parents might like to come into the setting and be involved in cooking activities, or might be able to provide recipes and recipe books for the setting.

Craft

There are many different craft activities that can be done with children. As in art, it is the process of being involved in craft activities that is more important than the finished product. Craft activities include cutting, sticking, collage, papier maché, junk modelling, modelling, making mobiles and much more.

Often old Christmas cards and birthday cards or pages from catalogues and travel brochures, are used for cutting activities. These may provide children with images that are mainly white European and Christian (e.g. white Father Christmas, models in smart clothes, holiday destinations). It is important when you are providing children with these types of cutting experiences, to think about the type of messages that children are receiving from these images. For example, a child who is a Jehovah's Witness does not celebrate Christmas or birthdays, but may be cutting out cards from these celebrations. Asking parents of different religions or cultural backgrounds to bring in cards, or finding other cards ensures that children have a variety of images to cut out. This needs to be done sensitively, as some parents may find it offensive for children to cut up cards that have religious significance, and this is something the setting may need to address. Instead of cards, pictures from magazines could be used, and they should be pictures of diverse things such as animals, landscapes, homes, buildings, elderly people and people's faces. Different styles of materials are also good for cutting as they provide a different experience from cutting paper. Some children, particularly children who have never used scissors before, may need some help in learning how to cut. Dual-handled scissors can be used to help with this. It is important to provide left-handed as well as right-handed scissors and tools, as it is very difficult for children who are left-handed to use right-handed scissors and tools.

In sticking activities the same holds true about the images being used as in the cutting activities. One sticking activity that extends children's awareness of themselves and others is to make a collage of people. This could include people in the setting, both children and adults. All the children in the setting could be involved in drawing a picture of themselves, or they could take photos and cut them out. The activity could be extended by cutting out as many different pictures of people from magazines as the children can find. Again ensuring that these images show people of different ages, colour of skin, cultures, religions, gender, disability, doing different jobs and much more.

The finished picture can then be mounted and displayed. Another activity that extends children's awareness of the world is making smell or touch pictures. This can be done by using spices such as nutmeg, fresh and dried herbs, or anything else that can be stuck down to make a picture that smells. Only use one smell at a time or it can get too overpowering and check that no one is allergic to the items you are using. Touch pictures can be made with any resources that have different feels to them such as carpet, different styles and types of materials, dried herbs, rice, different shaped pasta, and so on. Remember that touch pictures can be extended to make feely boards for feet as well. Children can be introduced to new smells and textures, and much discussion will come out of this. What does it smell or feel like? What do you think it is? What do you think it is used for? Where do you think it comes from? This activity is good for all children, and especially those who may need in help developing their senses. Work with papier maché is a very good craft activity that can be used to make all sorts of exciting things; moonscapes, landscapes, balloon mobiles, pintas, models and much more. When you are making papier maché, try and use papers in languages other than English, so that children see different scripts and styles of writing. Newspapers and magazines can now be bought in newsagents in many different languages, or perhaps parents or colleagues could bring some in. Another way of introducing children to different scripts and languages is through junk modelling. Try to use boxes and cartons that have different languages and scripts on them. This is now fairly easy, as most packets have more than one language on them. If necessary, ingredients for cooking can be bought from shops that stock packets in different languages. They can first be used for cooking and then saved for junk modelling. The table can also be covered in newspaper that is in a language other than English.

A Chance to Think 4.13

Craft activity

You have been asked to prepare and carry out a craft activity for a group of children age 6 and 7. One of the children, Veronique, is partially sighted. The things she sees are fuzzy and she has difficulty seeing things that are close up. This is the first time you have done an activity with this group of children. .

What do you need to consider when planning this activity?

What sort of activity will you do?

How will you ensure that all the children are able to participate in the activity?

What is your role when doing this activity with the children?

Compare your answers with the sample answers in Appendix 4.

Dance and music

Most adults enjoy some sort of music and dance, and so do children. There are many different styles of dance and music; ballet, jazz, tap, modern, ballroom, street dance, country and Western, reggae, soul, rap, calypso, garage and pop music to name but a few. It is important that all children have the opportunity to listen to, and appreciate, different kinds of music and dance and to dance or to move in different styles.

Children can be introduced to dance and movement by being allowed to move in the way the music makes them feel, as well as being shown and introduced too new and unfamiliar movements. If dance and movement sessions become too formal, children may feel inhibited. Dancing and movement sessions should be an enjoyable occasion for children. Movement is one way for children to express themselves though music. For some children, music and movement sessions can be very therapeutic. It is important during dance and movement sessions for different types of music from around the world to be played to children. Pictures of a variety of people from around the world dancing and moving in different styles can be displayed, and as used as a starting point for discussion.

Music can be played to help mark different parts of the routine so that children are aware of the changes in the day. Music can also influence children's behaviour. Try using music of different beats and tempos for different tasks for example, quiet soothing music at rest time. Music can also influence children's feelings and emotions and practitioners need to be aware of this and support children. Music from all around the world can be put on and used with headphones so that children can choose and listen to it on their own. Different styles of world music can be bought quite easily or parents and colleagues may be able to bring in music that they like. Practitioners need to try and evaluate the music and lyrics before playing them to the children to ensure they are suitable and do not contain any inappropriate language as some songs can contain words and messages that are very negative towards some individuals and groups. Sometimes this is difficult if the words are in a language not spoken in the setting.

Another way of making music is with voices or instruments. All settings sing songs almost every day. It is important to introduce children to a variety of songs and different styles and languages. These need to be introduced with a positive attitude, with practitioners showing they are valued and enjoyed. Children and adults may not understand the words of a song, for example, 'Frère Jaques' is commonly sung, but some adults, as well as children, do not understand what they are singing. However it can still be sung and enjoyed and translated where possible. Parents may be able to teach practitioners short songs in their own language. This makes parents feel valued and gives children the opportunity to experience and value a variety of languages. Some parents in the setting may want to know why children are singing songs in a variety of languages. Practitioners should feel confident about using different languages and be able to explain to parents why it is a positive experience for the children and the setting. One practical way of ensuring practitioners remember the words is to write them down and keep a song list handy so that a range of songs are sung. Another way is to make a song box with the children. This can be done by decorating an empty box and filling it with props for a range of songs and having the words written out and laminated. It is a good idea to start with songs you and the children like. Props could include a small doll for songs such as 'Miss Polly had a Dolly', frogs for '5 Little Specked Frogs', a rabbit for 'Little Peter Rabbit has a fly upon his nose' or sleeping bunnies and a small teddy bear for 'Round and Round the Garden'. Remember to ensure the props and laminated words and pictures provide positive images. A song box helps all children to participate in the session as they can hold a prop or pick one out of the box to choose a song.

Music sessions with instruments are also a good way of expanding children's musical experience, It is not very easy to buy a range of good quality authentic instruments from around the world, such as small steel drums, tablas, pan pipes and maracas. Because these are not made of plastic they introduce children to different sounds and ways of making music. It is not necessary for the setting to have lots of expensive instruments. Children enjoy making their own instruments and making music from everyday things, such as rulers, spoons and empty pits. Making and using instruments introduces children to concepts such as pitch, tone and volume and stimulates the senses.

A Chance to Think 4.14

Music

You are working in the toddler room in your setting with children age from 15 months to 2 years. You are organizing a music session involving some of the children, which includes instruments and songs. James, one of the children in the room, has a hearing impairment with moderate hearing loss.

How will you prepare for this session?

What sort of things will you do in it?

How will you ensure that James is able to participate in the session?

Compare your answers to the sample answers in Appendix 4.

Displays and interest tables

When displays or interest tables are used with children, one of the most important things to ensure is that they can see and be involved in them. One way of checking if children can see them is for practitioners to get down to a child's height and check. Displays can include large wall pictures done by the children, posters, photos or displays of children's work. It is important that whatever the display, practitioners check the images that are in it, to ensure they contain positive images of the groups that make up society. Images should be realistic and not exotic or caricatured. They should not marginalize people, or stereotype individuals. Displays should be labelled to introduce children to the written language. Displays can be labelled in a variety of languages, including symbol languages such as Bliss symbols, and parents might be able to help with this.

Children should be involved in putting together displays. Some children may be involved in getting the picture or display ready; other children can help practitioners to assemble it. Attractive displays of the 'work' children have done, something they have made, such a model from dough or a piece of art work, show that practitioners value what children do. Children's work should be displayed attractively where they can see it and show it to parents, carers or friends. All children should have the opportunity to display their work. It does not matter that it may be unrecognizable to an adult; it is what it represents to the child that is important.

Many things can be used as backing for displays, including sugar paper, newspaper (in a variety of languages) and textured backing such as corrugated card and other material. Local markets often have different styles of material for sale or parents may be able to lend material occasionally. Children's work should be labelled with their name. For children who use a language with a different script from English this can be done both in the script of their first language and also in English. Children's work can also be labelled with an explanation of what it is, using the children's own words. Displays should be maintained and changed regularly to keep everyone interested in them so that they do not become out of date, torn, dirty and unattractive.

Interest tables can be on a variety of subjects. They may be linked to a theme that is taking place in the setting or they may be nature tables or number or letter tables. Interest tables should be at child height, so the children can see them and be involved with them. Children can provide ideas for interest tables, bring things in from home for it or find things in the setting. Like all displays, interest tables should be labelled and laid out attractively. They should contain new and familiar things, for example, an interest table about fruit should have both new and familiar fruits. Children should be able to experience an interest table with all of their senses: looking at it; lifting things up and feeling them; tasting and smelling them and where appropriate, listening to them. This will both stimulate the sense and encourage discussion.

A Chance to Think 4.15

Interest tables

Your setting is going to work on a theme on 'Homes' and you have been asked to set up an interest table and display with the children. The children involved are between 2–5 years old. Some of the children live in bed-and-breakfast accommodation; others live in a variety of accommodation including, flats, houseboats and houses.

How would you involve the children?

What sort of things would you include in it?

Compare your answers with the sample answers in Appendix 4.

Drama and imaginative play

Imaginative play is a great way for children to explore roles in a safe and secure environment. They may play the part of a bus driver, a dentist, a parent or even a childcare worker. All children should have access to imaginative play and boys and girls should have equal access. It is perfectly natural for a boy to want to dress up in all kinds of clothes and act out roles, and this will not impede his development. Boys and girls may play with imaginative toys and role play in different ways, even if they have the same resources to start with and practitioners need to be aware of how children are playing and what they are interested in. There are many good things about imaginative play – children can do it on their own or with others, with equipment and resources, or without, and they can make pictures and stories in their head about new or familiar experiences. They can try roles out and see 'how they fit' and it enhances all areas of development.

Drama can be provided in a variety of ways. It does not have to be a big production for anyone in particular or for a special occasion. Children love to act out their favourite stories. Practitioners should try to ensure children have a wide choice of stories to choose from, including stories from a variety of cultures as well as stories depicting people in non-stereotypical roles, (e.g. 'Princess Smartypants' by Babette Cole is a funny story about a princess who does not want to get married). Children should be encouraged to act out the role they feel happy with, so that if a girl wants to act out the character in a story that is actually a boy, that is quite acceptable. All children should be able to take part in drama and role-play. It is important for children to interpret stories without adults making the activity too formal, so that children are not frightened of making mistakes. Practitioners need to provide children with the props, imagination and time to explore the world of drama.

Most settings provide some kind of imaginative play daily, from farm animals to home corners. How can anti-discriminatory practices be incorporated in this area of children's play?

The home corner

Home corners can be very versatile places and can be turned into many different things. The props and equipment should be as accurate as possible and reflect the variety of cultures that make up society. For example, as well as plates, knives and forks, the home corner could also have in it thali dishes, woks, Chinese bowls and chopsticks. If these have not been used by the children before, it is important that they should be introduced to them so that they know what they are called, what they are for and how to use them. As emphasized all through this book, they should not just be put in a home corner for special occasions, but should be available to the children the whole time. Calendars and newspapers or magazines in a variety of languages and styles, together with pictures and photos of families or people in the setting, can make the home corner very specific to the setting.

Earlier in this chapter we discussed the fact that children live many different types of homes and this can be reflected in the setting and home corner in how it is set up and through the equipment and resources put in it. Other props in the home corner could include dressing-up clothes that reflect the different styles of clothes and materials available worldwide for example, saris, shalwar kameez or kimonos. Some people may feel that using these types of dressing up clothes, which are in fact children's versions of clothes worn daily by adults, is not appropriate, as people's cultural backgrounds and traditions are being trivialized by being used as playthings. The only way for practitioners to discover whether this is so is to ask parents and colleagues for their opinions. Both boys and girls should be encouraged to dress up if they want to. Some parents may worry if they see their son dressing up in skirts and dresses, and practitioners need to think about their response if parents say they do not want their son to play with dressing up clothes.

Dolls are a popular prop in the home corner. There should be a variety of dolls available for children to play with, for example, black dolls, mixed parentage / dual heritage dolls, dolls with special needs, baby dolls, elderly dolls, boy dolls, soft dolls as well as white girl dolls. There should also be a variety of clothes available to dress them in. Practitioners also need to think about access to the home corner, who is playing in it and the types of play that is taking place. For example, are the younger children, or the children with special needs, playing the role of the baby or someone who needs caring for? If so, practitioners need to intervene to ensure they are not always seen in this role, but are also able to play other roles.

Sometimes it is appropriate for practitioners to join in the play taking place, or to encourage children who do not generally play in the home corner to use it. Sometimes some of the home corner props need to be taken out of the home corner and then used in different areas of the setting so that children can use them.

The hospital or dentist corner

If settings do not have much space, the home corner can be turned into other types of imaginative and role play areas such as a hospital or dentist corner. In settings that do have a lot of space, a hospital or dentist corner may be set out at the same time as the home corner. Changing the home corner into a hospital or dentist corner allows children to act out any fears they may have and enables them to ask questions about these scenarios in a safe and secure environment. Some children will have to go to hospital and they will know about it in advance, for example to have ear grommets inserted. Some children may attend hospital regularly for ongoing treatment; other children may attend because of an accident or emergency, for example, a broken bone. Whichever type of visit, having played in a hospital corner may help children with this experience. Many children will visit a dentist and some settings have dentists come visit them to check children's teeth. Again having played dentists may help children prepare for their visit to the dentist.

Both boys and girls should be encouraged to take the roles of doctors, dentists, oral hygienists and nurses and not see the roles as gender stereotypes. Practitioners need to ensure that they provide clothes and resources that enable children to do this, for example, not just providing dresses for nurses to wear.

Dolls or teddies can often take the role of patients and there should be several dolls provided that reflect different cultural backgrounds. Children with special needs, or younger children, should not always take the role of the role of the patient but be the dentist, nurse or doctor.

Children may like to make get-well cards to use in the hospital. These can be made in languages other than English. Books about hospitals and dentists may also be used to expand the activity, and these should be checked to ensure they are not depicting stereotypical roles.

Sometimes it is possible to visit hospitals or dentists surgeries with small groups of children. This is particularly good if a child is due to go into hospital or to the dentist. It is also possible to ask dentists to visit the setting.

A Chance to Think 4.16

Props

Some settings feel that children should not be playing with props that represent doctor's instruments. For example, some practitioners in an environment where children are exposed to illegal drugs feel that giving children a replica of a syringe might encourage children to see its use as acceptable.

What is your opinion about this?

The hairdressing corner

In settings that do not have much space it is possible to turn the hairdressing corner into a hairdresser's salon or to make use of it as a separate activity. A variety of equipment should be provided, including aprons, plastic scissors, mirrors, curlers, Afro combs, brushes, old hairdryers with the flex cut off, hair magazines showing people with different styles and types of hair, calendars, and notices for the door saying what time the shop opens and closes, a telephone and a diary to take bookings in, a till and some money. Empty shampoo bottles, conditioner bottles or empty boxes of hair products can be used. These should be washed carefully first, and should show pictures of people with different types and styles of hair. It is also possible to get both black and white toy heads with hair on that children can style. Hair extensions can also be used in the hairdressing corner as well as hair covers as some people keep their hair covered after it has been washed.

Both boys and girls should be encouraged to use the hairdressing corner. Practitioners should remember that not all children will have visited a hairdresser's salon. Some children may never have had their hair cut and some children may keep their hair covered for religious or cultural reasons.

Table and floor toys

There are many toys that promote drama and imaginative play, including animals, cars, trains dolls and dolls houses, shops, puppets, telephones and many more. Whatever is put out for the children to play with, or if they can choose activities themselves, all children should have access to them. Practitioners should be aware of who is playing with what, and when it may be necessary to intervene appropriately if some children are being denied access to activities.

Sometimes it will be appropriate to set out an activity on the floor and other days it will be appropriate to put the same activity on a table. Practitioners need to monitor this as sometimes some children are unable to access toys on a table. It is also exciting for children when activities are mixed and matched. For example, putting the bricks and play people out with the train track, or cars and animals out with empty boxes in the sand tray. This ensures activities are kept fresh and different, and means that is acceptable to play with toys in a context different from that which they may have been intended.

Growing activities

Not all children will have the opportunity to grow things at home as they may not have an outside space and parents may not want to grow things indoors. Growing can take place outside and inside and children gain a lot from seeing things grow. If settings have a garden, even if it is just a small one, it is fairly easy to grow things. Practitioners need to think about what they are able to grow.

Herbs are very easy to grow and once established are also easy to maintain. They can make a lovely sensory garden for children to experience as they all have different smells, textures and tastes. They can then be picked and used in cooking. Flowers are also great but are seasonal and need more looking after. Practitioners can talk about where the flowers originated from and there are many songs about flowers that can be sung with the children.

Even if settings do not have anywhere to dig in their outside space it is still possible to grow things using pots or containers, even a tyre lined with newspaper can be used for growing things. It is possible to grow many things in containers including herbs, flowers, carrots, tomatoes, potatoes, peppers and many other things. It is also possible to grown things inside as well including herbs, mustard and cress and mung beans. These can then be used in cooking, sometimes introducing children to tastes they have not tried before.

Growing and looking after plants can introduce children to activities they may not have experienced previously and they can use tools during the activity that may be new to them, for example, a dibber. Practitioners need to be aware of, and provide for, children's individual needs such as skin care and allergies.

Heuristic play

Heuristic play was originally developed for children between 10–20 months but older children can participate in it as well. It was developed to enrich settings, not to replace work already taking place.

Heuristic play materials can include: woollen pom-poms, (not to big or in primary colours), smalls bags and boxes, cardboard cylinders of all kinds, ribbons, wood off-cuts, old keys tied together in small bunches, curtain rings (wooden and metal), wooden pegs, hair rollers, varied lengths of chain (fine to medium size links) and 3 tins per child. Because the materials are accessible 'every day' objects it means that this activity can be undertaken by all settings and by parents as well. The materials are laid out attractively on the floor in a large space for the children to explore.

In Heuristic play children learn from what objects will 'do' or 'not do'. There is no right or wrong way of doing things. This means that all children will gain a sense of achievement from taking part in this activity.

Malleable play

The Concise Oxford Dictionary defines 'malleable' as '(of metal etc.) able to be hammered or pressed permanently out of shape without breaking or cracking; adaptable, pliable, flexible'. The malleable activities that take place in settings usually involve clay, Plasticine and dough.

There are many ways to ensure that anti-discriminatory practices are incorporated into malleable play activities. These include putting out thali dishes, chapatti pans or Chinese bowls and chopsticks with the activity, instead of rolling pins, saucepans, and cutters. Dough can be made by the children with a variety of flours, including chapatti flour or wholemeal four. It can be made warm or cold, with different smells in it, for example, adding a few drop of vanilla or lavender essence, with different textures, using porridge oats, for example. This gives children different experiences when they touch it and try and mould it. We have discussed in this book the need for teams to be clear about their settings policy on using food as a play material as some parents may find it offensive.

Other types of malleable play include setting things in jelly, and then letting children pull them out. This is particularly good for younger children and children who need additional support developing their manipulative skills. Practitioners can also mix porridge oats or wallpaper paste with warm water and food colouring to make a sticky, pliable mixture. Cooked pasta is also good for this. If cannelloni is cooked with some oil and food colouring until it is just soft, and then left to cool, the children can use it like a construction toy, as it sticks together. Spaghetti cooked with oil and food colouring, cooled and put out and played with, will eventually form a dough that can be cut with scissors.

Some children like malleable play activities; they may find them soothing, relaxing or a way of releasing frustrations or emotions. Other children are not quite so keen on them; they may feel inhibited, not like the look or feel of them or be afraid of getting dirty. Protective clothing should be available for children so that their clothes do not get dirty.

Practitioners also need to be aware of skin care needs. A child who has sensitive skin, or eczema, may be reluctant to play with malleable material. It is possible to buy gloves for children to wear, or to make malleable material that will not aggravate the skin. Some children are allergic to some substances and smells so practitioners need to talk to parents to find out what it is their child can, and cannot, play with, and what action needs to be taken in the event that they accidently come into contact with it. If a child in the setting has an allergy that has harmful results then the setting may have to stop using certain things.

Manipulative play

Manipulative play involves such things as jigsaws, threading, pegs and peg boards, stacking toys, activity centres, sorting games, post boxes and many more. Like all toys, they should be checked to ensure they are suitable for the children in the setting. Jigsaws should contain positive images of all individuals and groups of people. Touch jigsaws, which are good for all children but particularly good for those who have a visual impairment, can be bought or made. It is possible to make jigsaws using photos to ensure that the puzzles have personal relevance to the setting. Puzzles can be made of festivals 'people who help us', outings and of individual children and groups of children in the setting. It is not just enough for practitioners to put out jigsaws, they need to sit with them with the children and talk to the children about the images in a positive way.

A variety of manipulative activities can be made which ensures that at least some are suitable for every child in the setting. This may be particularly necessary when you are working with children with disabilities or special needs, as some commercially available material may be expensive or not meet the needs of individual children. Threading activities can be made using pictures of buildings such as places of worship or pictures of food. Their size will depend on the abilities of the children for whom they are being made. Postboxes can also be made using boxes with one or two shapes to put in, or with more shapes as needed.

Outdoor play

Not all settings have an outside space in which children can play, but it is important that all children are able to go outside and play. Some children experience outdoor play only in the setting. This may be particularly true of children who live in high rise flats or alongside busy roads. Indeed the EYFS says that, 'if a setting does not have direct access to an outdoor play area then they must make arrangements for daily opportunities for outdoor play in an appropriate nearby location'. All of the things children play with indoors should be available outside as well, for example, sand, water and construction toys.

Outside play has exciting experiences of its own that cannot be replicated indoors, such as experiencing the weather (and the vitamin D from sunlight which helps bones develop and become strong), mud, digging in soil, plants and worms. These may be new experiences for some children, and they may need an explanation of what they are and encouragement to play with them. All children should be encouraged to explore the outside environment, which adults need to ensure is safe. Some children do not like getting dirty and, if necessary, protective clothing, including hats, for sand play, should be provided.

Children can do things on a much large scale outside than they can inside, for example, use large constriction equipment, use louder voices, move and use their body in a different way. Outside play can be damaging to the skin, especially in the summer, with the risks associated with exposure to the sun. All children, whatever their skin colour, can and do burn, and it is important that their skin is protected when they are outside with sun screen and by wearing sun hats. Parents should be asked to provide sun screen that is suitable for their child's skin that is labelled and kept in a safe place.

Climbing frames, bikes, wheeled toys and urban junk such as milk crates, old tyres and planks are great fun outside and can be turned into many exciting games. All children should have access to this type of play. Children with special needs, such as impaired mobility, may need to have some outside equipment adapted.

Outdoor play does not just have to take place when the weather is fine. It is possible to go outside in the wind, rain and snow if children and practitioners have appropriate outdoor clothing. As with all activities, practitioners need to supervise children effectively and also join in with their play. As with indoor play, children should be encouraged to tidy up and have containers to put things in can be labelled with words and pictures so that children know where to put items.

Outings

Outings into the environment away from the setting are a good way for children to learn about the world in which we live and are a good way of involving parents in the setting if they are able to help. There are many places to visit and outings do not just have to be for a special occasion. It is possible to take children on a trip to the shops or market where they may see things they do not possess or use at home. Indeed, they may not get the chance to go shopping other than when at the setting.

Swimming can be a regular outing. Practitioners need to be aware of religious and cultural issues concerning removing children's clothing and of individual needs regarding hair and skin care, for example, some children may need to wear swimming caps and other children may need to have their hair styled in a particular way to keep it tidy. Children with long straight hair may need their hair combed after swimming, whereas children with locks or weaving may not. Swimming can dry out the skin and it may be necessary to have some body lotion or cream for children to use. Black skin can get very dry after swimming, (or water play) and may need moisturizing regularly. Parents should be asked to provide lotions which should be labelled with their child's name and kept in a safe place.

Outings can be organized to extend any theme the setting is undertaking. A theme on 'buildings' could include a visit to a mosque, church, synagogue or other religious buildings. A theme on 'people who help us' can include a visit to a hospital, dentist or fire station.

It is also possible to visit other settings where children may have friends, or to play with a special piece of equipment such as a ball pool. Art galleries or museums often have scheduled activities that children can take part in and are good places to visit to introduce children to new experiences and to widen their view of the world.

Parents may like to join in outings if they are able to. Parents who work may not be able to join in as much as they might like to, and practitioners need to ensure that parents are given as much notice as possible, if the outing is to affect them, for example, if it is an outing that involves the whole setting, or if children need special clothes, or if children are going to return late.

Persona dolls

Persona dolls were fist used in the 1950's in the United States. In the United Kingdom Persona doll training has been in existence since 2002. Persona dolls are large dolls with 'personas' and personalities. They each have their own background that can include were they are from, how old they are, family details, cultural and religious backgrounds and, very importantly, their name.

The persona doll is used by the practitioner to introduce children to new experiences, and help them deal with feelings and develop positive attitudes towards the individuals and groups that make up the society in which we live. This can be done at circle time or at other times in the day. A persona doll becomes a member of the setting. The persona doll training website says the persona doll approach

> encourages children to develop empathy and challenge discrimination and unfairness. It helps counter the prejudices and misinformation they pick up even if they have no personal contact with black and mixed parentage families, with lesbian, gay, traveller, or refugee families or with families in which adults or children are disabled. And they absorb these negative attitudes whether they live in small villages with mainly white adults and children, in middle class leafy suburbs or in run-down inner city areas.

Persona dolls are a very useful way to help all children and all settings to work within an anti-discriminatory framework.

Problem solving, reasoning and numeracy

Problem solving, reasoning and numeracy is not just about numbers and counting. It also includes calculating, shape, space and measure. Jigsaws introduce children to space, size, shape, number and pattern. We have already seen how jigsaws need to be evaluated.

Children find patterns in the world round them, as everywhere they look there are patterns. Practitioners can also find examples of Arabic patterns, Indian patterns and many more to introduce children to a variety of patterns. These can be used in many ways, as part of a display, as a starting point for discussion or as a starting point for a creative activity. Children can also make patterns using the equipment in the setting, both indoors and outdoors. Butterfly painting is a great example of pattern and symmetry.

The water tray or other water activities provide a good place to undertake problem solving reasoning and numeracy activities; sinking and floating, volume and capacity; numbers and much more. All children should have access to the water tray; some children may need help and support to do this. Again it can be used indoors and outdoors, for example, measuring the rainfall.

Sorting and classifying can be done using thali dishes, Chinese bowls, wooden bowls or wicker baskets as containers. Baskets from a variety of cultures can be brought from Oxfam and UNICEF shops or local markets.

Counting and number work can be done orally and in writing in a variety of languages. Some children may be able to count and do complex number work in their home language but not in English, and their ability should be recognized and valued. Likewise some children may be able to do quite complex number work orally, but not in writing.

Some cultures have traditional games that help children to learn numbers, for example, in Tigray (in Ethiopia) a game called 'nagash' is played which involves moving shells or stones around a board. This game can now be bought from Oxfam and used with children.

A Chance to Think 4.17

Problem solving, reasoning and numeracy

You are supervising Anna, a student in your setting. The college has set Anna a project called Problem solving, reasoning and numeracy for the under 2s, and she has come to you for advice.

Where will you suggest Anna looks for information?

What practical activities can you suggest to Anna that can be undertaken with children under 2?

Compare your answer to the sample answers in Appendix 4.

Science and technology

Science and technology are just one part of the area of knowledge and understanding of the world. Science is about exploration and problem solving, ourselves and living things, forces and energy, and materials. Technology is about identifying needs and opportunities, designing, planning and making things and using technology and tools. Girls and boys should have equal access to these activities, which are often split, either consciously or unconsciously, along gender lines, with girls doing science activities such as cooking or gardening and the boys doing woodwork. Practitioners need to be aware that this may happen and develop strategies to ensure equality of access for all children.

Science and technology does not have to be 'high tech' and expensive with computers and suchlike although, these can be used. It should be as everyday and accessible as possible: exploring nature and the weather outside; making ice cubes and watching them melt in the water tray; mixing things so that they change, for example, cooking, mixing paints or making dough.

A Chance to Think 4.18

Science and technology

In your setting you have observed that a new member of staff is just doing science and technology activities with the boys.

What would you do in this situation?

What would you do if the member of staff said this was done deliberately, as they felt it was wrong to do these activities with girls?

What messages is this sending to all the children in the setting?

Compare your answers with the sample answers in Appendix 4.

Treasure baskets

Treasure baskets are baskets full of treasure designed for use by babies between 6–9 months old but older children can enjoy them and benefit from them as well. A treasure basket is not a 'regular toy' nor does it contain toys or anything plastic. It is a natural basket containing a variety of objects including objects that are natural, for example, fir cones, objects made of natural materials, for example, little baskets, wooden objects, for example, small boxes, metal objects, for example, keys, objects in leather, textile, rubber paper and cardboard.

Children explore the objects either on their own or sitting with other babies. The adult is quiet and observes the children. This is a wonderful activity for all children as there is no right or wrong way of exploring, and all children can do this.

Videos, DVD, television, computers and game consoles

Many children and settings have computers, televisions, videos or DVDs and game consoles. As with any other resource, practitioners need to plan and evaluate how these are used. Some children get a great deal of pleasure from these and can learn new skills, for example, how to operate technology. Some children do not have access to this type of equipment for all kinds of reasons, including financial, or parents consciously choosing not to use them. Often using this type of media can be a very solitary activity, and we have seen how television can portray discriminatory images of both groups and individuals.

This is also true of videos, DVDs and some computer games and the games on games consoles. If practitioners are using these, then they need to choose how to use them and use them carefully. In these days of rapid technological advances, children can benefit from having access to these resources with adult supervision. Computers, for example, can provide, for some children ways of communicating. For some children computers may need to be adapted so that they can use them, for example, providing a larger keyboard than standard, using brighter graphics, making the facilities wheelchair accessible. It is particularly important that if computers are linked to the internet then they have a relevant security features installed on them to prevent children from accessing inappropriate material.

Supporting parents and others with play

Parents may have many different views about play including; it is what children do; it is not real learning; play is fun and harmless; it is expensive; we do not have room for play activities and many other views. We have seen how important play is for children and how it can influence and support them to develop both positive and negative attitudes. It is part of the role of the practitioner to talk to parents about play and how influential and important it is for children and support them with this.

References and useful resources

Abbot, L. and Moylett, H. (1997). *Working with the Unders-3's; Responding to Children's Needs.* Open University Press.

Anning, A. and Edwards, A. (2000). *Promoting Children's Learning from Birth to Five; Developing the New Early Years Professional.* Open University Press.

Bailey, R. and Bailey, R. (2008). *Foundations of Literacy* (3rd edition). Continuum.

Bilton, H. (2009). *Outdoor Play in the Early Years Management and Provision.* (2nd edition). Routledge.

Bradford, H. (2008). *Communication, Language and Literacy in the Early Years Foundation Stage.* Routledge.

Campbell, R. (2009). *Reading Stories with Young Children.* Trentham Books.

Dcsf. (2007). *Confident, Capable and Creative: Supporting Boys' Achievements.*

Dcsf. (2008). *Early Years Foundation Stage.*

Dcsf. (2008). *The Play Strategy.*

Drake, J. (2008). *Planning for Children's Learning and Play.* Routledge.

Duncan, J. and Lockwood, M. (2008). *Learning through Play: A Work-based Approach for the Early Years Professional.* Continuum.

Early Childhood Forum (2008). *It's All about Play.* Continuum.

Else, P. (2009) *The Value of Play.* Continuum.

Featherstone, P. and S. (2008). *Like Bees, Not Butterflies.* A&C Black.

Filer, J. (2008). *Healthy, Active and Outside.* Routledge.

Garrick, R. (2009). *Playing Outdoors in the Early Years* (2nd edition). Continuum.

Goldschmied, E. and Jackson. S. (1997). *People Under Three: Young Children in Day Care.* Routledge.

Hughes, A. (2006). *Developing Play for the Unders 3s.* Routledge.

Hughes, A. M. (2008). *Problem Solving Reasoning and Numeracy in the Early Years Foundation Stage.* Routledge.

Kellner-Pringel, M. (1980). *The Needs of Children.* Hutchinson.

Lee, A. (2007). *Childminder's Guide to Play and Activities.* Continuum.

Lindon, J. (2000). *Helping Babies and Toddlers to Learn: A Guide to Good Practice with Under-threes*. National Early Years Network.

Lindon, J. (2001). *Growing Up: From Eight Years to Young Adulthood*. National Children's Bureau.

Lindon, J. (2007). *Understanding Children and Young People Development from 5– 18 Years*. Hodder Arnold.

Louis, S. (2008). *Knowledge and Understanding of the World in the Early Years Foundation Stage*. Routledge.

May, P. (2008). *Creative Development in the Early Years Foundation Stage*.Routledge.

Newell, P. (1991). *The UN Convention and Children's Rights in the UK*. National Children's Bureau.

Nurse, A. D. (2009). *Physical Development in the Early Years Foundation Stage*. Routledge.

Play England. (2009). *Charter for Children's Play*.

Pound, L. (2008). *Thinking and Learning about Mathematics in the Early Years*. Routledge.

Pre-School Learning Alliance. (2007). *Listening Together*. Pre-School Learning Alliance.

Pre-School Learning Alliance. (2007). *Being Me*. Pre-School Learning Alliance.

Pre-School Learning Alliance. (2007). *Mark Making and Representation*. Pre-School Learning Alliance.

Pre-School Learning Alliance. (2007). *Music and Dance*. Pre-School Learning Alliance.

Pre-School Learning Alliance. (2007). *Playing and Learning Outdoors*. Pre-School Learning Alliance.

Roe, J. (2009). *Let's All Play*. Continuum.

Sangster, M. and Catterall, R. (2009). *Early Numeracy*. Continuum.

Sheppy, S. (2008). *Personal, Social and Emotional Development in the Early Years Foundation Stage*. Routledge.

Smidt, S. (2005). *Observing, Assessing and Planning for Children in the Early Years*. Routledge.

Smidt, S. (2009). *Planning for the Early Years Foundation Stage*. Routledge.

Whitebread, D. and Coltman, P. (2008). *Teaching and Learning in the Early Years*. Routledge.

Useful websites

www.afrotoys.com – a supply a range of ethnically diverse toys, games and accessories.

www.earlyyearsequality.org.uk – website for early years equality.

www.festivalshop.co.uk – resources and equipment to support festivals, information about religions and diversity.

www.letterboxlibrary.com – suppliers of books celebrating equality and diversity.

www.persona-doll-training.org – information about persona dolls and training available.

www.positive-identity.com – resources to support the development of positive identities.

www.rompa.com – suppliers of resources meeting the needs of all generations.

www.specialdirect.com – resources and equipment to support inclusion, motor skills and communication.

www.theequaloppshop.co.uk – suppliers of resources and equipment to support equal opportunities.

www.xtra-cat.com – supplies of equipment and resources to help workers to manage the challenge of social diversity.

Useful DVDs

Basic Skills Agency. (2006). *Language and Play Songs and Rhymes to Share Together* (DVD).

Dcsf. (2007). *Playing and Learning Together* (DVD).

Goldschmied, E. and Hughes, A. (n.d.). *Heuristic Play with Objects.* (video and DVD). National Children's Bureau.

5 Development, Identity and Self-Esteem

This chapter examines the areas of development, identity and self-esteem, their meaning and how they impact on anti-discriminatory practice. It will look in more depth at the importance of understanding development; in particular, the development of language and communication and the impact and influences different areas have on how practitioners work with children and families.

The development of communication and language

Practitioners are continually communicating with children and other adults. This communication may either be conscious or unconscious, may be planned and thought about, or may be an immediate response to another person.

Practitioners never stop communicating. Children and adults pick up messages from practitioners even when they think they are not communicating. Practitioners give out constant messages through the body language they use as well as through spoken language and other communication media. It is through language and communication that individuals are able to make themselves understood and also to understand others. Communication skills and language form a vital part of social interaction. It is therefore important that practitioners are aware of how they communicate and use language and they are aware of how children learn to communicate and use language.

All children develop ways of communicating. This is an important skill, as it enables individuals to interact with one another and not be isolated. There are many ways of communicating. Everybody communicates using gestures and body language and Chapter 2 looked at how race, religion and culture may influence language, including body language. Sometimes individuals communicate through a spoken language or languages. At other times it may be through a sign or symbol language, that is, British Sign Language, Makaton or Bliss symbols. It may be through written language, including Braille. Some individuals communicate using communication passports, photos or by using technology. Practitioners must be aware of the communication systems and needs of individual children in the setting, and provide the necessary equipment, support and encouragement for its use and development.

In this section of the chapter we examine the development of communication and language skills. The terms used with regard to communication and language are defined. Theories of speech and language development are examined. This section will also discuss how practitioners can support language and communication skills. A list of useful resources and publications is given at the end of the chapter for practitioners wanting more information on communication and language development.

We know that children use many different ways to communicate, both with one another and with adults. The systems children use to communicate will be influenced by their individual development, any special needs they may have, for example, a hearing impairment, the communication skills they possess, the situation they are in and the relationship they have with the person they are communicating with. Not all children develop the use of a spoken language and some children will develop and use more than one spoken language or ways of communicating.

The Concise Oxford Dictionary defines the word 'Communicate' as 'transmit or pass on by speaking or writing', and 'Language' as 'the method of human communication, either spoken or written, consisting of the use of words in an agreed way; the language of a particular community or country etc.'.

A Chance to Think 5.1

Communication

Think about the children in your setting. Think about different times of the day; when children arrive in the setting, at sleep and waking up time, outside play and quiet time.

How do children communicate with one another at these times?

Do children use different communication methods with one another and with adults?

How many different ways of communicating and how many different languages are used in your setting?

Theories of language development

Not all children will develop spoken language skills. This may be for reasons that affect development, for example, a hearing or speech impairment or a learning disability. Later on in this chapter we will look at communication skills other than spoken language, but this section focuses on the development of spoken languages.

The majority of children will develop some form of spoken language. It is amazing to think that when children are born they are able to communicate only through crying and movement but by the time they are 4 or 5 they can communicate very effectively through one or more spoken languages. Language development takes place in stages, or a sequence, with one stage being followed by another. The age at which a child reaches these stages varies because all children are different and develop at different rates. Psychologists have discovered that language development is consistent across a large variety of cultural groups and that the sequence of language development is the same across cultures.

There are many theories of language development. One theory is that the environment children are in will influence how they learn a language, together with its accent and dialect. So as well as learning language, children will also develop and use dialects and accents. Accents and dialects were discussed in Chapter 2. A child who is brought up hearing Arabic spoken will learn Arabic, and a child who is brought up hearing English spoken will learn English. Children's communication and vocabulary will also vary depending on whether they are talking to an adult or friend, and whether they are at home, in a setting or elsewhere. Distinct vocabularies and ways of speaking are used in the classroom or setting (formal), the playground or outside play (slang), and the home (informal or familiar).

Another theory put forward by psychologists is that children learn language through imitation (Ervin-Trip) and conditioning (Skinner). Imitation is where children imitate the language they hear around them. Conditioning takes place when adults reward or praise children for something they have said that is funny or right, or tell them that it is rude or wrong. If children are encouraged or praised, they will want to say what they said again, or say something new in order to be further rewarded.

Some psychologists and linguists (Chomsky, Lenneberg) believe that language development is innate and that children are pre-programmed to learn language. This means that they are born with the ability to learn language. Chomsky believes that there are many common features of all languages, that is, whatever language children are learning, they use the same systems of rules to do it. He called these rules 'universal grammar'. He said that this is because humans possess a 'language acquisition device' that enables them to learn language. Piaget believed that there is a relationship between language and a child's intellectual activities. Vygotsky believed that interaction in the social environment is important for language development and that adults need to 'scaffold' a child in order to help him or her develop.

The development of one spoken language

People who speak one language are called monolingual. We will now spend some time looking at how children with no special needs develop one language. This is done in stages, and although for the purpose of this section ages are put against these stages, it is important to remember that all children are individuals and develop these skills at different rates. Practitioners working with children of different ages need to be aware of the stages of language development and the needs of children in order to provided appropriate help, support and encouragement for them birth to 1 month. Newborn babies' use of their voice will consist of crying. The cry may sound different depending on whether they are hungry, uncomfortable, in pain or needing some company. As babies gets older they will make other sounds with their voice including gurgling, cooing and noises made in their throat.

1 month to 3 months
A baby may stop crying when they hear familiar soothing voices. They will gurgle and coo. Babies begin to smile when spoken to and they are developing more control over their lips and voice.

3 to 6 months

A baby will now turn their head in the direction from which a voice is coming. They will make many more sounds with their voice, including 'ka' and 'ba' sounds, and will practise making sounds, including laughing and shouting.

6 to 9 months

Between 6 and 9 months the babies makes more sounds inkling 'adad', 'der' and 'amem', and will be trying to copy sounds. They will now begin to use their voice deliberately to gain people's attention.

9 to 12 months

By now babies are is beginning to 'talk' to people in their own language or jargon. They show enjoyment in familiar words and can carry out simple instructions, for example, 'wave to granny'. Babies are now also beginning to recognize their own names. Babies may say two or three words, for example, 'dad dad' or 'mum mum'.

12 to 15 months

Children practise talking a lot, much of it still in their own particular language or jargon. They may use four or five recognizable words, but understand much more than they can say. By this age children are learning to recognize the word 'no' and its meaning.

15 to 18 months

At this age children show a great deal of interest in words and vocalizing. They particularly enjoy trying to join in singing and have a vocabulary of around 6 to 20 words. They may often use the word 'no'. Children of this age understand much more than they can say. They may echo words they like the sound of, or those that come last in a sentence. This is called echolalia.

18 months to 2 years

Children can understand what people are saying to them. Their vocabulary has grown to 50 or more words that they can use in short sentences. They are beginning to ask 'what's that?' as well as joining in songs. They use their names to talk about themselves, for example, 'Jamie want'.

2 to 2½ years

Children will start to use the pronouns 'I', 'me' and 'you' instead of names to talk about themselves and others. They also ask a great many questions, especially 'what' questions.

2½ to 3 years

Children hold simple conversations with people and may talk to themselves. They enjoy talking and will still be asking many questions at this age, including 'who' and 'where' questions. They enjoy words in any form, including rhymes, stories and conversations.

3 to 4 years

By now children are talking quite fluently and they possess a very large vocabulary. They may be beginning to recognize swear words and use them to see the effect this has on people. At this age children have learnt how to use grammar accurately, although they still make mistakes. They may know their own name, age and address. Their speech sounds much more adult and they use tone and pitch to vary it.

4 to 5 years

Children's vocabulary is now very extensive, up to about 300 words. They still ask many questions, particularly about the meaning of words they do not understand. Their speech is now much more like adults and they generally use grammar accurately. Children may be able to recognize words in writing, particularly their own name.

5 to 6 years

Children's vocabulary continues to expand and they are interested in new words. They may be able to write words and will be beginning to read.

6 to 8 years

Children's speech and language is now very sophisticated. They have a very large vocabulary and are generally capable of reading and writing.

The development of more than one language

A great many people in the world are bilingual or multilingual. Much of the vocabulary used when talking about more than one language is confusing and may be used in the wrong context. A short definition of the most commonly used words is given to try and ease some on the confusion.

- Bilingual; able to speak two languages;
- Multilingual; able to speak more than two languages;
- First language; the first language learnt;
- Mother tongue; the language spoken in the family;
- Majority language; the major language spoken in a country.

Many people worry about a child learning to speak two or more languages will be confused or unable to communicate effectively. This should not the case. We saw earlier in this section that the same system is used when learning all languages. Research has shown that children who are bilingual learn their first words at the same time as children who are monolingual, and that children who are bilingual, and children who are monolingual, often have a similar range of vocabulary.

Research also shows that there are no negative effects, only positive effects, regarding development when a child learns two or more languages. Siraj-Blatchford and Clarke say, 'Babies and toddlers are cognitively advantaged by growing up in two or more language environments'. Being bilingual or multi-lingual is very positive. However, some people still see bilingual skills differently depending on the languages being spoken, for example, a person who speaks French and English may be viewed more positively than a person who speaks Amharic and Arabic. In Chapter 1 we looked at attitudes people hold. Differentiating between languages are attitudes. All languages are equally impor-tant and valid. A person who speaks two or more languages has developed many skills which will be of great benefit, as language helps children to learn and develop in all other areas. As children learn two or more languages they will develop fluency in all languages. They may at times switch between languages in the same sentence. This is called 'code switching' and was discussed in Chapter 2. Children may also use the languages they speak in different situa-tions, for example, their home or first language at home, and English in the setting. Being able to speak more than one language is extremely advantageous. It can enhance an individual's sense of self-esteem and identity, (which will be discussed later in this chapter), as well as developing and enhancing cognitive, problem solving and thinking skills. When a child becomes an adult, being able to speak more than one language may even have an economic advantage. Practitioners need to support, value and respect these language skills.

Children can develop bilingual skills in two ways, either simultaneously or successively. Simultaneous bilingualism is when children learn both languages at the same time from birth. Successive or Sequential bilingualism is when children learn one language first and then learn a second language latter.

Simultaneous bilingualism

Children who learn two languages at the same time have the same pattern of language development as children learning one language. The rate at which they learn the languages may be different from that of a child learning one language as they have two languages to learn. At first children may use both vocabularies together as though one language, but gradually they begin to separate them and use them as two languages. Children then begin to recognize which adults and settings speak which language, and begin to use the languages in the correct situation. In order to be able to do this, children need to hear languages being spoken and used consistently. They also need opportunities to practise their language skills and encouragement and support to do so.

Successive or sequential bilingualism

In successive or sequential bilingualism the same patterns or stages of development occur as in learning a second language. Children learn one language first and then a second language. Children learning a second language need help, support and encouragement to do this.

Practitioners in settings may be in a position where they are caring for children who speak just one language at home, and then have to learn English or another language when they come into the setting. Children need the opportunity to keep practising their home, or first language, as by doing this it helps them to develop their second language. A child between 18 and 24 months who goes to a setting where practitioners do not speak his or her home (or first) language many have a period where development of both languages appears frozen. Some children may have a silent period when they do not speak in the language they are learning, but they are taking in the language and are beginning to understand it. Suddenly, in their own time when they feel confident in how to use the language, they begin to use it.

Practitioners need to support children, and not force them to speak, until they are ready. They also need to provide active language support though planning and play to support individual children with their language development.

A Chance to Think 5.2

Supporting children who are bilingual

Alexandra, a 2½-year-old Spanish child, is due to start in your setting. Alexandra's first language is Spanish and she does not speak any English. Her mother has arranged to take a few days off work to settle Alexandra into the setting, but then she has to return to work. You are going to be Alexandra's key person.

What could you do before Alexandra starts in the setting to prepare for her arrival?

When Alexandra starts in the setting, how will you help her to feel welcome and settled?

How will you prepare Alexandra and her mother, and support them both when she has to return to work?

Compare your answers with the sample answers in Appendix 5.

Special needs

Some children have special needs that affect their communication and language skills. They may be using systems to communicate that do not involve a spoken language, for example, sign or symbol languages, communication passports, photo books or other ways of communicating. These are known as Alternative and Augmentative Communication Systems (AAC). Alternative systems replace speech and augmentative systems support speech. Other children use a spoken language. Whatever form of communication is being used, it is important that practitioners recognize it, value it, use it and support children with it. Ways of supporting communication and language development are discussed later in this chapter.

Hearing impairment

There are different degrees of hearing impairment that affect the way children hear and communicate. A child may be born with a hearing impairment and some may develop a hearing impairment later in life. Sometimes this may be due to an injury or illness, for example, meningitis or 'glue ear'. If a child has a hearing impairment, this needs to be recognized as early as possible, so that help and support can be provided for both child and parents. Children may have mild, moderate or severe hearing loss. A child with mild hearing loss may find it hard to hear people speaking clearly. They may develop spoken language, but it may be delayed. A child with moderate hearing loss might need some support with language development. Some children may need to wear hearing aids. Children with severe hearing loss will need help and support with communication and language development, and because they are unable to hear spoken language, they may use other forms of communication such as sign language.

Speech impairment

Some children do not develop speech or speak in their own individual language. Some children with autism or cerebral palsy may not develop spoken language. Some children with Down's syndrome may be delayed in developing language, but may understand more than they can say. All children are individuals and practitioners should not make assumptions about a child's language development, or lack of it. Practitioners should observe children's communication and language skills and base their knowledge on that and what information parents have provided, and support and encourage children's communication and language skills. Some children develop a stutter or stammer. These two words mean the same. The British Stammering Association (BSA) has a definition by Enderby that says stammering is

> characterised by stoppages and disruptions in fluency which interrupt the smooth flow and timing of speech. These stoppages may take the form of repetitions of sounds, syllables or words, or of prolongations of sounds so that words seem to be stretched out, and can involve silent blocking of the airflow of speech when no sound is heard.

The BSA goes on to say that

> difficulties in speaking fluently between 2–4 years affects about one child in 20 and evidence shows that most children outgrow this phase over a few weeks or months, but up to a quarter of these children are at serious risk of developing chronic stammering which may persist into adulthood without intervention during the pre-school years.

No one knows why some children may develop a stutter / stammer, but it may be due to genetic factors. It may be because a child is in a hurry to talk, and his or her brain gets ahead of the language coming out. In the under 5s twice as many boys stammer as girls. Stammering can happen in any culture and in all social groups. A stammer often disappears, but if it does not, a child may need the specialist help of a speech and language therapist.

Body language

Body language is just what it says it is; the way we communicate with our bodies. Many messages can be given silently with the body. Some practitioners, when they see children doing something they are not supposed to, can just look at them in a particular way and the children will alter their behaviour. Children learn to 'read' body language. Just as language alters according to the situation people find themselves in, so do body language and the distance people choose to stand apart from one another. Edward Hall, a psychologist, discovered that there are four zones of proximity. The zone of intimacy is where people stand who know each other well. This can be from as close as bodily contact to about 18 inches away. Personal distance is for friends, people we trust or people we have something in common with. This is from 18 inches to 4 feet. The third zone is that of social distance, which is from 4 to 12 feet.

The last zone is the public zone, which is anything over 12 feet. The distance alters and varies across cultures.

In some cultures standing close to someone is considered impolite, and in other cultures it is quite acceptable to stand very close to people and have bodily contact with them. Likewise, in some cultures it is considered impolite for children to look at adults when they are talking to them. Body language is also discussed in Chapter 2. Practitioners need to consider body language and the messages given when working with children, parents and colleagues.

Supporting children's communication and language skills

All children need support and encouragement in order to help their communication and language use and development. This support needs to meet the individual needs of each child. All children need the opportunity and time to practise their communication and language skills in a supportive and non-threatening environment with both their peer group and adults. It is important for practitioners to listen to what children are saying and respond accordingly. As well as listening to children, practitioners need to provide them with opportunities to practise their listening skills. Children developing communication and language skills will make mistakes in the way they say things and in the vocabulary they use. When this happens, it is important that practitioners do not ridicule children, draw everybody's attentions to their mistake, or laugh at them. Children should not be expected to 'perform' or 'show off' their language skills in front of others as this may result in them feeling self-conscious and lacking in confidence. One effective way of helping children's language development is to repeat things back to children rephrased correctly, rather than saying, 'that is wrong, say it like this'.

Children need opportunities to practise their communication and language skills in a positive and supportive environment. They need to feel secure in themselves and the environment and trust practitioners in the setting. Children need to see and hear communication and language used naturally and be able to use their own communication and language skills in many different situations and with a variety of people. Children benefit from hearing language and vocabulary used consistently in the setting. It can be confusing when there are so many words for the same thing for example, some people may describea drinking vessel as a 'cup', others as a 'mug', and yet others as a 'beaker'. It also helps children if practitioners communicate with parents and share information about communication and language development. Parents can tell practitioners what vocabulary they use at home and whether they have any special words for particular things.

It is also useful to reflect and evaluate the environment. Background noise can be distracting for all children so try not to have the radio, music, or in a home situation, the TV on as background noise. Think about where activities are put out in settings, for example, do not put the book corner next to the water tray or next to an activity that you know will be very loud. Also plan the most suitable time of day to carry out activities so that children are ready for them. This should all be linked to the observation, assessment and planning cycle which was discussed in Chapter 4.

When talking to children or trying to get their attention, say their name at the beginning of a sentence so that they know who it is you are talking to. Ensure children are able to see displays that are labelled and that they are at 'child height'. These may include pictures and labels on the floor for children who are crawling or even on the ceiling over the nappy changing area (ensuring health and safety at all times). The Department for Children Schools and Family (Dcsf) launched the Every Child a Talker (ECAT) programme in 2008. Its document for lead practitioners says, 'A child's ability to develop language depends on being immersed in a rich environment of words, sounds, rhythm, and verbal and non-verbal expression from birth'. However, there are still many children starting school without the extended vocabulary and communication abilities which are so important for learning and for making friends. ECAT is designed to lead practitioners and their colleagues to create a developmentally appropriate, supportive and stimulating environment in which children can enjoy experimenting with, and learning, language. It can be implemented whether children are in early years settings, with a childminder, or at home with their parents.

Practitioners should plan and use a variety of activities to enable children to hear and practise communication and language. These can include stories, rhymes, songs and music, poems, drama, role play and props, conversation and listening games undertaken in a sensitive and supportive manner. These can all help children to develop confidence in themselves and in their communication and language skills. Practitioners need to provide a natural environment that is rich in communication in both verbal and written languages. This should include languages other than English, and can include welcome posters, labelling of objects in the environment, interest tables, books in single languages other than English, as well as dual language books, picture books, sign and symbol books and books in English. Settings should also provide opportunities and activities that encourage mark making and writing. Practitioners may also need to seek the advice and support of speech and language therapists or other relevant professionals. It is important to seek advice as early as possible in order to help and support children and families. This means observing children so that you are clear why you need to seek help and support and that when you talk to parents you are able to give clear examples of what you mean. These observations, examples and clear information will also be needed by speech and language therapists or other relevant professionals. Chapter 4 gives further suggestions about play and activities that practitioners may find useful.

Children who speak more than one language

Monolingual practitioners can support and facilitate the communication and language development of all children, including children who speak more than one language. Practitioners should acknowledge, value and respect the skills children have developed in speaking more than one language. Sometimes practitioners can feel threatened when children speak together in a language they do not understand, and they ask children to speak in English. If children are speaking to each other in their home language, or first language, in the setting then this should be encouraged, as otherwise children may feel that only English is valued in the setting.

Many children will choose not speak in the setting until they feel confident in both the setting and in their language skills. They may go through a silent period, as discussed earlier in this chapter. Children should not be forced to speak or be 'told off' if they do not get things right when they speak. Practitioners need to speak to children naturally using regular speech patterns and expressions. It is important not to speak in 'pidgin English' or baby talk, or to talk slowly and loudly, as this will not help a child's language development. Tone, gesture, facial expression and visual clues all help a child to understand what is being said.

Practitioners should also ensure that they know how to pronounce and spell all children's names and ensure that they are using the child's correct name. Some children may use their second name. Names should not be shortened, or altered to make it easier for practitioners to say them, as this is not valuing the person. A person's name is important; it is part of their identity. Asking parents is the only way to ensure that the correct name is being used. Names are discussed later in the chapter in the section on identity and self-esteem.

Settings could also begin to keep 'language books'. These are books, one for each language, where common words used by children are recorded for example, toilet, drink, hello, goodbye and so on. If this is done each time a child with a 'new' language to the setting begins to attend the setting will soon have a useful reference tool that can be added to. This ensures that even if practitioners who speak a variety of languages leave the setting, it still has the information it needs, and all practitioners can use the books so that no one practitioner has all the information. It is also possible to add words that can be used for displays or notices, such as 'welcome', or the names of colours and numbers.

Children need to see and hear their own language together with a variety of languages used in the setting. This can be done through books, displays, music, stories, rhymes and conversations. Chapter 4 gives more examples of activities that support and encourage language development.

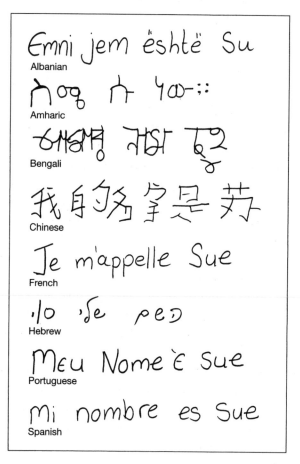

Figure 5.1 My name is Sue

Children with special needs

It is important not to make assumptions about communication and language skills of children with special needs. Practitioners should talk to parents and observe children to ensure they are aware of the individual communication and language skills of each child. Often a child will start in a setting and parents and practitioners may not be aware that he or she has any special needs; it is only by observation that this becomes apparent. If this is so, parents must be informed sensitively so that appropriate help can be obtained, for example, a child may develop a hearing impairment that may require help from a speech and language therapist or medical intervention, for example, 'glue ear'.

Children who have a hearing impairment will need particular help depending on the amount of hearing loss they have. Practitioners need to face children, as they may 'lip read'. Children also need to sit 'face on' to practitioners, or other children, so that their lips can be clearly seen. This may mean sitting in the front of a group. This should always be done in a sensitive manner so as not to make the child feel embarrassed. The other children in the setting will generally respond positively if practitioners explain why the child with the hearing impairment needs to sit near the front.

Children with a hearing impairment may also need non-verbal clues such as a gentle touch, to gain their attention or to encourage them to look and listen at the same time. Another prompt children find helpful is when practitioners say a child's name before they start a sentence; then the child will be aware that it is they who are being spoken to and not anyone else.

Listening games such as sound lotto, will help a child to develop listening skills. One of the most important things to remember is to speak clearly and naturally with hands away from the mouth. If a child is using a hearing aid it will pick up all the sounds around, not just the sounds he or she wants to hear.

Practitioners need to think about sound levels in the environment and what they can do to minimize them where possible, for example, putting down rugs on floors, closing windows, not having background noise such as radios on. If the environment is noisy to practitioners it will be doubly noisy to children using a hearing aid.

Children with other special needs also need to be encouraged and supported to use their communication and language skills. Some children may be able to vocalize, even if they cannot say particular words. Practitioners should encourage children to use their voice and learn what each sound means. Practitioners may need to learn sign or symbol languages or other alternative and augmentative communication methods in order to be able to communicate effectively with children. This may mean that practitioners need to attend training courses and practise using these communication methods. Once signs or other methods of communication are being used regularly in the setting, it is possible for other practitioners and children to be able to learn how to use them.

It is important for practitioners to acknowledge, value and respect the many different ways that children have of communicating and not make derogatory remarks about them in front of the children. It is also important that practitioners talk to children naturally. It may help children if practitioners use short sentences and try and use everyday words consistently.

Body language and gestures also help to convey meaning. It is important to play and have fun when communication and language with songs, rhymes and stories. This can be done using story sack and song boxes. Information about these is given in Chapter 4. It is possible to get books in many sign and symbol languages and even to make things more personal is to use or make books for children featuring the communication systems they use. It is helpful to children if they know what is happening in a setting, this can be done by making a visual timetable featuring pictures or photos so that children can see what is happening. When asking children questions, or giving choices, it can be helpful to use pictures or objects of reference to help them, as they can point to the one they want.

A Chance to Think 5.3

Supporting individuals around communication

David, a little boy with Down's syndrome, attends your setting. He has been attending for some time and is happy and settled in the setting and has made many friends. David is very independent. He has some speech that those that are close to him understand, and he uses sign language. Amanda, a student, has recently started in the setting. Amanda does not understand David's speech or sign language. You have noticed that she is actively avoiding David, and when she does have contact with him she laughs at his attempts to communicate with her and tells you she cannot understand him. David is beginning to lose his confidence and the other children have noticed this and have started to laugh at David.

What will you do in this situation?

How will you ensure that David regains his confidence and communication skills?

Compare your answers with the sample answers in Appendix 5.

Attitudes towards language and communication

We saw in Chapter 1 that we all possess attitudes towards a whole variety of things. People may also have attitudes towards communication strategies and language. Some people, wrongly, may feel that some languages are 'better' than others or have greater value. In particular, English and some European languages are often perceived as 'better' languages to speak than African or Asian languages. However, all languages are equally important and linguistically are of equal value. The same can also be said for accents and dialects. Some are seen as 'better' than others and some people make judgements about individuals based on the accent with which they speak. Practitioners need to be aware of their own attitudes towards communication strategies and languages and how these attitudes are reflected in their behaviour.

The way language is used can also shape people's attitudes. Words can be used, sometimes unintentionally, in an oppressive or discriminatory way. The word 'black' is often used in a negative way, for example, 'blackleg', 'black mood', and so on. Phrases can be used that exclude people with a disability, for example, 'stand on your own two feet'. English is, at present, a very male dominated language, for example, people still use words and phrases such as 'mankind' 'chairman' 'fireman', and so on. The way words and phrases are used can either intentionally, or unintentionally, marginalize, exclude, oppress and stereotype individuals and groups. Practitioners need to constantly think about and evaluate, how they use language and the message it conveys.

Language and communication strategies are not static implements. They are constantly changing and evolving. Some words and phrases that were used without thought at one time are now considered offensive or inappropriate. New words are constantly entering our vocabulary, and individuals and groups must now think about how language is used and the impact it has on individuals and groups. Words and phrases that are used today will change and evolve; new words will come into being and people's attitudes towards language will change. Practitioners need to discuss the use of language, its effects and their own attitudes to it within the team.

Development of identity and self-esteem

The final section of this chapter examines the development of identity and self-esteem. Practitioners need to understand how children develop their own self-identity and self-esteem, and try to ensure that this area of a child's development is positive. They also need to recognize if, and when, children are suffering from low self-esteem (for example, a child who is, or has been, suffering from abuse may have low self-esteem,) and be able to work to support a child to turn this around.

In this section we look at some of the signs of low self-esteem and the role of the practitioner in the development of identity and self-esteem. The Concise Oxford Dictionary defines 'identity' as 'the quality or condition of being a specified person or thing; individuality, personality'. 'Esteem' is defined as meaning 'having high regard for; greatly respect'. Gergen and Gergen, in their book Social Psychology, state that 'self-esteem refers to an individual's perception of his or her own adequacy, competence or goodness as a person'.

Psychologists and sociologists both agree that individuals are not born with any idea of who they are. A sense of self and identity is not innate. Individuals learn who they are and start to develop a sense of identity as they grow, because they start to interact with other people. Babies interact with people from their own families as well as people from society at large. It is only by interacting with others from the moment they are born that individuals develop a sense of self and identity. Individuals begin to become aware of who they are, and how they fit into the world, by the way people respond and react to them. Children are aware that people are reacting to them. People 'goo' and 'coo' at babies, talk to them, interact and respond to them. In the feature film 'Nell', starring Jodie Foster, the character Nell had been brought up without contact with other people. She developed her own language and sense of identity, which changed when she began to interact with other people.

A Chance to Think 5.4

Identity

Every individual has his or her own identity. This identity has to been formed, so that individuals know who they are. Once individuals have developed their identity, they also develop feelings about that identity. Some people feel good about themselves. This is known as having high self-esteem. Some people do not feel good about themselves. This is known as having low self-esteem.

What factors play a part in how people develop their sense of identity?

Why do some people have high self-esteem?

Why do some people have low self-esteem?

Compare your answers with the sample answers in Appendix 5.

Babies begin to learn that they are separate people with their own identities; they learn they are not physically attached to their mothers or any other person. Babies learn very quickly that if they cry, people will respond to them. They learn that they are part of a group of people (i.e. family and society) and that they have a particular place in that group. This might be in a single parent family, a gay or lesbian family, an extended family, a foster family or any other group of people.

We have seen that babies soon begin to learn a language and that they respond to language. Language has a very powerful part to play in how children develop their identity and self-esteem. People talk to babies and children. They tell them they are loved, beautiful, cute, clever, silly, naughty, bad, ugly and many other things. Children soon learn that these words mean something and that they have a value attached to them. If children are constantly told that they are beautiful or loved by people around them then they will believe that they are beautiful and loved and behave in a way that reflects that. If children are constantly told that they are bad or naughty and unloved, then they will come to believe that and behave in a way that reflects what they were told.

Children learn that they have a given name and a language and they respond to that name and language. A person's name is very important. It can be central to their identity; how a person sees themselves as well as how others see them and respond to them. A name can say much lot about a person's culture or even their religion. For some individuals it may provide a link to their family history. Naming traditions and systems may vary between cultures, religions and places, for example, in Tigray in Ethiopia, Christian children are given a name at birth and then a Christian or saint's name when they are baptized later. Surnames are not used; children take the names of their father and grandfather; they have four names; a birth name, a baptism name, their father's name and their grandfather's name. In the Sikh religion some children are given their names in a naming ceremony that takes place in the gurudwara, the Sikh religious building. They then take the Sikh family name, with boys taking the name Singh and the girls taking the name Kaur. Some given names are associated with religions; for example, Christian names come from the Bible, and many Jewish names come from the Old Testament section of in the Bible. Some Muslim names come from the Qur'an. Zoroastrians have a first name followed by their father's name as a second name with the last name being the family name. In some cultures, for example, the Arabic culture, some names are everyday words; in other cultures, names come from particular traditions associated with that culture. Chinese names start with the family name first, then a generational name and finally a personal name. Japanese people have two names. The first is the family name and the second is a given name. Some families do not use surnames. Other families may have a child where the two parents have different surnames, or they may share the same surname.

It is important that practitioners understand the naming systems used by the children and families they work with and not make assumptions about names. It is also important that practitioners are clear about how to pronounce and spell names. If necessary, practitioners should check with parents about naming systems, pronunciation and spelling. Practitioners should not shorten or change names, but use the name a child is given. Some families may use the second name they have given their child and not the one that is written first. Other children may have a 'given name' but be called by a derivative of it; for example, Henry may be known as Harry. The same is true for colleagues. Practitioners should not change or shorten colleagues' names, or use nicknames for them, unless they are invited to. Practitioners also need to check with parents about how they would like to be addressed. Some parents like to be addresses formally by their title and surname for example, 'Mrs Kaur'. Other parents prefer to be addressed informally by their first name.

Sometimes there may be children, practitioners or parents in the setting with the same name. It is possible to identify individuals in this situation without taking away from each person their identity. Names should not be changed or altered if there happen to be two people with the same name in the setting, nor should anything be added to a name that might be derogatory to the person, for example, 'Old Jane' is very offensive to both Jane and older people.

There are occasions when individuals may change their name. Sometimes a person has chosen to do this, for example, women sometimes change their surname when they get married and take their husband's surname. Sometimes they add the names together with a hyphen. Some people are not happy with their 'given name' or do not feel it reflects who they are, and they may then ask to be called by another name which they have chosen for themselves. Some people may change their name and have these changes made legal by deed poll. There may also be times when a child has their name changed without consultation, for example, on adoption. Some children who were born in one country and then adopted and subsequently come to live in a different country, may experience a name change. This can have an impact on them as names are central to a person's identity, and a child may feel that part of their identity has been taken away. Practitioners should not make assumptions about an individual's name and what they would like to be called. An individual's name plays an important part in the development of their identity and practitioners should recognize and respect names and what they may mean to people.

A Chance to Think 5.5

Names

Your name has had a big part to play in how you have developed your identity and how you feel about it. Think about your name and write it down. If possible talk to the people who gave you your name.

How and why did you get your name?

How do you feel about your name?

Have you changed your original 'given name' in any way?

If so why, and how did this make you feel?

Think about how you use children's names and how you help them feel proud of their name.

The development of identity is a complex process. A baby is not born with a sense of identity, but it is built up from birth from all that they experience and do not experience. Identity changes over time. It is not something that is static, but is constantly changing, evolving and growing. It can be influenced by many things, including age, culture, family background, religions, achievements, disability, self-esteem, country of residence, sexuality, gender, political beliefs, legal status, other people's perceptions, as well as all the life experiences a person has. Amin Maalouf in his book 'On Identity', when describing his own identity says:

> so am I half French or half Lebanese? Of course not. Identity can't be compartmentalised. You can't divide it up into halves or thirds or any other separate segments. I haven't got several identities: I've just got one, made up of many components combined together in a mixture that is unique to every individual.

While is it important not to compartmentalize identity, or put a label or type on a person, we will now examine how identity can be influenced or shaped. When discussing identity it is important to remember that every person is an individual, and no two people are ever the same. Some people may have many things in common, say a as result of their gender. They may even undergo the same experiences, but each person will react to them in their own way and these influences will be different for each individual. Even twins, who genetically have the most in common, will develop their own identity and sense of self. Everyone is unique and has their own identity. It is essential that practitioners recognize the importance of children developing a positive sense of their own identity and a strong sense of self-esteem.

Practitioners have an important part to play in this, and their very presence in a child's life will have an influence on this development, as will the other people with whom children have contact, together with the environment in which they live. Some children may receive many positive messages about themselves, which will help them develop a positive sense of identity and a strong sense of self-esteem. Other children may receive negative, stereotypical, discriminatory or oppressive messages, which may result in their developing low self-esteem and a poor sense of identity. Developing positive self-esteem and a strong sense of identity depends in part on children feeling accepted, valued and respected by others as worthwhile individuals.

Discrimination, prejudice, stereotyping and oppression all hurt people and may harm the development of a positive sense of self-identity and self-esteem. It must also be remembered that an individual feeling good about themselves does not mean them putting others down and making others feel negative about themselves. As Siraj-Blatchford said, 'A positive self-concept is necessary for healthy development and learning and includes feelings about gender, race, ability, culture and language. Positive self-esteem depends on whether children feel others accept them as competent and worthwhile'.

Dressing up helps children explore and 'try out' roles

Influences of ability on identity, self-esteem and development

Children all have different levels of ability. Some children will be gifted and talented. Directgov says, 'gifted and talented describes children and young people with an ability to develop to a level significantly ahead of their year group (or with the potential to develop those abilities)'. It defines gifted as 'those who have the ability on one or more academic subjects like maths and English'. It defines talented as 'those who have practical skills in areas like sport, music, design or creative and performing arts'. The National Association for Gifted Children says,

> Gifted children are often perfectionists and idealists and may equate achievement and grades with self-esteem and self-worth. This can lead to fear of failure and can interfere with their achievement in and out of school. The social and emotional development of a gifted child will probably not be at the same level as their intellectual development.

Quotes from children include 'I feel so lonely at school'; and 'why do they hate me for being clever?' Every child who is gifted and talented will have their own individual needs and no two children will be the same. Some children may 'play down' their abilities to 'fit in'; with their peers. Practitioners need to be aware of how to support children who are gifted and talented to develop a positive sense of identity and self-esteem.

A Chance to Think 5.6

Ability

A new child, Suba, is due to start in your setting next week. You have met with the parents who have told you they took Suba out of her last setting as she is very bright, but she was not having fun or being challenged and the staff could not cope with her asking lots of questions.

What are the issues for Suba and her parents?

What would you do and how would you support Suba and her parents?

Compare your answers with the sample answers in Appendix 5.

Influences of abuse on identity, self-esteem and development

We saw earlier in this book what is meant by child abuse and what constitutes child abuse. A child who has been abused may have low self-esteem and have issues concerning their identity. A child who has been abused may feel they are to blame for the abuse or that being abused is a part of life. Such feelings can have a profound effect on a child's sense of identity, Greff and Stuart say in *The RHP Companion to Foster Care*:

> the abuse can leave the child with feelings of having been damaged, of somehow being responsible for the fact the abuse happened, of guilt or shame and so on. All this will of course have a major impact on their sense of their own value and worth.

Practitioners need to work within their policies and procedure and work with children in a sensitive manner. They may need to seek help and advice when working with children who have been abused. Children need to be told that the abuse was not their fault and that they are not 'bad'. Some children may need the help of other professionals when working with issues related to the abuse. Practitioners may also need the help of other professionals when working with issues related to child abuse.

Influences of achievement on identity, self-esteem and development

In Chapter 1 we discussed research into teachers' perceptions of children at school and how they could be stereotypical. We also say how teachers' expectations of children may influence them and act as a self-fulfilling prophecy, and that children who are 'looked after' achieve lower results in school than children who are not looked after. Teachers and all practitioners who work with children are in a very powerful position. They are in a position of trust and influence. A child's achievements, or their sense of achievement, may have a great effect on the development of their identity and self-esteem.

Practitioners' assessments of children may also influence the way they behave towards children and consequently affect a child's achievements. Practitioners and parents are constantly assessing children both formally and informally. Parents may judge their child, either intentionally or unintentionally, in relation to things written in books or test scores, for example, developmental tests, or compare them with other children. Practitioners and parents will then talk to one another and compare information. This in turn influences practitioners because they learn information about children that they otherwise might not have known. This information is then used to make decisions about a child and their abilities. This informal assessment can be very subjective and may be based on a practitioners' personal beliefs and cultural 'norms'. This may lead practitioners to be biased towards an individual child or a group of children, particularly if practitioners are not aware of how their own personal frames of reference can influence their assessment of children. Indeed, Murphy said in the book 'Learners, Learning and Assessment', that there are 'no assessments that are culture fair, or culture blind'.

Formal assessments can include many aspects, for example, profiles, exams, statutory assessments, the common assessment framework and many more. Profiles are becoming more widely used. A profile may show where a child is at a given moment in time. Depending on the format used, a profile may include the skills and attitudes that a child has developed as well as what a child has learnt or knows. Because profiles are individual to each child, and children may be involved in helping to compile them, they can give a greater understanding of where a child has started from, and what they have achieved. Individuals are being compared, not with others, but against themselves. This is extremely positive for children ,as their achievements are being recognized, acknowledged and valued for what they are. Every child can do something and this needs to be acknowledged. Children who are able to can see and have an input into this process, which will help them develop a sense of achievement and self-esteem. A child with a sense of self and self-esteem may be motivated to learn and participate, for then they can understand what precisely they are achieving and that their individual efforts are therefore important. The Early Years Foundation Stage (EYFS) profile is used at the end of the Early Years Foundation Stage. The EYFS profile handbook says,

> The primary purpose of the EYFS profile is to provide year 1 teachers with reliable and accurate information about each child's level of development as they reach the end of the EYFS, enabling the teacher to plan an effective, responsive and appropriate curriculum to meet all children's needs.

Norm referenced assessments compare the achievements of individuals with those of other individuals, for example, they will rank class scores and there will be a first and a last. This can have a particularly strong influence on an individual's motivation and self-esteem. There always has to be a 'number one' and also an individual who comes last. For some individuals, no matter how hard they try, or what they learn or achieve, they will never come 'top of the class'. They may become de-motivated, or start to see themselves as 'not able to learn', which leads us back to the self-fulfilling prophecy. An individual who comes 'top of the class' may also be influenced by the results, They may feel they do not have to try, and consequently may acquire a false sense of themselves and of what they are capable. Norm referenced assessments may also give practitioners a false sense of children's achievements, for example, the individual who comes last may have actually learnt a great deal since the last assessment, but this may not be recognized in the results. They may feel they have put in a great deal of effort and it is not being recognized. To quote Murphy again, 'for effective learning, it makes a difference if pupils believe that the effort is more important than ability, that mistakes are an inevitable part of learning, and that they have control over their own learning'. Even the way practitioners work together and the records they make and keep can influence both themselves and the achievements of a child. Drummond says in the book 'Assessing Children's Learning',

> I like to make up my own mind. I like to start with a clean slate, children can be too easily labelled, teachers are always biased. I leave the records alone until I have had a chance to see for myself.

We can see that achievement can, and does, play a part in the development of self-esteem and identity. Practitioners need to be aware of the large role they play in this and how their day-to-day work and behaviour may have a huge impact on children and their achievements. Practitioners need to communicate with one another and constantly evaluate their own actions, behaviour, assessment methods, assumptions and biases. They need to recognize the achievements and efforts of all individual children and to support, encourage and value the efforts and achievements of each child. Practitioners need to know where a child started from and what they can do, so that they are clear about what a child has achieved.

Influences of adoption on identity, self-esteem and development

Some children are adopted. They leave their birth family and live with another family who become legally responsible for them. For some children this will happen soon after they are born. They may go straight to live with their adoptive family or they may spend some time with foster carers or in a residential setting prior to their adoption. For other children it will happen later, and they will spend a greater amount of time with other carers, before being adopted. Some children may have been born in one country and be adopted by families living in another country. Some children may be adopted by families who have a different racial or cultural identity from them. Children may be told at different ages that they are adopted. Some will have been told they are adopted at a young age, other children may be told at a later age, some individuals will find out as adults, and a few individuals not be told at all that they are adopted. Being adopted may raise issues for children about their identity and development of self-esteem. Children may feel that they do not know who they are, or what their roots and history are. They may wonder who they 'fit in' or why they do not look like other family members. Children may worry about telling their friends they are adopted and how they will react to this information. Some children who are adopted may retain some contact with their birth family, others may not. Research in 2009 titled 'Beyond Culture Camp: Promoting Healthy Identity in Adoption', found that 'Adoption is an increasingly significant aspect of identity for adopted people as they age, and remains so even when they are adults'.

Influences of bereavement on identity, self-esteem and development

It is often difficult to think about and work with the issue of bereavement but Winston's Wish, the childhood bereavement charity, say 'it is estimated that every 22 minutes in Britain, a child or young person in the UK is bereaved of a parent and approximately 1 in 25 children and young people have experienced bereavement of a parent or sibling' – that's about the same as one child in every school classroom in the country. This means it is likely that at some stage of their career practitioners will work with a bereaved child and family.

Bereavement is going to have an effect on a child's development, behaviour and feelings. Children of different ages will have differing understandings of death and different reactions to it. Children under 5 do not fully understand time and so do not have a concept of 'forever', but they will react to the feelings and emotions of the people around them. Children between 5 to 8 years of age begin to understand that death is final and that they will not see the person again. They may experience feelings such as guilt or confusion. This may come out in their behaviour as anger, tantrums or aggression. They may become withdrawn or clingy, or manifest other behaviour changes. From 9 upwards children understand that death will happen to everyone and is the end of bodily life. This may again be reflected in much of their behaviour. They may withdraw, become clingy, be tearful or aggressive, they may start to bully other children or become very emotional.

All children may feel lost and alone. They may feel guilty in that they have somehow caused this. The relationship that they had with the person is gone and this can result in a feeling of emptiness. If it is the loss of a sibling, parent or other significant person in their life then this is going to have a profound effect on their identity and self-esteem. Settings can provide a familiar routine, stability and a supportive key person at this difficult time in a child's life. Practitioners may find it difficult to deal with issues around bereavement and may need to seek support, advice or training to help them work with this subject and so be able to support children and families. Winston's Wish reports,

> One young person told us, "*My Mum died and my life changed for ever, it was the biggest thing that ever happened to me. My teacher never mentioned it.*" Stories like this are not uncommon. The teacher had acted no doubt, with good intentions, but the message that their pupil received was not a caring or helpful one.

They go on to say that children need 'Information and education, opportunities to express their feelings, communication, opportunities to remember and meeting others'.

Settings also need to remember that different religions will have different beliefs, traditions and practices around death and bereavement that may influence how they work with children and what information they are given. There are some useful books that settings can use with children including *No Matter What* by Debi Gliori, *Drop Dead* by Babette Cole and *The Frog Ballet* by Amanda McCardie. Before reading them practitioners need to read them first and be confident in what they contain and their own response to them. They also need to consider when, and how, to use them with children. Children need support to express their feelings about how bereavement has affected them.

Influences of being bullied on identity, self-esteem and development

Many children are the victims of bullies and some children bully other children. Childline says that:

> Bullying can happen to anyone at any age. Being bullied at school, home or online might involve someone pushing you, hitting you, teasing you, talking about you or calling you names. No one has the right to hurt you or make you feel bad, and if you are being bullied you don't have to put up with it, you can talk to someone about it.

Children who are bullied face issues around the development of their identity and self-esteem. Children who are bullied may feel isolated or scared, they may not want to attend setting. They may feel it is their fault. Some children may become depressed or self–harm and in some cases children may attempt suicide. Often children do not report being bullied. Bullying can have many long-term effects on children. The NSPCC study in 2000 titled 'Child maltreatment in the United Kingdom: A study of the prevalence of child abuse and neglect' says 'A quarter of children bullied by their peers reported that they suffered long term harmful effects lasting into adulthood'.

Children who bully also face issues around the development of their identity and self-esteem. Indeed, research shows that some children who bully have high self-esteem. Children may have experienced violence at home or may be being bullied themselves. They may not be able to express their feelings or control their anger. Practitioners need to be aware of, and working with issues around bullying in order to support all children. They need to observe both individual children and groups of children to see what is happening in the setting. Settings should have an anti-bullying policy that everyone is aware of and which children, parents and practitioners, are all working within. Practitioners need to listen to children, and respond to what they are being told. They also need to act as positive role models for children and be aware of the messages that their own behaviour is giving to children. It is extremely important to work with parents. Some practitioners may need additional information, training and support to help work with this issue.

Influences of disability and special needs on identity, self-esteem and development

There are many types of disability. The Disability Discrimination Act defines disability as 'a physical or mental impairment, which has a substantial and long-term adverse affect on a person's ability to perform normal day-to-day activities'. The type and influence of the disability on an individual's life may have differing effects on the development of that individual's identity and self-esteem. There are two different models of disability. The first is the 'Medical Model' of disability. In this model the disability is seen to be a 'problem' that the person with the disability needs to be able to find ways to 'cope' with the disability. Disability is seen as a medical issue. The responsibility is on the person with the disability to adapt in order to 'fit in'. The other model of disability is the 'Social Model'. This model was greatly influenced by people with disabilities. While is accepts the need for medical help and care, it focuses on the way that society causes the barriers that discriminate against people with disabilities. The social model of disability sees the person first and the disability second. It is useful for practitioners to reflect on these models of disability and how they may influence their own values and behaviour and the values and behaviour of the setting as a whole, as they have a huge impact on the development of identity and self-esteem of the children they work with. Some people see children with disabilities as 'sad' or to be 'pitied' as they will never 'get well'. This in turn may influence how an individual with a disability is perceived and consequently how they may then perceive themselves. A child will pick up messages they receive from people and their surroundings about themselves. If an individual is unable to gain access to a particular place, they may feel marginalized. If a child is unable to communicate with others who do not understand, or use the same communication systems as they use, they may feel frustrated or rejected. With all disabilities there may be a spectrum for example, a person with a hearing loss may have a cold or 'glue ear' that affects their hearing slightly and may be temporary. At the other end of the spectrum a person may be completely deaf. Some children may have a disability that is not immediately obvious. It is important that practitioners do not make assumptions about children, their disability or their identity. They need to see the child first and take into account their individual needs dependent on their development, and not see the disability first. Some children with disabilities may be very confident, outgoing and have a strong sense of identity; others may be lacking in confidence, and have a low sense of self-esteem or poor sense of identity. Often children react to people whose appearance is different from theirs. This can be true if a child sees an individual with a disability who looks different from them. Children often ask questions that embarrass the adults accompanying them. The reaction of the adult in this situation will have an effect on the identity and self-esteem of both the child asking the question and the person with the disability. A child who has a disability may find it hard to develop a positive sense of self-esteem and identity. As we saw earlier in this section, people often see the disability first before they see the individual; or perhaps the identity of the individual gets caught up with the disability and that is all people focus on. Micheline Mason says in the book *Good Practice in Caring for Young Children with Special Needs*.

> We (disabled people) reject the inhumanity of the 'medical model' of thinking, involved in labelling and identifying people by their impairing conditions. Calling

someone a 'Down's child' or a 'spina bif' makes the child no more than their condition . . . the social model of disability identifies prejudice and discrimination in institutions, policies, structures and the whole environment of our society as the principle for our exclusion . . . we must reject the legacy of the past that has excluded us and see children as they really are – not 'categories; but as citizens and with contributions to make if we let them.

We have already seen how powerful language can be. Being referred to as a 'disabled person' means the disability comes first. The example above a gives a very powerful message about how language may be used in a negative way and can influence how individuals are perceived. Terms such as 'the disabled' depersonalize people. As with all issues concerning identity, it is important to recognize that disability is only one area that may affect how an individual sees themselves. A child with a disability will also have other areas that affect their identity, for example, gender, family composition, colour and culture, to name but a few. Each will overlap and make a contribution as to how an individual perceives themselves and their identity. All children can do something and are able to achieve things. Practitioners need to build on what a child can do and not what they cannot do. Children need to feel secure, loved, respected and valued. Practitioners need to ensure a child with a disability is able to develop a strong sense of self-esteem and identity and to be able to participate in the setting. This may be done working by with parents to find out what needs their child have; by making changes to layout of the setting, for example, putting carpet or mats on the floor to improve listening conditions; giving children the space and time they need; ensuring children can access resources and activities, this may mean putting them on the floor and having the resources children need to enable them to participate; ensuring all children can see images of children with disabilities in the resources and in the wider environment.

A Chance to Think 5.7

Disability

Hisham has just started in your setting. He wears glasses indoors and has to change into sunglasses when he goes out and he cannot go out in very bright sunlight. The other children have started referring to him as 'the boy who wears glasses', rather than his name 'Hisham'. Hisham is starting to get upset by this.

What are the issues for Hisham and his parents?

What would you do and how would you support Hisham and his parents?

Compare your answers with the sample answers in Appendix 5.

Influences of domestic violence on identity, self-esteem and development

Like child abuse, domestic violence can take place in any family, across all cultures, and religions. The Home Office define domestic violence as:

> any threatening behaviour, violence or abuse between adults who are or have been in a relationship, or between family members. It can affect anybody, regardless of their gender or sexuality. The violence can be psychological, physical, sexual or emotional. It can include honour based violence, female genital mutilation, and forced marriage.

Many children can be affected by domestic violence. The Home Office statistics for 2002 found that 'at least 750.000 children a year witness domestic violence'. Children be affected in many ways and can have many responses to seeing and hearing domestic violence take place. These can include behaviour patterns, emotional and cognitive effects, such as copying what they have seen and heard; inability to express emotions; stress; powerlessness; low self-worth and other responses. These not only affect children as they grow but these effects can also influence their lives as adults.

  This is a sensitive subject for all practitioners. Sometimes they will not know that children and families are experiencing domestic violence. It is possible that some practitioners may themselves be experiencing domestic violence at home. Sometimes children and parents will disclose that they are experiencing domestic violence. It is essential that practitioners listen to children and families and support them. It is also essential that practitioners observe all aspects of a child's development and provide for and support it. Like abuse, domestic violence can have a profound effect on how a child feels about themselves, their identity and self-esteem. Practitioners may need help, support or training, in working with this and they should raise this with their manager or the person who supports them.

Influences of families on identity, self-esteem and development

Family composition

Families are made up of many different permutations, as we saw in Chapter 1. Some children are being brought up in single parent families. The Gingerbread report, 'Family finances', published in 2010 says that

> one in four families are headed by just one parent. These families are more likely to be below the poverty line; over half (52%) of children in single parent families

is poor . . . Family poverty, whether in a one- or two-parent household, damages children's experiences of childhood, impacts on their future prospects.

Both single parenthood and poverty can raise identity and self-esteem issues for children. Children want to 'belong', and in these days of ever-growing commercialization, having and owning items is becoming important for more and more individuals be it the latest trainers or other items that children in their peer group possess. Peer pressure can influence how individuals feel about themselves and how they see themselves fitting in or belonging to a group. Being part of a one-parent family can also influence a child's identity and self-esteem. Some people stereotype or make assumptions about lone parents and their circumstances. As with all stereotypes and assumptions these may be incorrect. The reasons a family is headed by a lone parent are as many and varied as the reasons for other family structures. A person may have made a conscious decision to be a lone parent, for example Jodie Foster, the Hollywood film star. Two parents may have lived together and then separated, with a child living with one parent and having contact with the other parent. A parent may have died, leaving the remaining parent to bring up any children alone. A child may be brought up by a lone foster parent. In every case the parent may be either male or female. Each of these differing situations may have a different impact on the life of a child. Families may also be made up of two heterosexual parents, or one or both parents may be gay or lesbian. Some practitioners may not have considered this family composition and may feel uncomfortable with it, depending on their own values and feelings concerning sexuality. Other families attending the setting may be discriminatory, as they may feel homosexuality is wrong or contrary to their religious beliefs. Children may ask questions about why their friend has two mothers or two fathers, and practitioners need to think about how they would respond to these situations. We have seen that not all families are 'nuclear' families made up of a mother, father and 2.4 children. Many children live in reconstituted or extended families. Every family member, fathers, mothers, children, grandparents, uncles, and all other members have an important role to play in the family. This whole book is about the issues that affect and influence a child's development. How a child is brought up, and by whom, is one of the major influences that will shape a child's identity and self-esteem. Practitioners needs to ensure they value and respect all the different types of family composition and ensure they provide a variety of images of the various family structures and compositions. They need to be aware of the impact of particular celebrations such as Mother's day and what this may mean to children who do not live with their mother. Practitioners also need to be prepared to discuss and respond to comments and questions about families in a sensitive and non-discriminatory manner.

Fathers have an important role to play in the lives of their children

Place in Family

A child's identity, self-esteem and how they see themselves may also be influenced by their place in the family. Are they the youngest, eldest, middle or only child? There is much research into birth order and how it may affect and influence a child's personality. As with all research findings, some of this will be true for some children and not for others. Only children may enjoying being the centre of attention. Eldest children can often develop responsible behaviour traits. Second children may be a 'bit of a rebel'. Middle children of three may be adaptable and get on with older and younger siblings, and the youngest child often remains the 'baby' of the family. Research into self-esteem and birth order shows that the eldest and youngest children tend to have higher self-esteem than middle born children. This may be because older children have all of their parent's attention and resources until siblings are born. The youngest child may get lots of attention from both parents and older siblings.

Practitioners may wish to reflect on their own position in their family and how it has influenced who they are, how they see themselves and how this then influences their work with children.

Parenting styles

Much has been researched and written about the role parents play in the development of their children. Psychologist Diana Baumrind identified and developed the concept of parenting styles that play a part in how a child develops. These parenting styles are used to define 'normal' variations in parenting, which are seen to be about how parents help their child to learn how to behave and react in social situations, and how parents control children. They are not used to define parenting styles that may be abusive or neglectful. The parenting styles reflect two important parts of the parenting role; parental responsiveness and parental demandingness. Parenting styles can influence a child's behaviour, how they get on socially, their performance at school, and their confidence and self-esteem. The four parenting styles are:

Indulgent (Permissive) parents – Baumrind say indulgent parents are 'more responsive than they are demanding, they are non-traditional and lenient, do not require mature behaviour, allow considerable self-regulation and avoid confrontation'.

Authoritarian parents – Baumrind says authoritarian parents are 'obedience – and status oriented, and expect their orders to be obeyed without explanation'.

Authoritative parents – Baumrind says authoritative parents 'monitor and impart clear standards for their children's conduct. They are assertive, but not intrusive and restrictive. Their disciplinary methods are supportive, rather than punitive. They want their children to be assertive and socially responsible, and self-regulated as well as cooperative'.

Unloved parents – make few demands and have little communication with their children. May be generally detached from their children's lives.

Research shows that children of parents who have authoritarian parenting styles rank lower in happiness, social competence and self-esteem. Children of parents who have unloved parenting styles generally have low self-esteem and are less competent than their peers. Children of parents who have an indulgent parenting style may find they cannot cope with demands of school, but they have better self-esteem than children of authoritarian or unloved parenting styles. The children who have high self-esteem are the children of parents who have an authoritative parenting style. Parenting styles may vary because of the way parents themselves were raised with culture, personality and many other reasons playing a part. Settings have a responsibility to work with parents and help and support them. Many settings offer parenting support groups and parenting programmes that help parents reflect on and develop their parenting skills and styles in order that they may develop confidence as parents and are able to support children in all areas of their development. Practitioners may also find that they recognize their own parenting style and this can influence how they work with children and families.

Influences of gender on identity, self-esteem and development

In Chapter 1 we saw how gender can influence and affect identity development. There are differences between men and women. Boys and girls are equal but different. Babies soon learn if they are a boy or a girl and what behaviour might be expected of them. Boys learn how to be a boy and what characteristics and qualities are deemed to be male or masculine. Girls learn how to be a girl and what characteristics and qualities are deemed to be female or feminine. We saw in Chapter 1 that this varies between cultures. It also varies between individuals. What the differences are, how they came about and how they influence identity have long been debated and will continue to be debated for many years to come. Carrie Paechter in the book 'Being Boys Being Girls' says:

> A person's masculinity or femininity is not innate, it is not natural, but instead is something that is learned, constantly reworked and reconfigured, and enacted to the self and to others. Masculinity and femininity are active states; they are not just what we are, they are what we do, how we appear, how we think of ourselves, at particular times and in specific places.

It is very important for practitioners to be aware of their own attitudes and values around gender, masculinity and femininity, and not to stereotype boys and girls into specific gender roles and identities.

We saw earlier in this chapter that language has a significant influence on gender and the development of identity, and we have seen how achievement can influence self-esteem and identity. We saw in Chapter 1 that boys and girls are treated differently, and every year when exam results are published there is a great debate in the media about the grades and differing gender achievements. Indeed the EYFS profile attainments for 2009 show that girls outperformed boys in 11 of the 13 scales of the EYFS profile.

Girls and boys are equally important but there are differences between the genders. Children learn about gender and what they learn affects their identity and self-esteem. As we have seen, attitudes and values also develop regarding gender, and stereotypes and discrimination occur. Parents will have views about how children should behave based on their gender and these will be passed on to their children who may, or may not conform to them.

Practitioners need to consider their own values and attitudes, and those of the setting, towards gender and how they work with parents around gender issues. Parents may say that they do not want boys playing with 'girls toys', or girls playing rough and tumble as it is not 'lady-like'. If boys and girls are expected to behave in a particular way, then that will have an influence on their development and of their identity and behaviour.

It is important for boys and girls to see both male and female positive role models in their lives. There are male practitioners working with children and young people but they are in the minority. Children need to see men in the setting and this can be challenging for some settings. Practitioners also need to remember that boys and girls will play in different ways, even if they start with the same resources. Practitioners need to plan and provide for play and activities that allow both boys and girls to explore their identity and become secure in it. Giving children tasks to undertake so that they feel a valued part of the setting can help develop their self-esteem. Practitioners should have high expectations of all children who should be allowed to develop as individuals and find out what they are capable of. Practitioners need to consider their own behaviour and how it affects the identity development and self-esteem of the children they work with, for example, they need to consider the language they use, the resources provided and how they are used, the images seen and not seen in the environment and the messages they give, the roles children may be expected to conform to, and the expectations of parents and how practitioners communicate with parents.

A Chance to Think 5.8

Gender

A father has been bringing his daughter age 1 year and his son age 4 ½ years to your setting. You notice dad does not seem to interact or talk to his daughter but spends a lot of time interacting with and talking to his son.

What are the issues for the children and father?

What would you do and how would you support the children and father?

Compare your answers with the sample answers in Appendix 5.

Influences for Gypsy, Roma and Traveller children on identity, self-esteem and development

Travellers are classed as a racial group, and therefore the contents of the Race Relations Act 1976 and the Race Relations (Amendment) Act 2000 apply. Traveller families and the children of traveller families may experience discrimination, which may in turn affect their self-esteem and development of identity. Some travellers may have a nomadic lifestyle; others may live on sites and others in houses. Dcsf report 'The Inclusion of Gypsy, Roma and Traveller children' found that many Families from Gypsy, Roma and Traveller communities do not declare their ethnic backgrounds to settings for fear of bullying and prejudice. It says,

> Children from Gypsy, Roma and Traveller communities should feel safe and cherished in school and therefore parents and pupils will be proud to identify themselves. Schools now have a duty to promote community cohesion and this is a real issue for their attention.

It goes on to give reasons why it is important to declare ethnicity. For pupils, some of the reasons given are,

> It is good to be proud of who you are. It is a human right for the world to respect you for who you really are. There is nothing to be ashamed of in being a Gypsy, Roma or Traveller.

The reasons given for parents include: If your children go to school in fear of disclosing their ethnic identity they will find it hard to make friends and may feel socially isolated and lonely. This experience should not be part of a happy childhood at school and is seldom part of successful learning. and 'It is important to children's psychological, social and personal development to be proud of their family and its cultural heritage'. Schools and Local Authorities are also advised that 'Teachers know that for children to experience happy and successful learning, they need to be self-confident in their personal and family identity and that this is inextricably linked to their self-esteem as learners' and also,

> Schools and local authorities want pupils to achieve to their full potential and it is recognized that pupils who are fearful and who have to deny their identity in the school setting are destined to underachieve compared with pupils who do not suffer this unfair and needless disadvantage.

It is crucial that practitioners communicate with parents and children and develop a relationship of trust with them so that parents and children are able to share with practitioners their feelings and wishes. Setting can also participate in Gypsy, Roma, Traveller History Month which takes place every year as does the International Gypsy guitar festival. Setting also need to ensure they have resources that reflect Gypsy, Roma and Traveller life. These could include examples of art and music and the 'Tess the Traveller' story books for and about travellers for children between the age of 3 and 7. Many Roma, Gypsy and Travellers also wear jewellery that has great cultural significance and should not be removed by practitioners. Practitioners may also find it helpful to contact relevant professional organizations for help and support.

Influences of health issues and illness on identity, self-esteem and development

All children get ill at some point in their lives. For some children, illness or health issues may occur for a short period of time, for example, a broken arm or a cold. For others, illness or health issues may affect them for the whole of their lives. Chronic illness in the under 16 age group has been increasing over the last 20 years in Britain. A chronic illness is an illness that goes on for an extended period of time, for example, asthma or diabetes. A chronic or ongoing illness or health condition can affect all areas of a child's development, including the development of identity and self-esteem. If a child has to attend hospital appointments, or have time off school, they may miss out on their education and being with their peer group and friends. Many children have to take ongoing medication during the day while in the setting, for example, for asthma, eczema, diabetes, allergies and many other conditions. How practitioners in the setting manage this can greatly affect how a child feels both about themselves and their health condition. A child's health can impact on many areas of their life for example, what they can eat / not eat, where they can go / not go, what clothes they can wear / not wear, what they can participate in /not participate in. This can have a big impact on children and may affect how they feel about themselves and also how their friends perceive them. Parents may feel stressed or worried by their child's ongoing health issues and this can then impact on the child. Parents may worry about how practitioners in settings are coping with their child's health issues. Will they recognize when they need help or support and are they encouraging them to participate in the life of the setting as much as they are able to? Asthma UK says, that

> 1.1 million children (one in 11) are currently receiving treatment for asthma in the UK. Throughout childhood, asthma is generally more common in boys than in girls. This trend reverses during puberty when more girls develop asthma for the first time. By the age of 18 years, asthma is more common in girls than boys.

Allergies are becoming more and more common. Some children are allergic to certain foods, others to dust, latex or other substances. The allergic reaction that individuals have may vary in type and severity. Blossom, the children's campaign from Allergy UK, published a report in 2008 called 'The Impact Allergy Has On Their Lives And The Lives of Their Families.' It found that over 40 per cent of children are now suffering from allergy and that 47 per cent of the children in the survey they carried out had at some point in their life been excluded from activities which non-allergic children would regard as a commonplace activity. The day-to-day life of children with allergies can be hugely affected. This then has an effect on the development of their identity and self-esteem. Sometimes a child with allergy may be embarrassed about it. They not may be to get in to settings as settings are not able to cope with allergy, or, as confirmed by the blossom report, they are excluded from activities in settings. Other children may comment about the effects of the allergy and it has been known for parents to tell their children not to play with children with allergies or not invite them to parties as they are not able to cope if a child has an allergic reaction. Children may not be able to go to particular places for example, restaurants or the park. Parents may feel anxious or worried about their child and this may be picked up by the child.

Children, parents and practitioners need to feel safe in the setting and confident about what to do and how to support all children with illness or ongoing medical issues. This may include ensuring the environment is suitable for children, for example, ensuing carpets are clean and gloves or protective clothing are available for those children who need it; ensuring the setting has policies, procedures and protocols in place that all practitioners are aware of and are following; training for practitioners in health and safety and use of medication, for example, EpiPens; talking to children and explaining about allergies, illness, medical conditions and what they mean. This can be done at circle time as part of an activity, or responding to a child who has made a comment or asked a question; using resources and books; planning and ensuring children can join in activities. This may mean looking at alternatives so that children are not excluded; ensuring any medication is given sensitively. The World Health Organisation defines health as 'a state of complete mental, physical and emotional well-being and not merely the freedom from disease or infirmity'. It is essential that practitioners support children with illness and health issues to take part in all aspects of life in the setting and help them to develop a positive sense of identity and self-esteem.

A Chance to Think 5.9

Illness / allergy

Safa has been attending your setting for some time. She is a lively child and enjoys dancing with her friends. Recently Safa has developed an allergy to strawberries. She brings a packed lunch and she has been sitting with her friends to eat her lunch. You manager has told you that due to her allergy Safa must now sit by herself on a table away from the other children.

   What effect might this have on Safa?

   What could you do in this situation?

   Compare your answers with the sample answers in Appendix 5.

Influences of language on identity, self-esteem and development

We saw earlier on in this chapter the importance of language and communication strategies. Language and identity are closely linked. We have seen how language can be used to stereotype individuals and groups. We have also seen how language, particularly the English language, can be very male oriented, with the use of male pronouns in books and in describing some occupations, for example, when the word 'nurse' is used, some people tend to think about this as a female profession, where the word 'doctor' suggests to some people a male profession. Although both of these words are in fact gender neutral people's experiences have led to them becoming laden with gender inferences. The publication 'Women and Language' from the European Commission reports: 'In language in the social environment, women are rendered transparent, non-existent, invisible and there is an indirect message that they should keep quiet.' An example of this is how some professions can be given a male label, for example, policeman, fireman. If this language is used in settings it may prevent both genders from using resources and equipment to its full potential. Both children and adults pick up messages from the way language is used. Practitioners need to think about how they use words and language and the messages that they are giving. We have seen how the language, accent or dialect spoken by an individual may influence the way they are perceived by others and that people may make judgements about individuals depending on the way they speak. We also explored the development of language, including the development of more than one language. The Dcsf Publication, 'Supporting children learning English as an additional language' says 'Bilingualism is an asset, and the first language has a continuing and significant role in identity, learning and the acquisition of additional languages', It also goes on to say 'home languages are also vital for maintaining positive family connections'. It is therefore it is important to maintain the language of the home, particularly where older family members who care for the child do not speak English. Otherwise this may mean that they are no longer able to have proper meaningful conversations with each other. We have seen how important families are in developing and maintaining a child's sense of identity and self-esteem. If families are not able to communicate together this can be affected. Individuals who do not use a spoken language, but who may 'sign', use a symbol language or use technology as a means of communication may often miss out on some of the 'everyday' communication and conversations. They may feel isolated by this. Practitioners need to be aware of how the use of language and communication can impact on the development of identity. They need to think about how they use and respond to language and the messages thus portrayed. Practitioners also need to ensure that they are valuing and respecting an individual's first language and that all children are able to use their first language. If individuals are unable to use their first language they may feel that their language is not valued and in consequence feel that they too are not valued. Practitioners may therefore need to lean to sign, use symbol languages or use technology in order to communicate with children and parents. Children and parents also need to see and hear their own language used and reflected in the environment, It needs to be accessible to them and valued and respected by practitioners at all times.

A Chance to Think 5.10

Attitudes towards gender in language

You are sitting watching children's television with a small group of boys and girls when one programme finishes. The presenters between programmes, who are both male, start talking about what happened in the programme, and the first presenter asks the second presenter to copy something that has happened in the programme. He does this well, but the first presenter laughs and says, 'You were run running like a girl. Stop being such a girl'. One of the children, Gerald (a boy,) starts laughing and another child, Hazel (a girl), says, 'don't laugh it's not funny'.

What would you do in this situation?

Compare your answers with the sample answers in Appendix 5.

Influences of legal status on identity, self-esteem and development

Individuals living in the United Kingdom many have differing legal status. Some individuals will have full legal status and others may not. They may be refuges or be seeking asylum. The word 'refugee' is defined in the 1951 United Nations Convention Relating to Refugees. In the Convention, a refugee is defined as someone who: has a well-founded fear of persecution for reasons of race, religion, nationality, membership of a particular social group, or political opinion; is outside the country they belong to or normally reside in, and is unable or unwilling to return home for fear of persecution.

While someone is waiting for their application to be considered, they are known as an 'asylum seeker'. Many refuges will have experienced war or violence, spent time in hiding and had a long and dangerous journey to safety. This, and experiences like this, will have an effect on a child's self-esteem and identity. Children who are refuges may be experiencing discrimination, have physical and mental health needs, feel isolated, and may not be able to understand the language or the day-to-day systems in their new environment. They may feel loss of their country of origin and confused by what is happening to them. Their parents may feel traumatized which will have an impact on their ability to care for their children. They may have had to leave family members behind resulting in worry or guilt. Another issue that a family may have to deal with is the uncertainty about their legal status. When families arrive in the United Kingdom they are assessed in centres that are not designed for children. Some children, even children as young as 6 and 7, may be travelling by themselves and not have the support of family members. A 2009 report by the House of Commons reports that 'in 2007, 3,525 unaccompanied children aged 17 or under applied for asylum in the United Kingdom . . . and as of March 2008, 3,500 unaccompanied children were "looked after".' UNICEF UK said in an article in 2004 about child refuges that 'refugee children continue to face public stigmatization, racism and discriminatory polices. . . . Refugee children also have specific needs that require particular attention and are largely being ignored'. Every child who is a refugee will have their own individual and diverse needs and must be treated as a child first. Practitioners must ensure that their individual needs are planned for and met. Tina Hyder, in an article in *Nursery World* (2001) described STOP – a framework for working with refugee children: 'S – Space and structure. T – Trust and talking, O – Opportunities to play, P – Partnership with parents (and other carers).' Practitioners following this framework will be able to begin working with children and families in a supportive way. Some children may need specialist help in helping them to deal with what has happened to them and their family, while other children may need time, consistency and support to help them develop and resolve issues concerning their self-esteem, identity and development. Practitioners need to evaluate how they are using play, activities and opportunities for children to develop relationships and share their feelings and experiences in a sensitive and appropriate way. The use of persona dolls may be particularly helpful. A sensitive key person is essential to help children feel safe, secure, listened to and to support their development. Settings may find it helpful to find out about Refugee Week, held every year in June. Practitioners themselves may need to seek support, time, knowledge and help in working with children who are refugees.

Influences for children who are left-handed on identity, self-esteem and development

Initially babies will use both hands and from about 18 months some children will begin to show preference for using a particular hand, but some children will still not show a preference until after 4 years of age, and many children even later. One in 12 of the general population is left-handed and 1 in 4 twins is left-handed. Growing up in a world dominated and set up for right-handed people can cause issues for children who are left-handed. They may have difficulty dressing and learning to write, as well as difficulty using some of the tools and equipment designed for use in the right hand. This may affect how they feel about themselves and influence their self-esteem.

There are also many negative attitudes around towards people who are left-handed. Many of these are based around superstition. It is not fully understood why some people are left-handed. Some theories say it is due to genetics and others say it is due to the way the brain functions. Research has found that stuttering and dyslexia occur more often in people who are left-handed. There are many things that practitioners can do to support children who are left-handed and ensure they are able to participate fully in the setting and feel good about themselves. Initially practitioners need to observe children and make sure they offer children objects in both hands. Practitioners must never try and alter a child's preferred handiness. Thought needs to be given to the layout of the environment, for example, the position-ing of seating so that children do not 'clash elbows' when trying to do art and craft, writing or at mealtimes, and so on. Settings also need to ensure they have equipment and resources that children who are left-handed can use so that they are able to fully participate in all activities. This will include left-handed scissors as they have the blades reversed in them; pens and pencils with grips or left-handed pens and pencils; left-handed pencil sharpeners that have the blades reversed and rulers that go from right to left. Most importantly practitioners need to consider their attitudes to children who are left-handed and how these attitudes are reflected in their work with children.

Influences for 'looked after' children on identity, self-esteem and development

Not all children live with their birth family. The Dfes statistics for March 2009 show there were 60,900 looked after children as on 31 March 2009. Some children may spend time in short-term foster care and then return to live with their family. Some children may spend a longer period with foster carers and then be adopted, and some children will spend time in a residential setting. Children who are 'looked after' will have different experiences of family and being cared for from those children who live with their birth families. Some children may know their birth families, others may not. This in itself may have a deep impact on an individual's sense of self and identity. Some children may feel a sense of loss, some may feel rejected and confused, some may feel they have done something wrong and others may wonder about their origins and background. An awareness and acknowledgment of a person's origin is an important part of that individual's identity development. Greff and Stuart in 'The Companion to Foster Care' quote 'The Who Cares?' Group, which said that young people in the care system should be given

> the right to know who we are . . . to have factual information about our family origins and background . . . [we must] makes sure that every young person really understands [their] situation and why [they] cannot live with [their] family.

Children who are 'looked after' may have several different professionals involved in, and knowing about, their lives and making decisions about them. They may regularly experience situations in their lives that children who live with their birth families do not, for example, moves between care settings and people, regular reviews, medicals and the involvement with a variety of professions and a wider number of people having personal information about them. Contact with birth families can help children who are looked after to develop and maintain a strong sense of identity and self-esteem. Contact may be through regular meetings, phone contact, letters, or via technology such as face book. The Ofsted publication 'Keeping in Touch' found that 'The longer a child had been in care, the more likely they were to have lost contact with their parents, brothers or sisters'. It can also be difficult and harmful for some children to keep in contact with their birth family and this can also have an effect on their sense of identity and self-esteem. National Institute for Health and Clinical Excellence publication Draft Guidance The physical and emotional health and wellbeing of looked after children and young people reports that ' about 60 per cent of those looked after in England were reported to have emotional and mental health problems. It also reported that a high proportion of looked after children and young people experience poor health, educational and social outcomes after leaving care' (Department for Children, Schools and Families 2009c). It also found that for children from birth to 5 years of age that

> The absence of a permanent carer at such a young age can jeopardise children's chances of developing meaningful attachments and have adverse consequences for their long-term wellbeing. Carers can unwittingly contribute to the development of insecure attachment patterns. For example, they may withdraw when the child appears not to need them – rather than making it clear that they are always there to help, so ensuring the child feels secure. It is difficult for children to join nurseries and other early years settings if they have not experienced secure relationships with care givers.

It goes on to say that:

> All looked-after children and young people need to develop a positive identity, emotional resilience and self-esteem. Achieving and maintaining a sense of security may be more difficult for children and young people from black and minority ethnic, multiple heritage backgrounds, or who are unaccompanied asylum seekers – they may also face racism and isolation. Care plans for these children need to capture the environmental circumstances for each child – where identity and cultural heritage is acknowledged and addressed.

Some practitioners, depending on the setting they work in, may or may not know that a child is 'looked after'. Many practitioners for example, foster carers or those working in residential settings will be working with children who are 'looked after'. All practitioners should work equally with all children to develop a positive sense of self and identity. If practitioners are aware that a child is 'looked after' they should not make assumptions or judgements about why that is the case or label individual children. Some children may have contact with their birth family, some may be involved in life story work and practitioners need to participate sensitively and support them with that. Practitioners need to be alert to the needs of individual children and work with them sensitively and accordingly.

Influences of mental health on identity, self-esteem and development

Mental health is an area about which some practitioners feel uncomfortable as they may know little about it, may have read or heard things about it, or be unsure what it is and what it means. The Department for Education and Skills publication Promoting Children's Mental Heath within early years and School Settings says:

> Mental health is about maintaining a good level of personal and social function-ing. For children and young people, this means getting on with others, both peers and adults, participating in educative and other social activities and having a positive self-esteem. Mental health is about coping and adjusting to the demands of growing up. It does not all happen at one point in time, and appears to result from an interactive process to which all can contribute, based on the child's environment, social and cultural context.

It goes on to say that some of the problems children can face

> are emotional disorders; conduct disorders; hyperkinetic disorders; developmental disorders; attachment disorders; eating disorders; habit disorders; post-traumatic stress syndromes; somatic disorders; psychotic disorders.
>
> When a problem is particularly severe or persistent over time, or when a number of these difficulties are experienced at the same time, children are often described as having mental health disorders.

The Office for National Statistics (ONS) survey found that in 2004, one in ten children and young people (10%) aged 5–16 years had a clinically diagnosed mental disorder.

Children who are experiencing poor mental health may have low self-esteem and self-worth. It may affect the development of their identity, as people may see and label 'the problem' before they see the child. Some children may be bullied or teased. They may feel rejected and isolated, and some may self-harm.

Settings need to ensure that children (and parents) have a key person who knows, and can support them and understands the needs of the child and family. This requires practitioners to have a good grounding in child development in working effectively with parents in order to carry out this role effectively. Practitioners need to be able to promote positive behaviour management and have effective policies and procedures in place to underpin this. Practitioners also need to plan and carry out activities that promote the all areas of development and in particular social and emotional development.

Some children may have parents who have a mental health illness. This may mean that, at times, a parent is not able to provide the care a child needs, resulting in a child feeling upset or not able to understand what is happening. This may also mean that at times, a parent, is unable to support any aspect of their child's development, including the development of identity and self-esteem. If a parent is not feeling good about who they are, then this can impact on their child. Some children who have a parent with a mental illness may be teased or bullied. It may be that the mental health problems of parents impact on their children in many different ways. The publication 'Think child, think parent, think family: a guide to parental mental health and child welfare' by The Social Care Institute for Excellence says that 'An estimated one-third to two-thirds of children whose parents have mental health problems will experience difficulties themselves (ODPM 2004).'

Practitioners may need to seek advice from relevant professionals as to how best to support and work with children experiencing mental health difficulties.

Issues for mixed parentage / dual heritage children on identity, self-esteem and development

We will see how race and colour may influence and affect a child's identity. As we saw at the beginning of this section, every individual has many different components that go to make up their identity, every one of which is important. Children who have two parents from different backgrounds may have different issues that affect the development of their identity and self-esteem from children who have parents of the same background. We have seen how powerful language is and how it can affect people's perceptions. This is particularly true when using words describing children who have parents from two different backgrounds. Children of mixed parentage /dual heritage may be from many different backgrounds and cultures. Children of mixed parentage / dual heritage need to feel that the background and heritage of both parents is equally valued and respected. We saw in Chapter 1, and also above, that children may be discriminated against and that there are stereotypes of many individuals and groups. Children of mixed parentage / dual heritage may also experience discrimination and stereotypes that can be damaging. It is important to recognize that these stereotypes are not accurate, and being of mixed parentage / dual heritage is indeed very positive as seen in the titles of two publications on the subject: *The Colour of Love: Mixed Race Relationships* (Alibhai-Brown and Montague, 1992) and *The Best of Both Worlds: Celebrating Mixed Parentage* (Early Years Anti-Racist Network, n.d.).

Tizzard and Phoenix, in their book, *Black, White or Mixed Race?* reported on the research they had undertaken. Parents with dual heritage children, when interviewed, felt that they needed to provide a strong sense of identity for their children and to encourage confidence and self-esteem. One parent said,

> I have always said to x, 'it is not that the world is divided into black and white people; that is not the conflict. It is divided into prejudiced and non-prejudiced people, and they can be of any colour'.

Ilan Katz and Almal Treacher in their chapter titled 'The Social and Psychological Development of Mixed Parentage Children' in the book *Working with Children of Mixed Race* say 'we need to go beyond identity to understand the social reality of mixed race children and see it as a social phenomenon. A holistic theory of identity development in mixed race children would have to take into account;

- The global development of the child and their overall identity development.
- Cultural issues (food, music, etc.) how they are brought into the family and how they interact with race.
- Family structure and dynamics, including the unconscious racialization of family processes.
- The extended family and their acceptance of difference within the family.
- The community and neighbourhood context.
- The wider social context and how it changes from time to time.
- Moral or ethical views on the politics of race'

Practitioners need to recognize that children of mixed parentage / dual heritage may be from many different backgrounds and cultures and every child will be a unique individual. Some children may have some things in common and some may not have anything in common in the formation of their identity. Practitioners also need to recognize that every child needs to develop a positive sense of their own identity and the components that go together to make them the person they are. As we saw earlier in this chapter, identity is made up of many parts and all need to be recognized and valued. Mixed parentage / dual heritage children need to be able to recognize, value and feel proud of all the various facets of their heritage that come from both parents. Practitioners need to talk to parents so that all are working together to enhance children's self-esteem and identity.

A Chance to Think 5.11

Mixed Parentage / Dual Heritage

Jason is a child of mixed parentage attending your setting. In the staff room you hear a colleague refer to Jason as a 'half-caste' and say, 'It's a shame because he is neither one thing or another'.

How would you react in this situation?

What can you do to try and change your colleagues language and way of thinking?

What can you do to give Jason a positive sense of himself and his identity?

Compare your answers to the sample answers in Appendix 5.

Influences of poverty on identity, self-esteem and development

The number of children living in poverty is rising. The Save the Children report 'Measuring Severe Child Poverty in the UK' published in 2010 found that

> the number of children living in severe poverty has risen over the period 2005/ 05 – 2—7/08 from 11% to 15% of all children. This means living on less than £12,220 a year (for a couple with one child,) leaving families around £113 a week short of what they need to cover food, electricity and gas, phones, other bills, clothes, washing, transport and healthcare; not to mention furnishings, activities for children and other essential items. Children and their parents are missing out to everyday essentials such as food and clothing, They cannot afford things that most families take for granted, such as celebrating a birthday or having a short family holiday.

This is going to have an effect on a child's development and is linked to how they see themselves, their identity and self-esteem. For families who live in poverty, day-to-day living can be a struggle. If families cannot afford 'essential items' children may be hungry. They may have to wear 'second hand' clothes and not be able to afford the latest fashion or trends in toys and equipment. This may result in children feeling they 'do not fit in'. Children may feel embarrassed inviting friends round to their house to play or may not even be able to afford to invite them round for tea. They may not be able to take part in some of the activities provide by settings if a charge is made for it, even if it is a voluntary charge. Parents and children may feel they are being judged by other families or the setting. Some children may say they do not want to do the activity rather than say they are not doing it as they cannot afford it. Families and children may not be able to participate in family celebrations, for example, birthdays, religious festivals and so on, and they may feel particular pressure at these times with media advertising and when other children and families are talking about what they are doing or buying.

The child action poverty group reports that 'Children do not leave social and economic inequality at the school gates – they bring them into the classroom'. Being poor harms their well-being and limits their ability to learn. Poorer children are more likely to be tired, hungry and disengaged from the educational process. . . . Poverty makes people's lives shorter and more brutal than they need to be. Poverty is not simply about being on a low income and going without – it is also about being denied power, respect, good health, education and housing, basic self-esteem and the ability to participate in social activities . . . By 3 years old, poor children may be up to a year behind the wealthiest children in terms of cognitive development and 'school readiness'.

Settings and practitioners need to be sensitive to the economic status of families and not make assumptions about families. Settings that are free to children and families at point of entry but with expensive uniforms may prohibit some families from attending. Practitioners also need to be aware of how they speak to families and what they are requesting, and not take it for granted that all families will be able to afford to contribute to the setting or for outings. Many families and children say they feel judged by settings and by other parents and children. Practitioners need to be aware of the powerful use of language and the impact of prejudice and discrimination and aim to eliminate it in their setting. Practitioners need to ensure that children who are living in poverty feel comfortable in the setting and that practitioners support their development, particularly the development of their identity and self-esteem. Some practitioners may feel they themselves need additional help, support and training in this area.

A Chance to Think 5.12

Poverty

Jane and Tom are siblings who attend your setting. They are living on the fourth floor in a bed and breakfast hotel as the family are homeless. They have to share a bathroom with four other families on the same floor. They do have access to a washing machine but it is in the basement and is often being used by other families. Jane and Tom's parents are on income support. Jane is 4 years old and very independent. She is always clean and well dressed. Tom is 15 months old and wears nappies. Sometimes when he comes into the setting he smells of stale urine and is wearing the same nappy he went home in.

What would you do in this situation?

Compare your answers with the sample answers in Appendix 5.

Influences of race on identity, self-esteem and development

We know that every child has a racial background and we have seen that children receive messages about their identity from many sources. Jocelyn Emama Maximé in the book *How and Why Children Hate*, says that in order for children to develop a positive identity they need to be aware of their racial identity and have a positive image of it. She argues that some aspects of identity are common to all children, for example, self-esteem, self-concept, pride and social awareness, but that racial identity is not the same for all children. Children come from different racial backgrounds and need to have a positive image of their own racial background in order to develop a strong personal identity and self-esteem. This is particularly true for black children who grow up experiencing prejudice, discrimination and stereotyping. Maximé says 'I have argued that the nurturance of black children's development of racial identity is fundamental to sound psychological well-being.' Jane Lane in her book *Young Children and Racial Justice*, writes 'in a society where racism is endemic, it is particularly important to give positive messages about being black, being different (for example being a traveller, being Jewish, Polish or Irish) and learning to be, or being, bilingual'.

We saw in Chapter 1 that children do experience racism and that the media can perpetuate this. The Machperson report in 1999 defined a racist incident as 'any incident which is perceived to be racist by the victim or any other person'. It is not just children who may experience racism; parents, family members, practitioners and many other individuals may also experience it as well. If a parent or practitioner is experiencing racism then this may influence how they feel about themselves. This can affect how individuals relate to and work with children about developing a sense of identity and self-esteem.

We also saw in Chapter 1 that children do notice skin colour and make value judgements about it. We also saw that teachers make judgements and treat children differently depending on their background and colour. There has been much research into how children develop their racial identity. We know that children experience many different environments, for example, home, settings and so on. Dena Phillips Swanson et al. reported in their research titled 'Racial identity development during childhood' found 'children whose parents socialize them regarding their racial history and values report more positive self-concept than children who lack an intervention that protects them against unchallenged and pervasive stereotypes'.

Practitioners need to recognize that individuals and groups are discriminated against on account of their colour or perceived racial identity. Very young children can and do experience racism. This may lead them to having a low sense of self-esteem and a damaged sense of identity. Practitioners need to challenge their own perceptions and values as well as those of others. They also need to constantly review and evaluate their own practice to ensure that they are not being discriminatory and that they are enabling children to develop a strong and positive sense of identity.

Influences for children who stammer on identity, self-esteem and development

We discussed earlier in this chapter what a stammer is and how it can affect children's communication. Having a stammer can affect other areas of development as well. The National Stammering Association says,

> stammering is not simply a speech difficulty but is a serious communication problem. For the child or adult who stammers it can undermine their confidence and self-esteem, and affects their interactions with others as well as their education and employment prospects.

It goes on to talk about the use of terminology. It says,

> some people consider the phrase "person who stammers" (or PWS) or "child who stammers" preferable to "stammerer". Stammering is something a person does. It is by no means the most important thing about the person, let alone who he or she is.

It is important to support and help a child who has a stammer in order to help their language and communication development for as we have seen this can have a direct impact on their self-esteem and identity. This can best be done by communicating with parents and working with a speech and language therapist. It is also helpful to support children by not criticizing them and helping them by giving them time to communicate and think about what they want to say. Try not to 'take over' and finish a child's sentences for them.

Influences for twins on identity, self-esteem and development

Twins and multiple births have been rising in the UK in the last 20 years and it is anticipated that this trend will continue. Twins can be identical or non-identical. Identical twins (monozygotic twins) share the same chromosomes and genes. They are formed when one fertilized ovum that has been fertilized by one sperm splits into two. About one-third of all twins are identical. Non-identical twins (dizygotic or fraternal twins) are formed when two separate ova are fertilized at the same time by two separate sperm. Non-identical twins (dizygotic or fraternal twins) will share 50 per cent of their genes. They may be the same sex or a boy and girl. They are no more alike than any other brother or sister. Much research has been carried out on twins, including research into the nature / nurture debate into health and disease , twins in the classroom and much more. Indeed, Kings College, London, has a department of Twin Research & Genetic Epidemiology. Many settings will, at some time, have siblings who are twins attending it. Often schools, after discussion with parents, will advise that they are placed in different rooms or classes. Whatever arrangements are made it is important to treat each child as an individual and call them by their correct name. It is also important to support each child's individual interests and spend time with each child alone. Parents may also ask for advice and there are now many organizations that parents of twins can join for support. Just as in a setting it is important that parents spend time with each of their children alone, and where possible to try and dress them as individuals. Children who are twins have very particular issues to deal with regarding the development of their identity, especially if they are identical twins and people have difficulty in telling them apart.

Practitioners need to be aware of how they are responding to and treating children who are twins, so that they treat them as individuals and not as 'part of a pair'. This is essential for all areas of their development, and in particular the development of their identity and self-esteem. There are some useful story books available including *T is for Twins*, by Mary Bond, Ralph Homan and Margaret Viles and *Little Miss Twins*, by Roger Hargreaves.

A Chance to Think 5.13

Twins

Louise and Amelia attend your setting. They are identical twins. All the children are playing outside. Louise is riding a bike with Amelia sitting on a trailer attached to it. Amelia gets off the trailer and goes to play with a group of children. Louise stays on the bike. You overhear an adult supervising say, 'one is still on the bike, but where has the other one gone?'

What would you do in this situation?

Compare your answers with the sample answers in Appendix 5.

Identical twins share the same chromosomes and genes

Other factors that may influence identity, self-esteem and development

While we have explored some issues that may affect a child's self-esteem, identity and development it is important to remember that this is not an exhaustive list. Identity can also be influenced by many other things for example, sexuality, religion, culture, class, age, economic status, and so on. As we saw at the beginning of this section on identity, each child is an individual. All children will have several facets to their identity that overlap, change and develop over time. Identity and its development is not static. It is important that practitioners do not make assumptions about children, label them or try to fit them into categories or make assumptions about children and families.

Signs of low self-esteem

Practitioners must acknowledge that not all children feel good about themselves and who they are, and that some children in the setting may be suffering from low self-esteem. Children who have been abused, or affected by domestic violence, may have low self-esteem. Children who consider themselves not valued and respected for who they are because of for example, their colour, culture, race, religion, language, abilities, disabilities or any other facet of who they are, may also suffer from low self-esteem. Signs of low self-esteem in children may be seen in a variety of ways including by what they say, how they play, and through their behaviour.

Signs of low self-esteem can include:

- not mixing with other children, or wanting to be by themselves;
- not wanting to be cuddled and avoiding physical contact;
- withdrawn or aggressive behaviour;
- not wanting to do things in case they get it wrong;
- say they are no good at anything, that they are ugly or bad;
- harming themselves, for example, cutting, or trying to remove skin colour by bleaching or burning themselves;
- not having any pride in their appearance;
- antisocial behaviour for example, disrupting other children;
- poor concentration;
- lack of confidence;
- issues around food, for example, over eating, not eating.

It is important that when looking at signs to remember that they are not 'tick lists' and that practitioners must carefully observe children to gain a full picture of what is going on for that child.

A Chance to Think 5.14

Self-Esteem

So far in this section we have talked about children's identity and self-esteem. It is also possible for adults to have low self-esteem. Practitioners may know colleagues or parents who have low self-esteem.

What effect might a parent with low self-esteem have on his or her children?

Compare your answers with the sample answers in Appendix 5.

The role of the practitioner

Much has been written about the role of the practitioner in working with children to enable them develop a positive sense of identity and self-esteem. All practitioners have a vital role to play in their day-to-day contact with children. They need to constantly evaluate and reflect on their practice. We have seen all the way through this section, and all the way through this book, that adults have an important and influential part to play in the way that children grow and develop. Nowhere is this more important than in the development of identity and self-esteem. Practitioners who work with children have a particularly important role to play, as they are seen as role models by both children and parents. Practitioners have a role to play in the development of all children in their setting, not just those who have the same cultural, racial, religious or linguistic background, abilities or disabilities as themselves. The settings are all inclusive, or should be.

It is often not possible for practitioners in settings to represent the backgrounds of all the children and families attending the setting. Practitioners will need to ensure that they are providing positive adult role models by inviting other adults to visit the setting for example, inviting parents to come in and help, or other adults to come in and be with the children. If this is not possible, then practitioners could take children out into the community to see positive role models. Practitioners also need to ensure that their resources reflect positive role models of all backgrounds. Practitioners need to take a proactive approach to ensure that all children are developing a positive sense of identity and self-esteem. There are times when practitioners may need to ask other professionals for help, advice and support in this area. This should not be seen as a sign of weakness or failure, but as a gap that other people may be more experienced or qualified to fill. By talking to other professionals, practitioners will enhance and build on their knowledge and skills in this area. There are many things that practitioners can do to help develop a child's identity and self-esteem including:

- respecting and valuing children as individuals and all the things that go to make them individuals, including their colour, disability, language, culture, gender and all the other factors that go to make who they are;
- respecting and valuing the parents and families of children in the setting;
- ensure everyone in the setting feels welcome and 'at home' in the setting;
- providing opportunities for children to explore their identities;

- not using derogatory, discriminatory or negative language, or talking about individuals and groups in a negative way;
- providing children with opportunities to grow and develop as individuals, but not consciously or unconsciously set them up to fail;
- acknowledging children's efforts and achievements;
- help and support children to get on together;
- allowing children to make mistakes and learn from them;
- not doing everything for children, but encouraging them to do things for themselves;
- providing equipment, resources and activities which promote positive images of all groups in society;
- evaluate equipment, resources and activities;
- spelling and pronouncing names correctly;
- ensuring everyone knows people's correct name;
- acknowledging that prejudice, stereotypes, discrimination and oppression exist and challenge them;
- have polices, procedures and practices in place that are implemented, reviewed, evaluated and updated;
- start with what a child can do, not what they cannot do;
- ensuring the environment is as accessible as possible;
- recognizing that language is powerful and being aware of how it is used;
- not categorizing or labelling individuals;
- working proactively with colleagues to discuss and evaluate practice;
- attend training and take part in development to keep up to date with
- issues, practice, knowledge and new developments;
- reflect on attitudes, values and behaviour;
- recognize that one person cannot know and do everything;
- learn from mistakes;
- listen to children and allow them to share their experiences;
- ensure children are able to make choices;
- work with parents and families and support them as needed;
- communicate with children, parents and families effectively;
- work with other professionals;
- ensure there is specialist equipment and resources for those who need it;
- observe; assess and plan to meet all children's individual needs;
- keep up to date records;
- use interpreters and translators and ensure things are translated where needed.
- provide services for parents as required and recognise that all families are unique;
- try not to make assumptions;
- do home visits were possible;
- share and enjoy time with children; give children their own space to place to put things;
- be a positive role model.

We started this book by examining both good practice and the legislation relating to anti-discriminatory practice. The EYFS practice guidance says,

> Practitioners must plan for the needs of the children from black and other minority ethnic backgrounds, including those learning English as an additional language, and for the needs of any children with learning difficulties and disabilities. Providers must actively avoid gender stereotyping and must challenge any expression of prejudice or discrimination by children or adults . . . You must plan for each child's individual learning requirements. The focus should be on removing or helping to counter underachievement and overcome barriers for children where these already exist. You should also identify and respond early to needs which could lead to the development of learning difficulties. There must be appropriate challenges for gifted and talented children.

The statutory welfare requirements state that 'Providers must plan and organise their systems to ensure that every child receives an enjoyable and challenging learning and development experience that is tailored to meet their individual needs'. It is important to remember that all children are individuals who will have some things in common with others, and other aspects that are unique to them and practitioners need to plan and provide for them, so that they are meeting the needs of children and families.

References and useful resources

Aldgate, J., Rose, W. and Jeffery, C. (2006). *The Developing World of the Child*. Jessica Kingsley Publishers.

Alibhai-Brown, Y. (2001). *Mixed Feelings The Complex Lives of Mixed Race Britons*. The Women's Press.

Alibhai-Brown, Y. (2001). *Who Do We Think We Are? Imagining the New Britain*. Penguin Books.

Arnot, M. and Mac an Ghaill, M. (2006). *The Routledge Falmer Reader in Gender and Education*. Routledge.

Baig, R. with Lane, J. (2003). *Building Bridges for Our Future : The Way Forward through Times of Terror and War*. Early Years Equality.

Baumrind, D. (1991). 'The influence of parenting styles on adolescent competence and substance use'. *Journal of Early Adolescence*. 11 (1), 56–95.

Bayley, R. Broadbent, L. and Pullinger, D. (2006). *Help Your Young Child Succeed*. Continuum.

Bhavnani, R., Mirza, S. M. and Meetoo, V. (2005). *Tackling the Roots of Racism: Lessons for Success*. The Policy Press.

Biehal, N., Ellison, S., Baker, C. and Sinclai, I. (2009). *Characteristics, Outcomes and Meanings of Three Types of Permanent Placement – Adoption by Strangers, Adoption by Carers and Long Term Foster Care*. Social Policy Research Unit, University of York.

Biddulp, S. (2003). *Raising Boys*. Thorsons.

Brighouse, H., Howe, K. R. and Tooley, J. (2010). *Educational Equality*. Continuum.

Brown, B. (1999). *Unlearning Discrimination in the Early Years*. Trentham Books.

Brown, B. (2001). *Combating Discrimination: Persona Dolls in Action*. Trentham Books.

Cameron, R. J. and Maginn, C. (2009). *Achieving Positive Outcomes for Children in Care*. Sage.

Chakrabati, M. and Hill, M. (2000). *Residential Child Care: International Perspectives on Links with Families and Peers*. Jessica Kingsley Publishers.

Christensen, P. and James, A. (2008). *Research with Children Perspectives and Practices*. Routledge.

Connolly, P., Smith, A. and Kelly, B. (2002). *Too Young to Notice? The Cultural and Political Awareness of 3–6 Year Olds in Northern Ireland*. Community Relations Council.

Council for Disabled Children. (2008). *Inclusion Policy*.

Cumine, V., Dunlop, J. and Stevenson, G. (2009). *Autism in the Early Years*. Routledge.

Curtis, A. and O'Hagan, M. (2003). *Care and Education in Early Childhood: A Students Guide to Theory and Practice*. Routledge-Falmer.

Dare, A. and O'Donovan, M. (2002). *Good Practice in Caring for Young Children with Special Needs* (2nd edition). Nelson Thornes.

Dfee. (2001). *Promoting Children's Mental Health within Early Years and School Settings*.

Dfes. (2003). *Aiming High: Raising the Achievement of African-Caribbean Pupils – Guidance*.

Dfes. (2003). *Aiming High; Raising the Achievement of Gypsy-Traveller Pupils – A Guide to Good Practice*.

Dfes. (2003). *Aiming High; Raising the Achievement of Minority Ethnic Pupils*.

Dfes. (2005). *Talking about Adoption for Children under 10*.

Dfes. (2005). *Talking about Adoption for Young People over 10*.

Dfes. (2006). *Working Towards Inclusive Practice: Gypsy/Roma and Traveller Cultural Awareness Training and Activities for Early Years Settings*. Save the Children.

Dcsf. (2006b). *Bullying around Racism, Religion and Culture. How to Prevent It, and What to Do When It Happens – Advice to Schools*.

Dcsf. (2007). *Confident, Capable and Creative: Supporting Boys' Achievements*.

Dcsf. (2007). *Getting it Right: Exclusion of Black Pupils – Priority Review*.

Dcsf. (2007). *Supporting Children Learning English as an Additional Language. Guidance for Practitioners in the Early Years Foundation Stage*.

Dcsf. (2008). *Early Years Foundation Stage*.

Dcsf. (2008). *Early Years Foundation Stage Profile Handbook*.

Dcsf. (2009). *Statutory Guidance on Promoting the Health and Well-being of Looked After Children*.

Dcsf. (2009). *The Characteristics of Bullying Victims in Schools*.

Dcsf. (2009). *Improving Educational Outcomes for Gypsy, Roma and Traveller Pupils – What Works? Contextual Influences and Constructive Conditions that May Influence Pupil Achievement*.

Dcsf. (2009). *Where Next for Pupils Excluded from Special Schools and Pupil Referral Units*.

Dcsf. (2009). *Parental Experiences of Services for Disabled Children – Qualitative Research (Phase 2) Exploring the Findings from the National Survey*.

Dcsf. (2009). *Looked After and Learning Evaluation of the Virtual School Head Pilot*.

Dcsf. (2009). *Supporting Parents with Their Children's 'At Home' Learning and Development*.

Dcsf. (2009). *Working at the 'Edges' of Care? European Models of Support For Young People and Families.*

Dcsf. (2009). *Safeguarding Children From Emotional Abuse – What Works?*

Dcsf. (2009). *Outreach to Children and Families – A Scoping Study.*

Dcsf. (2009). *Identifying and Teaching Children and Young People with Dyslexia and Literacy Difficulties.*

Dcsf. (2009). *Aiming High for Young People.*

Dcsf. (2009). *Drivers and Barriers to Educational Success – Evidence from the Longitudinal Study of Young People in England.*

Dcsf. (2009). *Safe from Bullying: Training Resources.*

Dcsf. (2009). *Nurturing Parenting Capability – The Early Years.*

Dcsf. (2009). *Breaking the Link between Disadvantage and Low Attainment Everyone's Business.*

Dcsf. (2009). *Children Looked After in England (Including Adoption and Care Leavers) Year Ending 31 March 2009.*

Dcsf. (2009). *Early Years Foundation Stage Profile Attainment by Pupil Characteristics, in England 2008/2009.*

Derman Sparks, L. (1989). *Anti-bias Curriculum; Tools for Empowering Young Children.* National Early Years Network.

Derman-Sparks, L. (2004). 'Early Childhood Anti-Bias Education in the USA' in vanKeulen, A. (ed.) *Young Children Aren't Biased, Are They?! : How to Handle Diversityin Early Childhood Education and School.* B.V.Uitgeverij SWP.

Derman Sparks, L. and the ABC Task Force (1989). *Anti-Bias Curriculum : Tools for Empowering Young Children.* NAEYC, Washington, USA. Available from National Children's Bureau.

Derman-Sparks, L. and Brunson Phillips, C. (1997). *Teaching/Learning Antiracism: A Developmental Approach.* Teachers College Press.

Dewis, P. (2007). *Medical Conditions: A Guide for the Early Years.* Continuum.

Dickins, M with Denziloe, J. (2003). *All Together: How to Create Inclusive Services for Disabled Children and Their Families. A Practical Handbook for Early Years Workers.* National Children's Bureau.

Drury, R. (2006). *Young Bilingual Children Learning at Home and School.* Trentham Books.

Dwivedi, K., N. (ed) (2002). *Meeting the Needs of Ethnic Minority Children.* Jessica Kingsley Publishers.

Edwards, S. O., Derman-Sparks, L. and Ramsey, P. (2006). *What if All the Kids Are White? Anti-bias Multicultural Education with Young Children and Families.* Teachers College Press.

Elfer, P. Goldschmied, E. and Selleck, D. (2003). *Key Persons in the Nursery.* David Fulton Publishers.

Fitzgerald, D. (2007). *Co-ordinating Special Educational Needs: A Guide for the Early Years.* Continuum.

Gergen, K. J. and Gergen, M. M. (1981). *Social Psychology.* Harcourt Brace Javanovich.

Goldschmied, E. and Jackson. S. (1997). *People Under Three: Young Children in Day Care.* Routledge.

Gurian, M. (2002). *Boys and Girls Learn Differently.* Jossey-Bass.

Hill, D. and Robertson, L. H. (2009). *Equality in the Primary School Promoting Good Practice across the Curriculum.* Continuum.

Holland, P. (2003). *We Don't Play With Guns Here: War, Weapon and Superhero Play.* Open University Press.

Hyder, T. (2004). *War, Conflict and Play.* Open University Press.

Ifekwunigwe, J. (ed) (2004). *Mixed Race Studies : A Reader.* Routledge.

Katz. I. (2001). *The Construction of Racial Identity in Children of Mixed Parentage: Mixed Metaphors.* Jessica Kingsley Publishers.

Kehily, M. J. and Swann, J. (2003). *Children's Cultural Worlds.* Open University.

Ladson-Billings, G. and Gillborn, D. (2004). *The RoutledgeFalmer Reader in Multicultural Education.* Routledge.

Lalonde, R. N. Jones, J. M. and Stroink M. L. (2008). 'Racial Identity, Racial Attitudes, and Race Socialization Among Black Canadian Parents'. *Canadian Journal of Behavioural Science 2008*, Vol. 40, No. 3, 129–39.

Lane, J. (2008). *Young Children and Racial Justice. Taking Action for Racial Equality in the Early Years – Understanding the Past, Thinking about the Present, Planning for the Future.* National Children's Bureau.

Lindon, J. (2000). *Helping Babies and Toddlers to Learn: A Guide to Good Practicewith Under-Threes.* National Early Years Network.

Lindon, J. (2001). *Growing Up: From 8ight Years to Young Adulthood.* National Children's Bureau.

Lindon, J. (2006). *Equality in Early Childhood : Linking Theory and Practice.*Hodder Arnold.

Lindon, J. (2007). *Understanding Children and Young People Development from 5–18 Years.* Hodder Arnold.

Livingston, T. (2005). *Child of Our Time.* Random House.

Loreman, T. (2009). *Respecting Childhood.* Continuum.

Lucus, B. and Smith, A. (2009). *Help Your Child Success.* (2nd edition). Continuum.

Maalouf, A. (2000). *On Identity.* The Harvill Press.

MacIntyre, C. (2005). *Identifying Additional Learning Needs in the Early Years.* Routledge.

Macintyre, C. (2008). *Dyspraxia in the Early Years.* Routledge

MacNaughton, G. (2000). *Rethinking Gender in Early Childhood Education.* Paul Chapman Publishing.

Maximé, J. E. (1993). 'The therapeutic importance of racial identity in working with black children who hate'. In *How and Why Children hate. A Study of Conscious Sources.* Jessica Kingsley Publishers.

McGinnis, H., Livingston Smith, S., Ryan, S., D. and Howard J., A. (2009). *Beyond Culture Camp: Promoting Healthy Identity Formation in Adoption.* Evan B. Donaldson Adoption Institute.

Morris, J. (2002). 'A lot to say! A guide for social workers, personal advisors and others working with disabled children and young people with communication impairments'. Scope.

Myers, K. and Taylor, H. with Adler, S. and Leonard, D. (2007). *Genderwatch – Still Watching.* Trentham Books.

National Deaf Children's Society. (2003). *Deaf Friendly Nurseries and Pre-Schools. A Guide for People Working with Deaf Children in Early Education Settings.*

National Institute For Health And Clinical Excellence. (2010). *Draft Guidance The Physical and Emotional Health and Wellbeing of Looked-after Children and Young People.*

Newberger, E. H. (2001). *Bringing Up a Boy: How to Understand and Care for Boys.* Bloomsbury Publishing.

O'Hagan, M. and Smith, M. (1999). *Early Years Child Care and Education: Key Issues.* Bailliere Tindall.

Ofsted. (2003). *Provision and Support for TravellerPupils.*

Ofsted. (2005). *Race Equality in Education: Good Practice in Schools and Local Education Authorities.*

Ofsted. (2009). *Keeping in Touch: A Report of Children's Experience by the Children's Rights Director for England.*

Okitikipi, T. (2005). *Working with Children of Mixed Parentage.* Russell House Publishing.

Owen, C., Cameron, C. and Moss, P. (1998). *Men as Workers in Service for Young Children: Issues of a Mixed Gender Workforce.* Institute of Education.

Paechter, C. (2007). *Being Boys Being Girls: Learning Masculinities and Femininities.* Open University Press.

Palmer, S. (2009). *21st Century Boys: How Modern Life is Driving Them Off the Rails and How We Can Get Them Back.* Orion Books.

Parker, D. and Song, M. (2001). *Rethinking 'Mixed Race'.* Pluto Press.

Peacey, V. (2010). *Family Finances, Executive Summary.* Gingerbread.

Phillips Swanson, D. Cunninghamy, M., Youngbloodz, J. and Beale Spencer, M. (2009). *Racial Identity Development during Childhood.* GSE Publications.

Pre-School Learning Alliance. (2007). *Being Me.* Pre-School Learning Alliance.

Pre-School Learning Alliance QCA. (n.d.). *Respect for All: Valuing Diversity and Challenging Racism through the Curriculum.* Pre-School Learning Alliance.

Reed, V. (2009). *Developing Attachment in Early Years Settings.* Routledge.

Sage, R. (2004). *A World of Difference: Tackling Inclusion in Schools.* Network Continuum Education.

Save the Children/DfES. (2006). *Working towards Inclusive practice :Gypsy/Roma and Traveller Cultural Awareness Training and Activities for EarlyYears Settings.* Save the Children.

Sax, L. (2006). *Why Gender Matters.* New York: Broadway Books.

Sheppy, S. (2008). *Personal, Social and Emotional Development in the Early Years Foundation Stage.* Routledge.

Siraj-Blatchford, I. and Clarke, P. (2000). *Supporting Identity, Diversity and Language in the Early Years.* Open University Press.

Smidt, S. (2007). *Supporting Multilingual Learners in the Early Years.* Routledge.

Social Care Institute for Excellence. (2009). *Think Child, Think Parent, Think Family: A Guide to Parental Mental Health and Child Welfare.*

Sterne, A., Poole, L., Chadwick, D. and Lawler, C. (2009). *Domestic Violence and Children.* Routledge.

Sure Start. (2003). 'Sure Start for Everyone; Promoting Inclusion, Embracing Diversity, Challenging Inequality'. Inclusion Projects Summary Report.

Sure Start. (2004). *Promoting Race Equality in Early Years.*

Sure Start. (2004). *Working with Young Children from Minority Ethnic Groups: A Guide to Sources of Information.* National Children's Bureau.

Topping, K. and Maloney. (2004). *The RoutledgeFalmer Reader in Inclusive Education.* Routledge.

UNICEF UK. (2004). *Child Refugees.*

Walker, G. (2008). *Working Together for Children: A Critical Introduction to Multi-Agency Working.* Continuum.

Welch, S. and Jones. P. (2010). *Rethinking Children's Rights: Attitudes in Contemporary Society.* Continuum.

Wilson, G. (2008). *Help Your Boys Succeed.* Continuum.

Wood, E. (2008). *The Routledge Reader in Early Childhood Education.* Routledge.

Wright, M. A. (2000). *I'm Chocolate, You're Vanilla: Raising Healthy Black and Biracial Children in a Race-Conscious World. A Guide for Parents and Teachers.* Jossey-Bass.

Publications for children

Alko, S. (2009). *I'm Your Peanut Butter Big Brother.* Alfred A. Knopf.

Ashley, B. and Thompson. C. (2002). *Double the Love.* Orchard Picture books.

Aubrey, A. (2008). *Flora's Family Understanding Adoption.* QED Publishing.

Aubrey, A. (2008). *There for You: Understanding Divorce.* QED Publishing.

Aubrey, A. (2008). *A Place in My Heart: Understanding Bereavement.* QED Publishing.

Benjamin, F. (2007). *My Two Grannies.* Frances Lincon.

Brownjohn, E. (2002). *All Kinds of Bodies.* Tango Books.

Brownjohn, E. (2003). *All Kinds of Feelings.* Tango Books.

Brownjohn, E. (2006). *All Kinds of Fears.* Tango Books.

Cole, B. (1996). *Drop Dead.* Red Fox.

Damon, E. (1995). *All Kinds of People.* Tango Books.

Damon, E. (2005). *All Kinds of Homes.* Tango Books.

Damon, E. (2007). *All Kinds of Babies.* Tango Books.

Edmonds, L. (2005). *An African Princess.* Picture Corgi.

Fox, M. (1997). *Whoever You Are.* Harcourt Children's Books.

Fuller, R. (2010). *All Kinds of Families.* Tango Books.

Gliori, D. (1999). *No Matter What.* Bloomsbury Publishing.

Grimes, N. (2004). *A Day With Daddy.* Teaching Resources.

Hooks, B. (2004). *Skin Again.* Hyperion Books.

Humphrey, P. (2010). *I'm Special.* Evans Publishing Group.

Katz, K. (2002). *The Colors of Us.* Owlet Paperbacks.

Katz, K. (2001). *Over the Moon: An Adoption Tale.* Henry Holt and Co.

Manning, N. (2005). *What's My Family Tree?* Franklin Watts.

McCardie, A. (1997). *The Frog Ballet.* Red Fox.

McQuinn, A. (2009). *My Friend Mei Jing.* Annick Press.

McQuinn, A. (2008). *My Friend Jamal.* Annick Press.

Moore-Mallinos, J. (2007). *It's OK to Be Me Just Like You, I Can Do Almost Anything.* Barron's Educational Series.

Moore-Mallinos, J. (2007). *We are Adopted.* Barron's Educational Series.

Newman, L. and Thompson, C. (2009). *Daddy, Papa, and Me.* Tricycle Press.

Newman, L. and Thompson, C. (2009). *Mommy, Mama, and Me.* Tricycle Press.

Pinkney, S. L. (2002). *Shades of Black.* Scholastic Press.

Pinkney, S, L. (2007). *I Am Latino: The beauty In Me.* Little, Brown Young Readers.

Polacco, P. (2009). *In Our Mothers' House.* Philomel.

Powell, J. (2004). *Becky Has Diabetes.* Evans Publishing Group.

Powell, J. (2007). *Allergies.* Evans Publishing Group.

Powell, J. (2007). *Asthma.* Evans Publishing Group.

Powell, J. (2009). *Zac Has Asthma.* Evans Publishing Group.

Powell, J. (2009). *Aneil Has a Food Allergy.* Evans Publishing Group.

Powell, J. (2009). *Charlotte Has Impaired Vision.* Evans Publishing Group.

Powell, J. (2009). *Jordan Has a Hearing Loss.* Evans Publishing Group.

Powell, J. (2009). *Luke Has Down's Syndrome.* Evans Publishing Group.

Powell, J. (2009). *Sam Uses a Wheelchair.* Evans Publishing Group.

Richardson, J. and Parnall, P. (2007). *And Tango Makes Three.* Simon & Schuster Ltd.

Richmond, M. R. (2008). *I Wished for You: An Adoption Story.* Marianne Richmond Studios.

Thomas, P. (2002). *Don't Call me Special: A First Look at Disability.* Barron's Educational Series.

Thomas, P. (2001). *I Miss You A First Look at Death.* Barron's Educational Series.

Thomas, P. (2003). *The Skin I'm In.* Barron's Educational Series.

Walsh, M. (2004). *My World, Your World.* Corgi Childrens.

Wilkins, V. A. (1995). *Are We There Yet?* Tamarind Books.

Wilkins, V. A. (2003). *Boots for a bridesmaid.* Tamarind Books.

Willis Hudson, C. (1991). *Bright Eyes, Brown Skin.* Just Us Books.

Useful websites

www.afteradoption.org.uk – information on adoption.

www.allergyuk.org – information on allergies.

www.asthma.org.uk – information on asthma.

www.baaf.org.uk – British association for adoption and fostering.

www.bemyparent.org.uk – information about adoption.

www.cpag.org.uk – child poverty action group.

www.domesticviolencedata.org – information and data on domestic violence.

www.emaonline.org.uk – on line support for ethnic minority attainment.

www.fatherhoodinstitute.org –Fatherhood Institute.

www.gypsy-traveller.org – seeks to end racism and discrimination against Gypsies and Travellers.

www.ican.org.uk – information on supporting speech, language and communication skills.

www.kidscape.org.uk – information about child abuse and keeping children safe.

www.kidz4mation.com – suppliers of personal development children's books.

www.multiverse.ac.uk – site for teachers exploring diversity and achievement.

www.nace.co.uk – information about able, gifted and talented pupils.

www.nagcbritain.org.uk – National Association for Gifted Children.

www.naldic.org.uk – National Association for Language Development in the Curriculum, working for pupils with English as an additional language.

www.ncb.org.uk – National Children's Bureau.

www.nhs.uk – information on child development, mental health and much more www.nspcc.org.uk – NSPCC, information about child abuse.

www.ofsted.gov.uk – Office for Standards in Education. Useful publications and research.

www.parentingstyles.co.uk – information on parenting styles.

www.stammering.org – British Stammering Association.

www.twinsuk.co.uk – information about twins.

www.unicef.org.uk – UNICEF information and data.

www.womensaid.org.uk – Women's Aid.

Useful DVDs

Chatter Matters – for parents and children from 0–5. From I Can at www.ican.org.uk.

Learning to Talk Talking to Learn – a guide from early years practitioners. From I Can at www.ican.org.uk.

Appendix 1
Sample answers for Chapter 1

A Chance to Think 1.3

Skin Colour

Children may have attitudes that are racist, prejudicial or discriminatory. They may feel superior, feel inferior, have low self-esteem or have pride in their skin colour. Children may get their attitudes from their parents, other adults, the media, books or comics, the toys or equipment they play with, the environment around them and what they see and hear, or do not see and hear. Children's behaviour can include children using derogatory language about skin colour; children not wanting to play with children who have a different background from themselves; the way children play with and use resources; black children suffering from low self-esteem and poor self-image, and the behaviour that results from that; white children feeling they are superior to, or better than, black children.

A Chance to Think 1.7

Race

The situation seems not to reflect the true mix of the population. It is a false situation. It may be happening genuinely by accident; the administration policy may be at fault; it may be for racial reasons; parents may be asking for a particular session. The things that could be done about it are; ask the manager again; discuss it with the owner or management committee, and ask them to look at the admissions policy; monitor applications over the next few months to see why it may be happening.

A Chance to Think 1.8

Race, Religion, Culture and Language

Talk to parents about their needs and their child's needs, and find out what they are and how you can meet them. Provide resources, equipment and activities that contain positive visual images, for example, jigsaws, posters, wall displays, books, dressing up clothes, skin tone paints, paper and crayons. Provide diets that meet the needs of all children. Ensure notices and newsletters are translated and that languages other than English are used in the setting, for example, tapes, books, labelling. Acknowledge festivals and evaluate how this is done. Plan activities that meet the needs of all children. Invite people to visit and be with the children. Undertake visits into the community and the wider community. Evaluate policies and procedures. Provide training and development for all practitioners on race, religion culture and language. Challenge discrimination. Talk to children. Respect dress codes. Ensure that hair and skin care is provided for. Keep a book of useful words in languages spoken in the setting.

A Chance to Think 1.9

The Outcomes for Children

You could include the following information: The Outcomes for Children came from the Every Child Matters green paper in 2003; The Children Act 2004 gave them legal status. They cover the age range from birth to age 19. There are five of them. They can be remembered by the word SHEEP. Stay Safe, be Healthy, Enjoy and Achieve, Economic Well being, Positive Contribution. All 5 are equally important and all link together; their aim is to improve outcomes for all children and young people; Everybody who works with children and young people, for example, in hospitals, nurseries, residential settings, colleges, schools, child minders, foster carers, the police,and so on, must work to promote the outcomes for children. The five outcomes are linked to the Early Years Foundation Stage and can be found on the bottom of the 'Principles into Practice cards;' The Ofsted inspection process and self-evaluation form are linked to the five outcomes. You could give the team the five outcomes and do an exercise asking them to say, with evidence, what the setting does now to promote the five outcomes and what it could do to improve practice.

A Chance to Think 1.10

Early Years Foundation Stage

Many things can influence how a child develops and becomes the individual they are. These include: basic needs being met / not being met; type of setting attended; stimulation / lack of stimulation; place in family; health / illness; parenting styles; genes; the impact of society; the environment; culture; gender; age; expectations of adults and self; individual needs; disability;

ability; experiences; relationships; resources; abuse / violence; religion; time and place; legal status; economic status and many others.

A Chance to Think 1.11

Approaches to Work

Multicultural – Recognizing that children have different cultural backgrounds and, through planning, trying to meet the needs of the children; involving and recognizing everyone's culture; accepting and respecting people's cultural backgrounds; celebrating festivals and cultural events; providing resources that show people's cultures.

Anti-racist/anti-sexist – Providing an anti-racist, anti-sexist environment; allowing boys and girls to have equal access to experiences; treating people as individuals, not on the basis of race or sex; not stereotyping because of race or sex; being aware of the language used.

Anti-discriminatory practice – Incorporates and recognizes all groups in society, so that it is anti-racist, anti-sexist and also anti-ageist,and so on; recognizes all aspects that go to make individuals and society, for example, race, sex, disabilities, language, sexual orientation, culture, religion, economic statusand so on, and provides positive images, resources, environments and attitudes for all of them; does not just provide equipment, but explains and works on the injustices in society. Anti-discriminatory practice ensures that all groups in society are reflected. The other two are making a start, but both have important aspects missing.

A Chance to Think 1.13

Disability

Feelings might include embarrassment, feeling awkward, being unsure what to do, wanting to get the children to be quiet, feeling unable to handle the situation, feeling OK about the situation, knowing what to do and say. Explain to the children in your group about Down's Syndrome, using language appropriate to their understanding; explain how hurtful their remarks are making the father and daughter feel; ask the father and child to join your group for a story if appropriate; find a book, or books, to take back to the setting to use with the children about Down's Syndrome.

A Chance to Think 1.15

Working with Parents

Feelings might include embarrassment, no particular strong feelings, you may not like it, but be professional about it, feel it is positive for Claire as she is wanted and loved, put feelings to one side and work in partnership for the benefit of Claire. In the same way as when working with all the other parents; communication; welcoming Claire's mother and her partner into the setting; inviting them to be involved in the setting.

That some children have a mum and a dad, some have only one parent and some children have two mums or two dads, step-families,and so on; get books about families from the library to use with the children.

A Chance to Think 1.16

Language

Before Fasil and his parents start, contact an interpreter to learn a few key words; arrange for an interpreter to be present on the first day; smile; body language; gestures; welcoming atmosphere; say 'hello' in Amharic if possible.

Try to get an interpreter; use other parents who speak Amharic, (if appropriate and if information is not personal or confidential;) do not use an interpreter the family are not happy with.

A Chance to Think 1.17

Attitudes

Allow Jane to reply if she wants to; deal with the outcome of that; sensitively try to find out what the mother means by that remark and whether she understands what she has said; explain that the remark is offensive and why; explain the ethos of the setting and why the remark may have hurt Jane's feelings; try to deal with the hurt feelings and any other feelings that may be around; look for literature that will support the setting's point of view.

A Chance to Think 1.18

Students

Feelings might include shock, embarrassment, surprise, empathy, understanding; it might be appropriate not to say anything at the time but go away and plan what to say.

The supervisor could talk to George about why he wants to wear a dress to the setting; ask him about whether he thinks it is appropriate; take time to think about it and discuss it with others as appropriate; discuss it with the manager and the staff team to see how they feel; if not agreeing to let George wear a dress, explain why; if agreeing, discuss the dress code and what is appropriate and what is not; work out how questions from parents and children will be handle; talk to George's tutors if appropriate and find out what guidance he is being given by them.

A Chance to Think 1.19

Male Practitioners

Feelings may include anger or surprise after having tried to reassure parents; feeling upset at the parents' attitude; understanding how parents feel and trying to think about their rights. The manager could talk to James and the parents separately; James should be supported, as he as a practitioner and supervising children in the bathroom is part of this role; the manager should also discuss with James why he thinks the parent does not want him to supervise Lalita in the bathroom or change her; discuss the rights of James and the rights of the parents; the parents should have had this explained to them before they started in the setting; try and find out what the parents' concerns are and reassure them.

Appendix 2
Sample answers for Chapter 2

A Chance to Think 2.3

Inspection

The statement is incorrect and shows a narrow view of race issues. The setting is not complying with relevant legislation and good practice issues. All children are individuals and should be treated equally, not the same.

All practitioners in all settings need to be addressing issues of race.

By recognising the need to address the issue.

By realizing there is a legal obligation to do so.

Get training and development to help deal with their own feelings; ensure policies, procedures and practice are in place and regularly monitored and evaluated; ensure the curriculum and resources acknowledge and reflect individuals' backgrounds in a positive way.

A Chance to Think 2.5

Religion

By talking to parents and colleagues and finding out what their needs are. By providing activities, resources and positive images relating to religions; providing for dietary requirements; acknowledging festivals; respecting dress codes; not using negative or derogatory language when discussing religions.

A Chance to Think 2.6

Culture

Things that may be included a person's culture are dress, language, diet and food, way of eating, music, art, literature, hygiene practices, jewellery, traditions, discipline, attitudes, values, religious beliefs and many more.

Culture affects and influences all things that happen in the setting. The setting needs to be aware of these so that it can acknowledge them and provide for them for example, appropriate diets; hair and skin care; providing positive images, resources and activities that reflect cultural backgrounds; not using negative or discriminatory language.

A Chance to Think 2.7

My Setting

Acknowledge all cultures; talk to parents and colleagues and ask questions sensitively; provide for cultural needs as appropriate for example, dietary requirements; hair and skin care; providing positive images, resources and activities that reflect cultural backgrounds; not using negative or discriminatory language.

A Chance to Think 2.9

Safeguarding

Recognizing that people have different ways of disciplining children, and that some of these nay not be appropriate; cultural and religious variations in child rearing practices; what bruises and injuries look like on different skin colours and tones; Mongolian blue spot is a naturally occurring birth mark; different economic and cultural backgrounds may mean that people have different standards of care; child abuse can occur in any race, religion, culture, class, economic group, in any family; and in cities, towns and villages; man and women can abuse children.

A Chance to Think 2.11

Ways of Eating

The children and adults will gain experience of eating food with fingers; introducing thali dishes and using them correctly; introducing or practicing new skills and vocabulary; recognizing, acknowledging and respecting cultural variations in the eating of food.

A Chance to Think 2.12

Swimming

Upset that no one had been consulted about going swimming and the decision had been made by the manager; other practitioners and parents may have views about taking the children swimming; that if this happens that Shelan should go to the pool to help with the children but not go in the pool; if staffing is tight Shelan could stay in the setting and cover there, to allow another member of staff to go swimming with the children.

Talk to Shelan about how she would like to be supported and do this as much as possible.

A Chance to Think 2.13

Hair Care

Put the white cloth back on as well as possible; comfort Amarjit; explain to the children that it is possible for boys to have long hair; explain why Amarjit has long hair; explain his feelings have been hurt and this needs to be put right; find pictures of boys and men with long hair to show the children.

Appendix 3
Sample answers for Chapter 3

A Chance to Think 3.1

Buddhism

Talk to the family and ask them about their needs. Ask colleagues if they have any information or know anything about the Buddhist religion. Visit the library or such the internet for information. Visit a Buddhist temple.

A Chance to Think 3.2

Christianity

It is a good idea if planned well.

Some parents may not want their children to visit a church, so it is important to talk to them about the outing, the reasons for it and were else you are visiting; get the parents' permission; ask for parent volunteers to help on the trip; send letters home explaining the trip and what will happen; talk to the vicar before the trip about the reasons for the trip and what you want the children to get out of it; take photos during the visit to share with the children and parents; ensure everyone is dressed appropriately for the visit.

Talk to the children about the visit, where they are going, what the building is, what they are going to see, who they are going to meet; get books from the library about churches and different buildings; watch a DVD featuring churches; find out if any of the children have been to church and ask them to talk about what happens when they go to church: answer the questions children may have.

Talk with the children about where they went, what they saw, heardand so on, answer their questions; do some creative work for example, a collage or model of the church; create an interest table; use the photos to make a display or book; talk to parents about the visit.

A Chance to Think 3.3

Hare Krishna

Ask Krishna's parents what he can eat and not eat and ask them what the dietary requirements of Hare Krishna are. Do some research yourself by visiting the library or searching the internet. Pass on all the information to the cook and the other staff in the setting.

A Chance to Think 3.4

Hinduism

Find out about Divali; inform parents; some parents may object to this, so talk to them about it, what you will be doing and why. Make diva lights; tell or act out the story of Rama and Sita; ask parents to come in and help; cook Divali food or have a Divali meal; make Divali cards with appropriate scripts; visit a Hindu temple; make pictures, colourings and art of Rama and Sita; display some Hindu art; create a Hindu interest table; play Hindu music; create a wall picture or display; turn the home corner into a Hindu home; wear Hindu clothes.

A Chance to Think 3.5

Islam

It depends on the times at which Fatma has to pray; it might be disruptive until the practicalities are sorted out but it should not affect the smooth running of the setting; it will be good for parents, staff and children and broaden their experience.

The setting will have to ensure its routine allows for Fatma to pray; colleagues may have to take different breaks; talk to all workers to explain the importance of this; ensure Fatma can do the shifts that allow for greatest flexibility for her; provide a quite private space for her to pray.

A Chance to Think 3.6

Judaism

Be pleased that Elizabeth feels able to come in to the settings and glad that she has offered. Elizabeth will get to see the setting and the children; she will, it is to be hoped, feel valued and respected; the children will benefit from having another adult to tell them stories; the children, and staff, may hear stories they have not heard before; they will be able to learn about Hanukah and

Elizabeth will be able to answer questions; the staff may see Elizabeth in a new way; they will be able to talk to Elizabeth in the setting and learn more about her religion and beliefs.

A Chance to Think 3.7

Rastafarianism

Sensitively take the member of staff to one side and explain that Tafari keeps his hat on indoors and why. Follow up by giving some written material on Rastafarian dress codes.

A Chance to Think 3.8

Sikhism

Sensitively explain what the five Ks are, and that the dagger is one of them and not a symbol of violence. Ask Rajinder if he will talk to the parents to explain more about the five Ks.

Appendix 4
Sample answers for Chapter 4

A Chance to Think 4.2

Views

Eurocentric means a white European viewpoint.

The setting needs to address the issue as children are being given incorrect messages about the world and the people in it.

Practitioners may need training to begin to address why the setting needs to change and to address the issues, attitudes and feelings around this; visit other settings to examine and compare their approaches; evaluate the equipment and resources being used in the setting and, if necessary, get rid of the ones that are not appropriate and recommend buying new ones; advise practitioners on how to use equipment and resources and the importance of language; introduce new menus and foods into the setting.

A Chance to Think 4.3

Physical Skills

Feelings could include: feeling OK; slightly nervous having never worked with a child with cerebral palsy before; anxiety; you might try to find out as much about cerebral palsy before Magdy started in the setting to give you some information and to prepare you for talking to Magdy's parents about how you can meet his needs.

Treat Magdy as an individual, not making assumptions about his physical skills; he may have difficulty being able to control movements or may be unable to control movements depending on the severity of the cerebral palsy; he may be floppy, have poor balance, muscle stiffness and may have difficulty feeding himself.

Talk to Madgy's parents to find out about his needs and ensure the setting has all the information it needs; get support from Magdy's parents; get support from other agencies as appropriate; introduce Madgy to the children and staff; observe Madgy; take him to activities and carry him as needed; treat him as an individual; provided any equipment he may need to join in activities; adapt equipment, resources and activities as needed; find equipment, resources and activities that he likes to use and enjoys; give him the opportunity to try things and support him where needed; answer any questions from children honestly; constantly observe and evaluate your practice; continue to communicate with Magdy's parents.

A Chance to Think 4.4

Gender

The girls are not getting a chance to use the water tray.

Talk to the practitioner to find out if this is a planed use of the water tray; discuss the need for the girls to be able to play with this as well as the boys; plan how that can happen.

A Chance to Think 4.5

Communication

Go to the library; talk to parents and colleagues; contact relevant organisations and ask for information; search the internet. The setting could label thing in a variety of languages; dual language books; single language books in languages other than English; songs and rhymes in a variety of languages; music; ensuring children hear and see a variety of languages; acknowledging and talking about languages positively; doing activities that involve languages.

A Chance to Think 4.6

Feelings

Miriam may feel upset hurt, upset, confused. She may not understand why she has not been invited or she may feel hurt because she has not been invited because of her skin colour. Miriam's parent may feel hurt, angry and upset. You can do a variety of things; talk to Miriam and her parent about some of the reasons why Miriam may not have been invited; talk to Miriam and her parent about their feelings and ask how you can support them; if possible talk to Jane and her parents to find out why Miriam was not invited; use a persona doll to help talk about the scenario; have a tea party in the setting and invite everyone.

A Chance to Think 4.10

Mealtimes

Mealtimes and snack times link to and support all four themes in the Early Years Foundation Stage. A Unique Child is about how children develop, are included and kept safe and healthy. Children can find out about what they like to eat and what other people like to eat and eating together. They learn about how to hold and use utensils correctly and about making choices and learning about eating healthy food.

Positive Relationships – is about respecting each other, parents as partners, supporting learning and the key person. Mealtimes and snack times are something that is done together either with one adult (key person) and one child or one adult and a group of children this involves relationships and being together. Parents are involved in sharing information with settings about their child's dietary requirements and eating habits.

Enabling Environments – is made up of observation, assessment and planning, supporting every child, the learning environment and the wider contexts. Observing children at mealtimes can provide adults with lots of useful information about children for example, what do they like / not like? How do they use utensils? How confident are they? This information can then be used to help with planning and how adults and the environment can support children's learning. The environment can affect how children feel about mealtimes and eating. Food is linked to the emotions – is eating a pleasurable experience or a stressful one? The last aspect of the wider context is about how do we all work together for example, settings with parents, with the community for example, going out to local shops and buying food with working with and getting advice from cooks and health visitors.

Learning and Development – is about play and exploration, active learning, creativity and critical thinking and the six areas of learning and development. Children learn through experience and mealtimes need to be a pleasurable experience. For active learning to take place children need to feel at ease, secure and confident this will lead to them thinking, making connections and asking questions. The six areas of learning and development are all interconnected and linked to the four themes. Mealtimes supports all six areas in many different ways.

A Chance to Think 4.11

Planning Round a Theme

Personal, Social and Emotional Development	Communication, Language and Literacy	Problem Solving, Reasoning and Numeracy
1. Discuss where food comes from and how it is distributed.	1. Food interest table labelled and with cookery books (ask parents to help with labelling in various languages)	1. cooking food using a recipe, weighing and measuring, cooking times, amounts etc.
2. Turn home corner into a food shop or Chinese restaurant	2. Story tapes, stories and rhymes e.g. Hungry caterpillar, Chapattis not chips, 5 little peas in a pea pod pressed.	2. matching food e.g. length, weight, shape
3. Invite parent to come in a cook food with the children.	3. having conversations at meal times	3. cutting food into amounts and shapes e.g. do you want your toast in ½ or ¼'s, squares or triangles.
4. sharing food together and making choices	4. writing menus to put on the table at meal times	4. serving at meal times, how many would you like?

FOOD

Knowledge and Understanding of the World	Physical Development	Creative Development
1. growing food e.g. mung beans, cress	1. eating food with different types of implements e.g. knife and fork, chopsticks, fingers.	1. drama and music – the hungry caterpillar and finding food related music.
2. using the senses to identify food and tastes whilst having eyes closed.	2. opening food containers e.g. bags, tins, jars and measuring out food with different implements.	2. printing using fruit and vegetables, e.g. apple, mango, kiwi fruit, plantain, potato.
3. Examining cooking equipment and seeing how it works e.g. fridge, cooker, whisk, scales etc.	3. Learning about bodies, when am I hungry / thirsty / full? talking about food and keeping healthy	3. using food in the home corner and adding equipment and materials to extend play e.g. menus, cooking utensils.
4. identifying where food comes from, what is grown, manufactured etc and which countries do items come from?	4. having a pick-nick outside.	4. making place mats, menus, recipe books.

Figure A1 Planning on the theme of food

A Chance to Think 4.13

Craft Activity

You need to think about where you will carry out the activity; the seating and layout of the activity; the type of activity; the type or resources being used; protective clothing. A collage of bright-coloured materials with different textures. Only have a few children; ensure there is enough space to do the activity; ensure there is enough equipment and resources for the number of children; put things so children can reach them; help them as needed but do not do it for them; talk about what is happening and facilitate conversation; ensure all are able to participate but do not force participation; show things to Veronique as appropriate and describe things to her.

A Chance to Think 4.14

Music

Think about the individuals taking part; have a selection of songs and rhymes ready written on a list; use a song box; plan how long the session will last; organize the instruments with enough for everyone; organize the space where it is going to take place, so there is no background noise and distractions.

Finger rhymes; nursery rhymes action songs with parts of the body; quite and loud songs; playing instruments.

Ensure there is no background noise or distractions; sit facing the children; do things in groups and individually so that all children get a turn; use the props from the song box so all children can be involved; do things at different volumes; use body language and gestures as well as different tones of voice.

A Chance to Think 4.15

Interest Tables

Talk to the children about the interest table and display and explain what it is going to be about; ask them for ideas; talk about the types of homes they live in and how they can be incorporated into the display; talk about all the other kinds of home people live in; talk about the fact that some people do not have a home to live in; talk about animal homes; find and look at lots of pictures of different types of homes; design and build homes from construction toys, modellingand so on; paint pictures of homes; visit different homes if possible; ensure children help putting the interest table and display together.

A Chance to Think 4.17

Problem Solving, Reasoning and Numeracy

Anna can start by looking at the Early Years Foundation Stage documentation and CD Rom.

To support problem solving, reasoning and numeracy activities Anna can do include; sand play for example, is it heavy? You have made a star shape, water play for example, is it full? matching games for example, this circle is bigger than this circle, rhymes and songs for example, 1, 2, buckle my shoe, puzzles and talking about them as they are done, stories with numbers in for example, the three bears, making things of different sizes, posting boxes, stacking beakers, treasure baskets and heuristic play, music and movement for example, curling up small.

A Chance to Think 4.18

Science and Technology

Talk to the member of staff sensitivity about what you have observed. Ask them if they realize that this is what is happening.

Talk to them about the importance of girls doing science and technology activities; bring in research to back this up; explain the ethos of the setting and that, even if he thinks it is wrong, the setting has a policy of anti-discriminatory practice.; if necessary talk to the manager of the setting so that this can be monitored; recommend training courses.

All the children in the setting are getting messages that are gender stereotyped.

Appendix 5
Sample answers for Chapter 5

A Chance to Think 5.2

Supporting Children Who are Bilingual

Try and learn a few Spanish words, such as 'hello', 'toilet' and 'drink'. Start a 'Spanish Word Book' for the setting and write down words so you remember them. Colleagues can use the book and more words can be added as you learn them.

Smile; talk to Alexandra's mum so that Alexandra can see the setting is friendly and that her mother trusts everyone; show Alexandra and her mother round the setting; introduce them to children and staff; start Alexandra in the setting gradually, so that she can get used to spending more time each day without her mum; buddy Alexandra up with another child.

Reassure Alexandra's mother and ensure she has the phone number of the setting so that she can phone to see how Alexandra is; ensure the setting has Alexandra's mum's contact details and emergency numbers; ask her to write down any words that she things may be useful and add these to your 'Spanish Word Book'; have any comfort objects that Alexandra may use to hand; ask her to explain to Alexandra what is happening; ensure Alexandra can say goodbye to her mum and know when she will be returning; comfort Alexandra as appropriate, and encourage her to join in with the other children.

A Chance to Think 5.3

Supporting Individuals Around Communication

Talk to Amanda on her own and find out why this is happening; explain how damaging it is to David and the other children; explain to her how to communicate with David; discuss how you can support her to do this; discuss her feelings about working with David and how these affect her work with him; talk to her tutors if necessary; if this continues remove her from the situation and inform her tutors why this has happened.

Work with David on a one-on-one basis and support him; plan and develop situations where he can regain his confidence; acknowledge and praise his communication efforts and skills; talk to the other children and explain how he feels then they laugh at him.

A Chance to Think 5.4

Identity

Many thing affect how a person develops their identity including; their name; place in their family; how people treat them and react to them; what they hear being said about them; the images they see around them; the images they do not see around them and much more.

Because they feel good about themselves and have a strong sense of their own identity; they get positive reassurance about themselves from others and society at large. Because they have a poor self-identity; they do not feel good about themselves; they may be being abused or living in a home where domestic violence is taking place; they get negative messages about themselves from other people and / or society at large.

A Chance to Think 5.6

Ability

The issues for Suba and her parent's include; not being happy with the setting Suba attended; feeling that Suba is bright and needs to be challenged and have fun; needed to feel that staff can cope with being asked questions.

You could support Suba and her parent's by; talking to them and asking what they want from a setting and being clear about what you can offer; Ask what they mean by 'bright' and what they are doing to support Suba's development; observe Suba when she starts in your setting to find out where she is developmentally; plan activities and experiences that meet Suba's needs and interests; continue to observe, assess, evaluate, plan and work with Suba's parents; work with other professionals as needed.

A Chance to Think 5.7

Disability

This issues for Hisham include; settling into a new setting; remembering to change glasses when going outside; not being able to go out in bright sunlight; not feeling part of the setting and being singled out; not being called by his name and being known as the boy who wears glasses.

Issues for Hisham's parents include; trusting the setting and practitioners to remember Hisham's needs and meet them; remembering to take the sunglasses to the setting; hoping the glasses do not get lost or broken; wanting the best for Hisham and for him to 'fit in' and settle into the setting.

Support Hisham and his parents by: talking to the parents and find out as much as possible about Hisham's needs and what needs to be done in the setting to meet them; reassuring them that his glasses will be taken care of and they will be changed when going outside; ensuring all practitioners are aware of Hisham's needs and how to meet them; talk to Hisham and reminding him to change his glasses; involving him the activities; ensuring that all the children know Hisham's name and us it and remind them as needed; do an activity making glasses with the group; visit an optician as an activity; try and ensure there is a shady areas where Hisham can play outside; if unable to go outside ensure appropriate activities inside; find and use resources showing children wearing glasses, if necessary make some.

A Chance to Think 5.8

Gender

The issues for children and dad include; dad may be giving more time and attention to his son; the children may pick up that this means he values his son more. The son may feel he is valued and important; the daughter may begin to think that she is not worthy of his attention and is invisible; this may affect the development of self-esteem and identity of both children.

You can support dad by sensitively discussing this with him; he may not have realised he is doing it and what the implications may be; be a positive role model for dad in how to interact with boys and girls and children of different ages.

A Chance to Think 5.9

Illness / Allergy

Safa may feel excluded and wonder what she has done wrong; she may feel it is her fault, or that her friends do not like her any more.

You could talk to the manager about why this decision has been made; explain how it may affect Safa; ask if you can talk to the parents about what they feel Safa needs; find out more about the allergy and what the reactions might be; ensure that you put in place a treatment plan in case Safa comes into contact with strawberries; evaluate the policies and procedures of the setting and if necessary exclude strawberries from the setting and lunch boxes; ensure all parents know about not sending strawberries into the setting.

A Chance to Think 5.10

Attitudes towards Gender in Language

You could start by asking the Gerald why he is laughing and why he thinks it is funny; ask why Hazel says it is not funny and how the remark has made her feel. Talk to all children about how hurtful the remark is to both boys and girls because of the message it is giving; talk about why remarks like that should not be used. Contact the presenters and the television company to raise the issue with them and how discriminatory and hurtful it is.

A Chance to Think 5.11

Mixed Parentage / Dual Heritage

By asking if they realised that the word 'half-caste' was offensive and explaining what it means.

Talk to colleagues about the meaning of the word and asking if they meant it; talking about the positive benefits of having a mixed parentage / dual heritage background; ask the manager of training if appropriate; bring in literature for colleagues.

Provide positive images of mixed parentage / dual heritage children and adults; talk to Jason about his background; talk to Jason's parents; provide resources and activities so that Jason can feel positive about himself.

A Chance to Think 5.12

Poverty

Talk sensitively to the parents explaining the importance of washing and changing Tom as he is uncomfortable and may develop nappy rash; ensure that Tom has a clean new nappy on when he leaves the setting; try and find outs sensitively why this is happening and discuss with the parents how the setting can support them.

A Chance to Think 5.13

Twins

Gently say ask the adult who they are talking about. Explain that it does not sound very nice to say 'the other one'. If they say ' the twins' ask if they mean Louise and Amelia. Explain that it is important for Louise and Amelia that that they are treated as individuals and it is important to use names and not to label children as this can affect their identity and self-esteem. It is also important for the other children in the setting to hear all children be called by their names.

A Chance to Think 5.14

Self-Esteem

A parent with low self-esteem nay not be able to give their children the positive reassurance and support they need to develop their self-esteem; they may not understand why this is important; they may not be able to ask for help and support; their children may also develop low self-esteem.

Useful Organizations

Ability Net
PO Box 94
Warwick CV34 5WS
www.abilitynet.co.uk
Freephone Helpline: 0800 269545
Ability Net is a national charity helping disabled adults and children use com-
puters and the internet by adapting and adjusting their technology.

Ability Online
www.ablelink.org
Ability Online is a free internet community where young people with disabilities and illnesses and their parents can meet others like them, make friends
from all over the world, share their hopes and fears, find role-models and
mentors, and feel like they belong.

About Human Rights
Daresbury Point, Green Wood Drive
Manor Park
Cheshire WA7 1UP
www.abouthumanrights.co.uk
About Human Rights was formed to offer a unique reference point and com-
prehensive advice on human rights.

Action for Blind People
14–16 Verney Road
London SE16 3DZ
www.actionforblindpeople.org.uk
Freephone Helpline: 0800 915 4666
Action for Blind People provides free and impartial support and advice on
everything to do with visual impairment.

Action for Kids (AFK)
Ability House
15A Tottenham Lane
Hornsey
London N8 9DJ
www.actionforkids.org
Tel: 020 8347 8111
AFK is a national charity working with children and young people with
physical and learning disabilities and their parents and carers.

Action for Sick Children
32b Buxton Rd
High Lane
Stockport SK6 8BH
www.actionforsickchildren.org
Tel: 01663 763 004
Action for Sick Children is the leading children's healthcare charity.

Action on Rights for Children (ARCH)
www.arch-ed.org
Tel: 020 8558 9317
ARCH is an internet-based children's rights organization.

Adoption UK
Linden House
55 The Green
South Bar Street
Banbury
Oxfordshire OX16 9AB
www.adoptionuk.org
Tel: 01295 752240
Adoption UK supports adoptive families, before, during and after adoption.

Advisory Centre for Education (ACE)
1c Aberdeen Studios
22 Highbury Grove
London N5 2DQ
www.ace-ed.org.uk
Tel: 020 7704 3370
ACE is a national charity that provides advice and information to parents
and carers on a wide range of school-based issues including exclusion,
admissions, special education needs, bullying and attendance.

**Advisory Council of the Education of Romany and Other Travellers
(ACERT)**
Moot House
The Stow, Harlow
Essex CM20 3AG
www.acert.org.uk
ACERT works on several issues including equal access to education for
Gypsies, Romas and Travellers.

Afasic
1st Floor
20 Bowling Green Lane
London EC1R 0BD
www.afasic.org.uk
Tel: 020 7490 9410
Afasic was founded in 1968 as a parent-led organization to help children and
young people with speech and language impairments and their families.

Allergy UK
3 White Oak Square
London Road, Swanley
Kent BR8 7AG
www.allergyuk.org
Tel: 01322 619898
Allergy UK is a medical charity dealing with allergy, that represents the views
and needs of people with allergies, food intolerance and chemical sensitivity.

Alliance for Inclusive Education
336 Brixton Road
London SW9 7AA
www.allfie.org.uk
Tel: 020 7737 6030
The Alliance for Inclusive Education is a national network of individuals, families and groups working together to help change the mainstream education system, so that all young people can learn, play and live together.

Association for Spina Bifida and Hydrocephalus (ASBAH)
42 Park Road
Peterborough PE1 2UQ
www.asbah.org
Tel: 0845 450 7755
ASBAH is the leading UK-registered charity providing information and advice about spina bifida and hydrocephalus.

Asthma UK
Summit House
70 Wilson Street
London EC2A 2DB
www.asthma.org.uk
Tel: 020 7786 4900
Helpline: 0800 121 62 44
Asthma UK is the charity dedicated to improving the health and well-being of the 5.4 million people in the UK whose lives are affected by asthma. It has offices in London, Belfast, Cardiff and Edinburgh.

Asylum Aid
www.asylumaid.org.uk
Tel: 020 7354 9631
Asylum Aid is an independent national charity working to secure protection for people seeking refuge in the UK.

Audit Commission
1st Floor
Millbank Tower
Millbank
London SW1P 4HQ
www.audit-commission.gov.uk
Tel: 0844 798 2946
The Audit Commission is an independent watchdog, driving economy, efficiency and effectiveness in local public services to deliver better outcomes for everyone.

AVERT
4 Brighton Road
Horsham
West Sussex RH13 5BA
www.avert.org
AVERT is an international HIV and AIDS charity, based in the UK, working to avert HIV and AIDS worldwide, through education, treatment and care.

Barnardo's
Tanners Lane
Barkingside
Ilford
Essex IG6 1QG
www.barnardos.org.uk
Tel: 020 8550 8822
Barnardo's is a children's charity working with families in many ways including fostering and adoption, disability, and coping with domestic violence.

Beaumont Society
27 Old Gloucester Street
London WC1N 3XX
www.beaumontsociety.org.uk
Tel: 01582 412220
The Beaumont Society provides help and support for all transgender people.

Board of Deputies of British Jews
6 Bloomsbury Square
London WC1A 2LP
www.bod.org.uk
Tel: 020 7543 5400
The Board of Deputies of British Jews' 300 representatives, drawn from a broad
cross-section of the Jewish community throughout Britain today, are together
the chief voice of British Jewry.

British Association for Adoption and Fostering (BAAF)
Head Office
Saffron House
6–10 Kirby Street
London EC1N 8TS
www.baaf.org.uk
Tel: 020 7421 2600
BAAF works on family finding, publications, training, conferences, consul-
tancy, campaigning and advice.

**British Association for the Study and Prevention of Child Abuse and
Neglect (BASPCAN)**
17 Priory Street
York YO1 6ET
www.baspcan.org.uk
Tel: 01904 613605
BASPCAN was established to protect children from suffering, or likelihood of
suffering, significant harm, ill-treatment, impairment of health or development
by the encouragement and promotion of any methods, services and facilities
calculated to safeguard and promote the welfare of such children.

British Deaf Association
10th Floor, Coventry Point
Market Way
Coventry CV1 1EA
Textphone: 02476 550393
www.britishdeafassociation.org
The British Deaf Association is the home of the largest UK deaf organization
run by deaf people for deaf people.

British Diabetic Association (Diabetes UK)
Central Office
Macleod House
10 Parkway
London NW1 7AA
www.diabetes.org.uk
Tel: 020 7424 1000
Diabetes UK is the largest organization in the UK working for people with
diabetes, funding research, campaigning and helping people live with the
condition.

British Dyslexia Association (BDA)
Unit 8
Bracknell Beeches
Old Bracknell Lane
Bracknell RG12 7BW
www.bdadyslexia.org.uk
Tel: 0845 251 9002
BDA is a national charity. Their vision is that of a dyslexia-friendly society that
enables dyslexic people of all ages to reach their full potential.

British Epilepsy Association (Epilepsy Action)
New Antsey House
Gate Way Drive
Yeadon
Leeds LS19 7XY
www.epilepsy.org.uk
Tel: 0113 210 8800
Epilepsy Action aims to improve the quality of life and promote the interests
of people living with epilepsy.

British Humanist Association
1 Gower Street
London WC1E 6HD
www.humanism.org.uk
Tel: 020 7079 3580
The British Humanist Association exists to promote humanism and support
and represent people who seek to live good lives without religious or super-
stitious beliefs.

British Institute of Human Rights
King's College London
7th Floor
Melbourne House
46 Aldwych
London WC2B 4LL
www.bihr.org
Tel: 020 7848 1818
The British Institute of Human Rights is a human rights organization committed to challenging inequality and injustice working with organizations. They
do not work with individuals.

British Institute of Learning Disabilities (BILD)
Campion House
Green Street
Kidderminster
Worcestershire DY10 1JL
www.bild.org.uk
Tel: 01562 723 010
BILD is working to improve the lives of people in the UK with a learning disability.

British Nutrition Foundation
High Holborn House
52–54 High Holborn
London WC1V 6RQ
www.nutrition.org.uk
Tel: 020 7404 6504
The British Nutrition Foundation provides guidance on all aspects on nutrition,
and has a teacher centre providing information and resources linked to the
curriculum.

British Sikh Consultative Forum
2 Chignell Place
London W13 0TJ
www.bscf.org
Tel: 020 8579 8898
The British Sikh Consultative Forum was created in 2002 as a mechanism for
interfacing with the government. The forum allows for discussion within
the Sikh community and promotes consensus within the community wherever possible. They also seek to develop relations with other communities
and to bring issues of concern to Sikhs to the attention of government and
the wider political and administrative system.

British Stammering Association
15 Old Ford Road
London E2 9PJ
www.stammering.org
Tel: 020 8983 1003
The British Stammering Association is a national organization for adults and children who stammer, run by people who stammer.

Brittle Bone Society
Grant-Paterson House
30 Guthrie Street
Dundee DD1 5BS
www.brittlebone.org
Tel: 01382 204 446
The Brittle Bone Society is an organization providing support to people affected by the bone condition Osteogenesis Imperfecta (OI).

Buddhist Society
58 Eccleston Square
London SW1V 1PH
www.thebuddhistsociety.org.uk
Tel: 020 7834 5858
The Buddhist Society provides information on Buddhism.

Bullying UK
702 Windsor House
Cornwall Road
Harrogate HG1 2PW
www.bullying.co.uk
Bullying UK is charity working with children and parents around bullying issues.

Centre for Accessible Environments (CAE)
70 South Lambeth Road, Vauxhall
London SW8 1RL
www.cae.org.uk
Tel: 020 7840 0125
CAE is the UK's leading authority on inclusive design. They aim to help secure a built environment that is usable by everyone, including disabled and older people.

Centre for Studies on Inclusive Education (CSIE)
New Redland Building
Coldharbour Lane, Frenchay
Bristol BS16 1QU
www.csie.org.uk
Tel: 0117 328 4007
CSIE is an independent organization promoting inclusive education as a basic
human right of every child.

Challenging Behaviour Foundation
c/o The Old Courthouse
New Road Avenue
Chatham
Kent ME4 6BE
www.thecbf.org.uk
Tel: 01634 838 739
The Challenging Behaviour Foundation wants to see children and adults with
severe learning disabilities, who are described as having challenging behaviour, having the same life opportunities as everyone else, including home
life, education, employment and leisure.

CHANGE
19/20, Unity Business Centre
26 Roundhay Road
Leeds LS7 1AB
www.changepeople.co.uk
Tel: 0113 243 0202
CHANGE is a national rights organization led by disabled people. It campaigns
for equal rights for all people with learning disabilities.

Child Bereavement Trust
Aston House, West Wycombe
High Wycombe
Bucks HP14 3AG
www.childbereavement.org.uk
Tel: 01494 446 648
The Child Bereavement Trust is a charity that supports families and educates
professionals both when a child dies and when a child is bereaved.

Child Exploitation and Online Protection (CEOP) Centre

33 Vauxhall Bridge Road

London SW1V 2WG

www.ceop.gov.uk

Tel: 0870 000 3344

CEOP is dedicated to eradicating the sexual abuse of children. They are part of UK policing and very much about tracking and bringing offenders to account either directly or in partnership with local and international forces.

Child Growth Foundation

2 Mayfield Avenue, Chiswick

London W4 1PW

www.childgrowthfoundation.org

Tel: 020 8995 0257

The Child Growth Foundation is a charity relating to children's growth. It provides information of benefit to parents with a child who has a diagnosed or suspected growth problem, to people who have a growth problem and their families, and to people and medical professionals with an interest.

Child Poverty Action Group (CPAG)

94 White Lion Street

London N1 9PF

www.cpag.org.uk

Tel: 020 7837 7979

CPAG is the leading charity campaigning for the abolition of child poverty in the UK and for a better deal for low-income families and children.

Child Rights Information Network (CRIN)

c/o Save the Children

1 St John's Lane

London EC1M 4AR

www.crin.org

Tel: 020 7012 6866

CRIN envisions a world in which every child enjoys all of the human rights promised by the United Nations, regional organizations, and national governments alike.

Childline
www.childline.org.uk
Tel: 0800 1111
Childline provides a counselling service for children and young people.

Children are Unbeatable! Alliance
94 White Lion Street
London N1 9PF
www.childrenareunbeatable.org.uk
Tel: 020 7713 0569
The Children are Unbeatable! Alliance campaigns for the UK to satisfy human
rights obligations by modernizing the law on assault to afford children the
same protection as adults. It also has offices in Northern Ireland, Scotland,
Wales.

Children First
83 Whitehouse Loan
Edinburgh EH9 1AT
www.children1st.org.uk
Tel: 0131 446 2300
Children First has 125 years' experience of working with children and families. Their vision is a happy, healthy, safe and secure childhood for every
child and young person in Scotland.

Children in England
Unit 25, 1st Floor
Angel Gate, City Road
London EC1V 2PT
www.childrenengland.org.uk
Tel: 020 7833 3319
Children in England are the leading membership organization for the chil-
dren, young people and families voluntary sector. Their mission is to create
a fairer world for children, young people and families by championing the
voluntary organizations which work on their behalf.

Children in Northern Ireland (CiNI)

Unit 9, 40 Montgomery Road

Belfast BT6 9HL

www.ci-ni.org.uk

Tel: 028 9040 1290

CiNI is the regional umbrella organization for the children's sector in Northern Ireland. CiNI aims to enhance the lives of all children in Northern Ireland by promoting the work of the children's sector and maximizing positive outcomes for children, young people and their families.

Children in Scotland

Princes House

5 Shandwick Place

Edinburgh EH2 4RG

www.childreninscotland.org.uk

Tel: 0131 228 8484

Children in Scotland is the national agency for voluntary, statutory and professional organizations and individuals working with children and their families in Scotland.

Children in Wales

25 Windsor Place

Cardiff CF10 3BZ

www.childreninwales.org.uk

Tel: 029 2034 2434

Children in Wales is the national umbrella organization for those working with children and young people in Wales. Its aims are to promote the interests of these groups and take action to meet their needs. They are a registered charity and an independent non-governmental organization.

Children with Leukaemia

51 Great Ormond Street

London WC1N 3JQ

www.leukaemia.org

Tel: 020 7404 0808

Children with Leukaemia is a charity helping children affected by leukaemia. They fund research into causes and treatments, support families through welfare programmes and campaign on their behalf.

Children's Legal Centre
University of Essex
Wivenhoe Park
Colchester
Essex CO4 3SQ
www.childrenslegalcentre.com
Tel: 01206 877 910
The Children's Legal Centre is a national charity committed to promoting
  children's rights. Providing legal advice, information and representation for
  children and young people.

Children's Rights Alliance for England
94 White Lion Street
London N1 9PF
www.crae.org.uk
Tel: 020 7278 8222
The Children's Rights Alliance for England provides a national phone and
  email advice service for children in England on equality and human rights.

Children's Society
Edward Rudolf House
Margery Street
London WC1X 0JL
www.childrenssociety.org.uk
Tel: 0845 300 1128
The Children's Society is a charity working to make childhoods better for
  children in the UK.

Children's Workforce Development Council (CWDC)
2nd Floor
City Exchange
11 Albion Street
Leeds LS1 5ES
www.cwdcouncil.org.uk
Tel: 0113 244 6311
CWDC leads change so that the thousands of people and volunteers working
  with children and young people across England are able to do the best job
  they possibly can.

City and Guilds
1 Giltsper Street
London EC1A 2DD
www.cityandguilds.com/uk
Tel: 020 7294 2800
City and Guilds is the UK's leading vocational awarding organization.

CLIC Sargent
Griffin House
161 Hammersmith Road
London W6 8SG
www.clicsargent.org.uk
Tel: 020 8752 2800
CLIC Sargent cares for children and young people with cancer and their
families. It also has offices in Bristol, Glasgow and Belfast.

Communication and Learning Enterprises (CANDLE)
48 Station Road
Holywell Green HX4 9AW
Tel: 079 4627 4795
CANDLE provides training for practitioners and learning and commun-
ication support for young people and adults with disabilities.

Communication Matters
c/o The ACE Centre
92 Windmill Road
Oxford OX3 7DR
www.communicationmatters.org.uk
Tel: 0845 456 8211
Communication Matters is a national charitable organization of members
concerned with the augmentative and alternative communication (AAC)
needs of people with complex communication needs.

Community Insight
Avonbridge House
Bath Road
Chippenham SN15 2BB
www.communityinsight.co.uk
Tel: 0845 313 2600
Community Insight helps in developing services aimed at those working in childcare and education. These include a comprehensive range of books and related materials, and an annual training programme.

Community Playthings
Robertsbridge
East Sussex TN32 5DR
www.communityplaythings.co.uk
Tel: 0800 387 457
Community Playthings helps in providing products to support play.

Contact a Family
209–211 City Road
London EC1V 1JN
www.cafamily.org.uk
Tel: 020 7608 8700
Contact a Family provides support, advice and information for families with disabled children.

Council for Awards in Children's Care and Education (CACHE)
Apex House, 81 Camp Road
St Albans
Herts AL1 5GB
www.cache.org.uk
Tel: 0845 347 2123
CACHE is the UK's only specialist awarding body for the child and adult care sectors.

Council for Disabled Children (CDC)
NCB
Wakley Street
London EC1V 7QE
www.ncb.org.uk/cdc
Tel: 020 7843 1900
CDC is a semi-independent council of the National Children's Bureau.

Cruse Bereavement Care

PO Box 800

Richmond

Surrey TW9 2RG

Tel: 020 8939 9530

www.crusebereavementcare.org.uk

Cruse Bereavement Care is a national charity set up to offer free, confidential help to bereaved people.

Cystic Fibrosis Trust

11 London Road, Bromley

Kent BR1 1BY

www.cftrust.org.uk

Tel: 020 8464 7211

The Cystic Fibrosis Trust is the UK's only national charity dealing with all aspects of cystic fibrosis.

Daycare Trust

2nd Floor, Novas Contemporary Urban Centre

73–81 Southwark Bridge Road

London SE1 0NQ

Tel: 0845 872 6260; 020 7940 7510

The Daycare Trust is a national childcare charity that provides information for parents, childcare providers, employers, trade unions, local authorities and policy makers.

Deafblind UK

National Centre for Deafblindness

John and Lucille van Geest Place

Cygnet Road, Hampton

Peterborough PE7 8FD

www.deafblind.org.uk

Tel: 01733 358 100

Deafblind UK is a national charity offering specialist services and human support to deafblind people and those who have progressive sight and hearing loss acquired throughout their lives.

Department for Children, Schools and Families (DCSF)
Sanctuary Buildings
Great Smith Street
London SW1P 3BT
www.dcsf.gov.uk
Tel: 0870 000 2288; 0845 60 222 60
The purpose of the DCSF is to make this the best place in the world for children and young people to grow up.

Department of Health (DH)
Richmond House
79 Whitehall
London SW1A 2NS
www.dh.gov.uk
Tel: 020 7210 4850
DH exists to improve the health and wellbeing of people in England.

Diabetes UK
Macleod House
10 Parkway
London NW1 7AA
www.diabetes.org.uk
Tel: 020 7424 1000
Diabetes UK is an organization working for people with diabetes, funding research, campaigning and helping people live with the condition.

Disability Alliance
Universal House
88–94 Wentworth Street
London E1 7SA
www.disabilityalliance.org
Tel: 020 7247 8776
Disability Alliance provides a helpline for disabled people, their families and carers. It produces the Disability Rights Handbook every May.

Disability Information and Advice Line (DIAL) UK
St Catherine's
Tickhill Road
Doncaster
South Yorkshire DN4 8QN
www.dialuk.info
Tel: 01302 310 123
DIAL UK provides an information and advice service to disabled people and
others on all aspects of living with a disability.

Disability Information Trust
Nuffield Orthopedic Centre
Headington
Oxford OX3 7LD
www.abilityonline.org.uk
Tel: 01865 227 592
The Disability Information Trust is a registered charity that specialises in the
assessment and testing of disability equipment and the publication of
independent, verified and in-depth information on that equipment.

Disability Law Service (DLS)
39–45 Cavell Street
London E1 2BP
www.dls.org.uk
Tel: 020 7791 9800
DLS has provided high-quality information and advice to disabled and deaf
people for over 30 years.

Disabled Living Foundation (DLF)
380–384 Harrow Road
London W9 2HU
www.dlf.org.uk
Tel: 020 7289 6111
DLF is a national charity that provides impartial advice, information and
training on daily living aids.

Disabled Parents Network (DPN)

81 Melton Road

West Bridgford

Nottingham NG2 8EN

www.disabledparentsnetwork.org.uk

Tel: 0300 3300 639

DPN is a national organization of and for disabled people who are parents or who hope to become parents, and their families, friends and supporters.

Down's Syndrome Association

Langdon Down Centre

2a Langdon Park

Teddington TW11 9PS

www.downs-syndrome.org.uk

Tel: 0845 230 0372

The Down's Syndrome Association is a national charity covering all aspects of living with Down's syndrome.

Dyspraxia Foundation

8 West Alley

Hitchin

Herts SG5 1EG

www.dyspraxiafoundation.org.uk

Tel: 01462 455 016

The Dyspraxia Foundation is an organization that aims to support individuals and families affected by dyspraxia, to promote better diagnostic and treatment facilities for those who have dyspraxia, to help professionals in health and education to assist those with dyspraxia, and to promote awareness and understanding of dyspraxia.

Early Education

The British Association for Early Childhood Education

136 Cavell Street

London E1 2JA

www.early-education.org.uk

Tel: 020 7539 5400

Early Education is the leading national voluntary organization for early-years practitioners and parents with members and branches in England, Northern Ireland, Scotland and Wales. It promotes the right of all children to education of the highest quality. It provides support, advice and information on effective practice for everyone concerned with the education and care of young children from birth to eight years.

Edexcel
190 High Holborn
London WC1V 7BH
www.edexcel.com
Tel: 0845 618 0440
Edexcel is the provider of internationally recognized qualifications.

Education Otherwise
PO Box 325
Kings Lynn PE34 3XW
www.education-otherwise.org
Education Otherwise is a membership-based organization that provides
    support and information for families whose children are being educated
    outside school.

Eduzone
Cedar House
Sopers Road, Cuffley
Herts EN6 4RY
www.eduzone.co.uk
Tel: 0845 445 556
Eduzone are suppliers of educational resources and equipment for children.

Epilepsy Action
New Anstey House, Gate Way Drive
Yeadon
Leeds LS19 7XY
www.epilepsy.org.uk
Tel: 0113 210 8800
Epilepsy Action aims to improve the quality of life and promote the interests
    of people living with epilepsy.

Equal Opp Shop Ltd
33 The Crescent
Urmston
Manchester M41 5QR
www.theequaloppshop.co.uk
Tel: 0161 202 9499
The Equal Opp Shop Ltd are specialists in multicultural resources and toys,
    disability awareness resources and childminding resources.

Equality and Human Rights Commission
3 More London
Riverside Tooley Street
London SE1 2RG
www.equalityhumanrights.com
Tel: 020 3117 0235
The Equality and Human Rights Commission deals with all issues relating to
equality and human rights.

Families Need Fathers
134 Curtain Road
London EC2A 3AR
www.fnf.org.uk
Tel: 020 7613 5060
Families Need Fathers seeks to obtain, for the children, the best possible blend
of both parents in the lives of children; enough for the children to realize
that both parents are fully involved in their lives.

Family Action
501–505 Kingsland Road
London E8 4AU
www.family-action.org.uk
Tel: 020 7254 6251
Family Action is the leading provider of services to disadvantaged and socially
isolated families since its foundation in 1869. They tackle some of the most
complex and difficult issues facing families today – including domestic
abuse, mental health problems, learning disabilities and severe financial
hardship.

Family Rights Group
Second Floor, The Print House
18 Ashwin Street
London E8 3DL
www.frg.org.uk
Tel: 020 7923 2628
Family Rights Group is a charity in England and Wales that advises parents
and other family members whose children are involved with or require
social care services.

Fatherhood Institute
Horsingtons Yard, Tiverton Place
Lion Street
Abergavenny NP7 5PN
www.fatherhoodinstitute.org
Tel: 0845 634 1328
The Fatherhood Institute is the UK's fatherhood think-tank

Festival Shop Ltd
56 Poplar Road, Kings Heath
Birmingham B14 7AG
Tel: 0121 486 3569; Fax: 0121 486 4971; Email: info@festivalshop.co.uk
www.festivalshop.co.uk
The Festival Shop Ltd sells a variety of resources that promote anti-discriminatory practice.

Fostering Network
87 Blackfriars Road
London SE1 8HA
www.fostering.net
Tel: 020 7620 6400
The Fostering Network is the UK's leading charity for everyone with a personal or professional involvement in fostering. It also has offices in Cardiff, Glasgow, Belfast, North West England, North East England and South West England.

Gender Trust
Community Base
133 Queens Road, Brighton
East Sussex BN1 3XG
www.gendertrust.org.uk
Tel: 01273 234 024
Gender Trust is a charity which supports anyone affected by gender identity issues.

Gingerbread
255 Kentish Town Road
London NW5 2LX
www.gingerbread.org.uk
Tel: 020 7428 5400
Gingerbread is the leading national charity working to help the UK's 1.9 million lone parents and their children.

Gypsy Council
c/o Gypsy Roma Traveller Achievement Service Leeds
West Park Centre, Spen Lane
Leeds LS16 5BE
www.grtleeds.co.uk/information/GypsyCouncil
Tel: 0113 274 8050
The Gypsy Council is involved in a wide spectrum of support and liaison
work, supporting Gypsy families in planning applications and their fight for
decent legal places to live. They also offer an advice service to Gypsy people,
students and others on many different issues, and are a main point of contact for both national and local media. It has a large resource library for
academic work.

Home Office
Direct Communications Unit
2 Marsham Street
London SW1P 4DF
www.homeoffice.gov.uk
Tel: 020 7035 4848
The Home Office is the lead government department for immigration and
passports, drugs policy, counter-terrorism and police.

Home-Start
Head Office
The Home-Start Centre
8–10 West Walk
Leicester LE1 7NA
www.home-start.org.uk
Tel: 0116 258 7900
Home-Start helps to increase the confidence and independence of families.
It has 13 regional and nation offices supporting local Home-Starts across
the UK. It also supports Home-Starts in British Forces bases in Germany
and Cyprus.

Hyperactive Children's Support Group
71 Whyke lane
Chichester
West Sussex PO19 7PD
www.hacsg.org.uk
The Hyperactive Children's Support Group is a registered charity which has
been successfully helping ADHD/hyperactive children and their families
for over 30 years.

I Can
8 Wakley Street
London EC1V 7QE
www.ican.org.uk
Tel: 0845 225 4071
I Can is a children's communication charity.

Immigration and Nationality Directorate (UK Border Agency)
Public Enquiry Office
Lunar House
40 Wellesley Road
Croydon CR9 2BY
www.ukba.homeoffice.gov.uk
The UK Border Agency is responsible for securing the UK borders and controlling migration in the UK. They manage border control for the UK, enforcing immigration and customs regulations. They also consider applications for permission to enter or stay in the UK, and for citizenship and asylum.

Jain Samaj Europe
32 Oxford Street
Leicester LE1 5XU
www.jaincentre.co.uk
Tel: 0116 254 1150
Jain Samaj Europe is a network through which to share Jain heritage and religion.

Joseph Rowntree Foundation
Head Office
The Homestead
40 Water End
York YO30 6WP
www.jrf.org.uk
Tel: 01904 629 241
The Joseph Rowntree Foundation is an endowed charity that funds a large, UK-wide research and development programme. They seek to understand the root causes of social problems, to identify ways of overcoming them, and to show how social needs can be met in practice.

Just for Kids Law (JfK)
402 Harrow Road
London W9 2HU
www.justforkidslaw.org
Tel: 020 7266 7159
JfK provides advocates who act on behalf of young people in legal and quasi-legal proceedings.

KIDS National Development Department (National Training & Inclusion Projects)
6 Aztec Row
Berners Road
London N1 0PW
www.kids.org.uk
Tel: 020 7359 3073
KIDS National Development Department works with disabled children, young people and their families.

Kidscape
2 Grosvenor Gardens
London SW1W 0DH
www.kidscape.org.uk
Tel: 020 7730 3300
Kidscape works UK-wide to provide individuals and organizations with practical skills and resources necessary to keep children safe from harm.

Law Centres Federation
PO Box 65836
London EC4P 4FX
www.lawcentres.org.uk
Tel: 020 7842 0720
Law Centres are not-for-profit legal practices providing free legal advice and representation to disadvantaged people.

Learning Through Landscapes
Head Office
3rd Floor Southside Offices
The Law Courts
Winchester
Hampshire SO23 9DL
www.ltl.org.uk
Tel: 01962 846 258
Learning Through Landscapes helps schools and early-years settings make the
most of their outdoor spaces for play and learning.

Letterbox Library
1–73 Allen Road
Stoke Newington
London N16 8RY
www.letterboxlibrary.com
Tel: 020 7503 4801
The Letterbox Library is a social enterprise organization committed to cele-
brating equality and diversity in the very best children's books.

Liberty
21 Tabard Street
London SE1 4LA
www.liberty-human-rights.org.uk
Tel: 020 7403 3888
Liberty provides information on human rights issues and the UK Human
Rights Act.

Listening Books
12 Lant Street
London SE1 1QH
www.listening-books.org.uk
Tel: 020 7407 9417
Listening Books is a UK charity providing a fantastic selection of high-
quality audiobooks to over 7,000 people across the UK who find it difficult
or impossible to read due to illness or disability. They support the National
Curriculum from Key Stage 2 to A Level and have a huge range of fiction
and non-fiction titles for both adults and children.

Living Paintings
Queen Isabelle House
Unit 8 Kingsclere Park
Kingsclere
Newbury
Berkshire RG20 4SW
www.livingpaintings.org
Tel: 01635 299 771

Living Paintings helps blind and partially sighted people share in the visual images that colour and inform all our lives. For children their work specifically supports the development of essential life skills – touch and listening, language and vocabulary, reading and communication, as well as the understanding of visual concepts such as colours, relative size and the representation of objects as raised images.

London Friend
86 Caledonian Road
Islington
London N1 9DN
www.londonfriend.org.uk
Tel: 020 7833 1674

London Friend is a charity that has been serving the lesbian, gay, bisexual and transgender community since 1972.

London Lesbian and Gay Switchboard (LLGS)
PO Box 7324
London N1 9QS
www.llgs.org.uk
Tel: 020 7837 6768

LLGS provides an information, support and referral service for lesbians, gay men, bisexual, trans people and anyone who needs to consider issues around their sexuality.

Look
National Office
c/o Queen Alexandra College
49 Court Oak Road
Harborne
Birmingham B17 9TG
www.look-uk.org
Tel: 0121 428 5038
Supporting parents and carers of children with a visual impairment.

Makaton Charity
Manor House
46 London Road
Blackwater, Camberley
Surrey GU17 0AA
www.makaton.org
Tel: 01276 606 760
The Makaton Charity uses signs and symbols to teach communication, language and literacy skills to people with communication and learning difficulties. It provides training, support, research information and much more.

Mencap
123 Golden Lane
London EC1Y 0RT
www.mencap.org.uk
Tel: 020 7454 0454
Mencap is the UK's leading learning-disability charity working with people with a learning disability and their families and carers.

Mind
15–19 Broadway
Stratford
London E15 4BQ
www.mind.org.uk
Tel: 020 8519 2122
Mind is the leading mental-health charity in England and Wales working to create a better life for everyone with experience of mental distress.

Minority Rights Group International
54 Commercial Street
London E1 6LT
www.minorityrights.org
Tel: 020 7422 4200

The Minority Rights Group International campaigns worldwide with around
130 partners in over 60 countries to ensure that disadvantaged minorities
and indigenous peoples, often the poorest of the poor, can make their voices
heard.

Muslim Council of Britain (MCB)
PO Box 57330
London E1 2WJ
www.mcb.org.uk
Tel: 0845 262 6786

MCB is a national representative Muslim umbrella body with over 500 affiliated national, regional and local organizations, mosques, charities and
schools. MCB is pledged to work for the common good of society as a whole,
encouraging individual Muslims and Muslim organizations to play a full
and participatory role in public life.

National Aids Trust
New City Cloisters
196 Old Street
London EC1V 9FR
www.nat.org.uk
Tel: 020 7814 6767

The National Aids Trust is a charity dedicated to transforming society's response
to HIV. They provide fresh thinking, expert advice and practical resources,
and campaign for change.

National Association for Gifted Children (NAGC)
Suite 14, Challenge House
Sherwood Drive
Bletchley, Milton Keynes
Buckinghamshire MK3 6DP
www.nagcbritain.org.uk
Tel: 0845 450 0295

NAGC is a membership charity that deals with all aspects of giftedness in
children.

National Association for Special Educational Needs (NASEN)
Nasen House
4/5 Amber Business Village
Amber Close
Amington
Tamworth
Staffordshire B77 4RP
www.nasen.org.uk
Tel: 01827 311 500
NASEN is an organization for special needs information.

National Association of Toy and Leisure Libraries
1A Harmood Street
London NW1 8DN
www.natll.org.uk
Tel: 020 7428 2280
The National Association of Toy and Leisure Libraries has over 35 years' experience in helping toy and leisure libraries as well as working across the voluntary and statutory sector developing policy and using their expertise to promote the value of play and leisure opportunities for all. It also has offices in Scotland, Wales and Northern Ireland.

National Autistic Society (NAS)
393 City Road
London EC1V 1NG
www.nas.org.uk
Tel: 020 7833 2299
NAS champions the rights and interests of all people with autism and aims to provide individuals with autism and their families with help, support and services that they can readily access, trust and rely upon and which make a positive difference to their lives.

National Blind Children's Society
Central Office, Shawton House
792 Hagley Road West
Quinton
Birmingham B68 0PJ
www.nbcs.org.uk
Tel: 01278 764 770
The National Blind Children's Society helps enable children and young people with visual impairment to achieve their educational and recreational goals.

National Childminding Association (NCMA)
Royal Court
81 Tweedy Road
Bromley
Kent BR1 1TG
www.ncma.org.uk
Tel: 0845 880 0044
NCMA is a charity and professional association whose mission is to ensure that families in every community have access to high-quality, home-based childcare, play, learning and family support so they can help their children reach their full potential.

National Children's Bureau (NCB)
8 Wakley Street
London EC1V 7QE
www.ncb.org.uk
Tel: 020 7843 6000
NCB's mission is to advance the well-being of all children and young people across every aspect of their lives.

National Council of Hindu Temples UK (NCHT)
c/o 1 Hans Close, Stoke
Coventry CV2 4WA
www.nchtuk.org
Tel: 07805 054776
NCHT is the oldest and one of the largest Hindu umbrella bodies linking over 200 Hindu temples and faith organizations and works with them for the benefit of the Hindu community across the UK. It acts as a resource centre and one of the main consultative and advisory bodies on the matters relating to the British Hindu community, culture and religion and regularly interacts with many government and statutory departments.

National Day Nurseries Association (NDNA)
Head Office
National Early Years Enterprise Centre
Longbow Close
Huddersfield
West Yorkshire HD2 1GQ
www.ndna.org.uk
Tel: 01484 407 070
NDNA is a charity representing children's day nurseries across the UK.

National Deaf Children's Society
15 Dufferin Street
London EC1Y 8UR
www.ndcs.org.uk
Tel: 020 7490 8656; Minicom: 020 7490 8656
The National Deaf Children's Society is a charity dedicated to creating a world without barriers for deaf children and young people.

National Eczema Society
Freepost WC4049
London N19 5BR
www.eczema.org
Tel: 020 7281 3553
The National Eczema Society provides information and advice about eczema.

National Playbus Association
Head Office
Brunswick Court
Brunswick Square
Bristol BS2 8PE
www.playbus.org.uk
Tel: 0117 916 6580
The National Playbus Association supports mobile community work, enabling their members to work more effectively within their local communities around the UK.

National Portage Association
Kings Court
17 School Road
Birmingham B28 8JG
www.portage.org.uk
Tel: 0121 244 1807
The National Portage Association is a home-visiting educational service for pre-school children with additional support needs and their families.

National Society for Epilepsy
Chesham Lane
Chalfont St Peter
Bucks SL9 0RJ
www.epilepsysociety.org.uk
Tel: 01494 601 300
The National Society for Epilepsy is the leading medical charity working for
everyone affected by epilepsy.

National Society for Promoting Religious Education
Church House
Great Smith Street
London SW1P 3AZ
www.natsoc.org.uk
Tel: 020 7898 1518
The National Society for Promoting Religious Education has a wide member-
ship, including many Church of England and Church in Wales schools, as
well as individual supporting members.

National Society for the Prevention of Cruelty to Children (NSPCC)
Weston House
42 Curtain Road
London EC2A 3NH
www.nspcc.org.uk
Tel: 020 7825 2500
NSPCC campaigns for the end of child cruelty.

National Spiritual Assembly of the Bahá'ís of the United Kingdom
27 Rutland Gate
London SW7 1PD
www.bahai.org.uk
Tel: 020 7584 2566
The National Spiritual Assembly of the Bahá'ís of the United Kingdom provides information about the Baha'i faith and its website has links to Baha'i
agencies and local Baha'i community websites.

Network
811–7 Woodfield Terrace
Stansted
Essex CM24 8AJ.
www.network81.org
Tel: 0845 077 4056
Network is a national network of parents working towards properly resourced
inclusive education for children with special educational needs.

Network of Buddhist Organisations (UK)
PO Box 4147
Maidenhead SL60 1DN
www.nbo.org.uk
Tel: 0845 345 8978
The Network of Buddhist Organisations was founded to promote fellowship
and dialogue between Buddhist organizations.

Network of Sikh Organisations (UK)
Suite 405, Highland House
165 The Broadway
London SW19 1NE
www.nsouk.co.uk
Tel: 020 8544 8037
Network of Sikh Organisations is a registered charity that links more than 100
UK gurdwaras and other UK Sikh organizations in active cooperation to
enhance the image and understanding of Sikhism in the UK.

**Office for Advice, Assistance, Support and Information on Special Needs
(OAASIS)**
The Croft
Vicars Hill
Boldre
Lymington
Hants SO41 5QB
www.oaasis.co.uk
Tel: 0800 197 3907
OAASIS is a resource for parents and professionals caring for children with
Autism / Asperger Syndrome and other learning disabilities.

Office for National Statistics
Customer Contact Centre
Office for National Statistics
Room 1.101
Government Buildings
Cardiff Road
Newport
South Wales NP10 8XG
www.statistics.gov.uk
Tel: 0845 601 3034
The Office for National Statistics provides statistics on all areas of childcare
and equality.

Office for Standards in Education (Ofsted)
Alexandra House
33 Kingsway
London WC2B 6SE
www.ofsted.gov.uk
Tel: 0845 640 4045
Ofsted inspect and regulate to achieve excellence in the care of children and
young people, and in education and skills for learners of all ages.

Office of Public Information for Jehovah's Witnesses in Britain
Watch Tower Bible and Tract Society
The Ridgeway
London NW7 1RN
www.watchtower.org
Tel: 020 8906 2211
The Office of Public Information for Jehovah's Witnesses in Britain provides
information on the Jehovah's Witnesses religion, health and medical care
and its website has a section on additional publications.

Office of Public Sector Information (OPSI)
102 Petty France
London SW1H 9AJ
www.opsi.gov.uk
Operating from within the national archives, the OPSI is at the heart of
information policy, setting standards, delivering access and encouraging the
re-use of public sector information. It provides a wide range of services to
the public, information industry, government and the wider public sector
relating to finding, using, sharing and trading information.

Oxfam

Oxfam House

John Smith Drive

Cowley

Oxford OX4 2JY

www.oxfam.org.uk

Tel: 0300 200 1300

Oxfam is a registered charity; its website has information about Oxfam's work, a section on teacher resources with ideas, resources and support for developing the global dimension in the classroom and a shop to buy from.

Parentline Plus

520 Highgate Studios

53–79 Highgate Road

Kentish Town

London NW5 1TL

www.parentlineplus.org.uk

Tel: 020 7284 5500

Parentline Plus is a national charity providing help and support to anyone caring for children – parents, grandparents, step-parents, relatives – for families living together as well as apart.

Parents for Inclusion

336 Brixton Road

London SW9 7AA

www.parentsforinclusion.org

Tel: 020 7738 3888

Parents for Inclusion is a national charity that helps parents so that disabled children can learn, make friends and have a voice in ordinary school and throughout life.

People First

Unit 3

46 Canterbury Court

Kennington Park Business Centre

1–3 Brixton Road

London SW9 6DE

www.peoplefirstltd.com

Tel: 020 7820 6655

People First is an organization run by and for people with learning difficulties to raise awareness of and campaign for the rights of people with learning difficulties and to support self-advocacy groups across the country.

Physically Disabled and Able Bodied (PHAB)
Summit House
50 Wandle Road
Croydon
Surrey CR0 1DF
www.phab.org.uk
Tel: 020 8667 9443
PHAB's aim is to promote and encourage people of all abilities to come
together on equal terms, to achieve complete inclusion within the wider
community.

Play England
8 Wakley Street
London EC1V 7QE
www.playengland.org.uk
Tel: 020 7843 6300
Play England's website provides information about the work of this organization which promotes the adoption of the Charter for Children's Play and is
the leading publisher of play news, information and research.

Positive Identity
PO Box 17709
London SE6 4ZQ
www.positive-identity.com
Tel: 020 8314 0442
Positive Identity is a company which is able to offer comprehensive advice and
equipment regarding early years in the area of a multicultural society in
which we live. The equipment supports the foundation stage and is necessary for an effective curriculum which builds on the children's self esteem
and identity.

Prader-Willi Syndrome Association UK
125a London Road
Derby DE1 2QQ
www.pwsa.co.uk
Tel: 01332 365 676
The Prader-Willi Syndrome Association is the only organization in the UK
which is dedicated to supporting people with Prader-Willi syndrome (PWS),
their families, carers, and the professionals who work with them.

Pre-school Learning Alliance
The Fitzpatrick Building
188 York Way
London N7 9AD
www.pre-school.org.uk
Tel: 020 7697 2500
Pre-school Learning Alliance is a leading educational charity specializing in the early years.

Quakers in Britain
Friends House
173–177 Euston Road
London NW1 2BJ
www.quaker.org.uk
Tel: 020 7663 1000
Quakers in Britain provides information for and about Quakers in Britain.

Refugee Council
Head Office, 240–250 Ferndale Road
Brixton
London SW9 8BB
www.refugeecouncil.org.uk
Tel: 020 7346 6700
The Refugee Council not only gives direct help and support but also works with asylum seekers and refugees to ensure their needs and concerns are addressed.

Relate
Central Office, Premier House
Carolina Court, Lakeside
Doncaster DN4 5RA
www.relateforparents.org.uk
Tel: 0300 100 1234
Relate for Parents is a unique and innovative set of online media tools designed to cater for parents' needs by providing advice, support, guidance and techniques to enable them to understand and improve their family relationships, manage conflict and make change happen.

Research in Practice
Blacklers
Park Road
Dartington Hall
Totnes
Devon TQ9 6EQ
www.rip.org.uk
Tel: 01803 867 692
Research in Practice is the largest children and families research implementation project in England and Wales.

Rett Syndrome Association UK
Langham House West
Mill Street
Luton LU1 2NA
www.rettuk.org
Tel: 01582 798 910
The Rett Syndrome Association provides information on Rett Syndrome.

Royal College of Speech and Language Therapists
2 White Hart Yard
London SE1 1NX
www.rcslt.org
Tel: 020 7378 1200
The Royal College of Speech and Language Therapists is the professional body for speech and language therapists and support workers.

Royal National Institute of Blind People (RNIB)
Head Office
105 Judd Street
London WC1H 9NE
www.rnib.org.uk
Tel: 020 7388 1266
RNIB supports blind and partially sighted people.

Salusbury World
c/o Salusbury Primary School
Salusbury Road
London NW6 6RG
www.salusburyworld.org.uk
Tel: 020 7372 2244
Salusbury World provides educational, social and emotional support for refugee children, and supports parents and the wider refugee community by providing home/school liaison, family workshops and outings, and also a comprehensive social advice service.

SANE
1st Floor Cityside House
40 Adler Street
London E1 1EE
www.sane.org.uk
Tel: 020 7375 100
SANE was established in 1986 to improve the quality of life for people affected by mental illness.

Save the Children
1 St John's Lane
London EC1M 4AR
www.savethechildren.org.uk
Tel: 020 7012 6400
Save the Children works to ensure children get proper healthcare, food, education and protection.

Scope
6 Market Road
London N7 9PW
www.scope.org.uk
Tel: 020 7619 7100
Scope's vision is a world where disabled people have the same opportunities to fulfil their life ambitions as non-disabled people.

Sickle Cell Society
54 Station Road
London NW10 4UA
www.sicklecellsociety.org
Tel: 020 8961 7795
The Sickle Cell Society provides information and advice on sickle cell disease and thalassaemia.

Single Parent Action Network (SPAN)
Millpond Baptist Street
Easton
Bristol BS5 0YW
www.spanuk.org.uk
Tel: 0117 951 4231
SPAN is a uniquely diverse organization empowering one-parent families
throughout the UK.

Social Care Institute for Excellence (SCIE)
Goldings House, 2 Hay's Lane
London SE1 2HB
www.scie.org.uk
Tel: 020 7089 6840
SCIE is a source of good practice guidance, research and learning materials for
social care and social work.

Soldiers, Sailors, Airmen and Families Association (SSAFA) Forces Help
19 Queen Elizabeth Street
London SE1 2LP
www.ssafa.org.uk
Tel: 0845 1300 975
SSAFA help and support those who serve in the armed forces and those who
used to serve.

Speakability
1 Royal Street
London SE1 7LL
www.speakability.org.uk
Tel: 020 7261 9572
Speakability is a national charity dedicated to supporting and empowering
people with Aphasia and their carers.

Special Direct
Park Lane Business Park, Kirkby-in-Ashfield
Nottinghamshire NG17 9GU
www.specialdirect.com
Tel: 0800 318 686
Special Direct provides a range of resources to people working with children with
special needs.

Stonewall
Tower Building, York Road
London SE1 7NX
www.stonewall.org.uk
Tel: 020 7593 1850
Stonewall works to achieve equality and justice for lesbian, gay and bisexual
    people.

TALK Adoption
Head Office, Unit 5 Citygate
5 Blantyre Steet
Manchester M15 4JJ
www.afteradoption.org.uk
Tel: 0808 808 1234
General Number: 0161 839 4932
TALK Adoption is part of After Adoption, a voluntary adoption agency and
    one of the largest providers of adoption support services in the UK.

Terrence Higgins Trust
314–320 Gray's Inn Road
London WC1X 8DP
www.tht.org.uk
Tel: 0845 1221 200
Terrence Higgins Trust is the leading and largest HIV and sexual health
    charity in the UK.

TTS Group Ltd
Park Lane Business Park
Kirkby-in-Ashfield
Nottinghamshire NG17 9GU
www.tts-group.co.uk
Tel: 0800 318 686
TTS Group Ltd supplies high-quality educational resources to schools and
    parents across the UK.

Twins and Multiple Births Association (Tamba)
2 The Willows
Gardner Road
Guildford
Surrey GU1 4PG
www.tamba.org.uk
Tel: 01483 304 442
Tamba is a charity set up by parents of twins, triplets and higher multiples,
and interested professionals, in 1978. It is the only UK-wide organization
that directly helps parents and professionals to meet the unique challenges
that multiple-birth families face. It undertakes research, campaigns, and
provides information and support to over 10,000 members and supporters
each year.

Twins UK
1 Esther Court
Wansbeck Business Park
Rotary Parkway
Ashington
Northumberland NE63 8AP
www.twinsuk.co.uk
Tel: 01670 856 996
Twins UK was launched in September 2005 in response to the growing need
to provide appropriate information, advice, and good quality, practical
products for the increasing number of parents of twins and more.

United Nations Children's Fund (UNICEF)
UNICEF House
30a Great Sutton Street
London EC1V 0DU
www.unicef.org
Tel: 020 7490 2388
UNICEF is an organization that raises awareness of issues affecting children.

Vegan Society
Donald Watson House
21 Hylton Street, Hockley
Birmingham B18 6HJ
www.vegansociety.com
Tel: 0845 458 8244
The Vegan Society is an educational charity that promotes and supports the
vegan lifestyle.

Vegetarian Society
Parkdale, Dunham Road
Altrincham
Cheshire WA14 4QG
www.vegsoc.org
Tel: 0161 925 2000
The Vegetarian Society is an educational charity promoting understanding
and respect for vegetarian lifestyles.

Vitiligo Society
125 Kennington Road
London SE11 6SF
www.vitiligosociety.org.uk
Tel: 0800 018 2631
The Vitiligo Society exists to help people with vitiligo live positively with the
condition.

Voice
Head Office
320 City Road
London EC1V 2NZ
www.voiceyp.org
Tel: 020 7833 5792
Voice is one of UK's leading voluntary organizations working and campaign-
ing for children and young people in public care.

Winston's Wish

The Clara Burgess Centre

Westmoreland House

80–86 Bath Road

Cheltenham GL53 7JT

Tel: 01242 515 157

www.winstonswish.org.uk

Winston's Wish is the leading childhood bereavement charity and the largest provider of services to bereaved children, young people and their families in the UK.

World Health Organisation (WHO)

Avenue Appia 20, 1211 Geneva 27

Switzerland

www.who.int

Tel: +41 22 791 21 11

WHO is the directing and coordinating authority for health within the United Nations system.

World Organisation in Early Childhood Education UK (OMEP)

www.omepuk.org.uk

Email: omepuk@googlemail.com

OMEP is concerned for the welfare and education of children from birth to eight years. They are part of a worldwide organization and concern themselves with children everywhere, but are particularly involved with those in the UK.

Xtra

Goyt Side Road

Chesterfield S40 2PH

www.xtra-cat.com

Tel: 0845 880 1477

Xtra provides thousands of topical resources to help children and young people cope with modern social issues.

YoungMinds
48–50 St John Street
London EC1M 4DG
www.youngminds.org.uk
Tel: 020 7336 8445
YoungMinds is the UK's only national charity committed to improving the mental and emotional well-being of children and young people.

Zoroastrian Trust Funds of Europe
440 Alexandra Avenue
Harrow HA2 9TL
www.ztfe.com
Tel: 020 8866 0765
The Zoroastrian Trust Funds of Europe provides information about Zoroastrianism.

Useful Websites

www.begrand.net – a website especially for grandparents where they can find information and support on everything from fun, free things to do with their grandchildren, to serious issues like grandparents' legal rights.

www.c4eo.org.uk – the Centre for Excellence and Outcomes in Children and Young People's Services.

www.dadtalk.co.uk – a social networking site, encouraging dads to communicate with one another and to take up opportunities to learn from each other and develop the confidence to achieve more with their children.

www.gosh.nhs.uk – Great Ormond Street, information and podcasts on aspects of health.

www.gotateenager.org.uk – a social networking site, run by Parentline Plus, giving help and advice to the parents of teenagers.

www.nice.org.uk – National Institute for Health and Clinical Excellence.

www.open2.net/childofourtime – information following the child of our time series and lots of other useful information.

www.parentchannel.tv – a free website for parents of 5–19 year olds that offers expert advice on parenting through a collection of helpful short videos.

www.teachers.tv – a TV experience on your computer. Watch themed videos selected to match your interests, including great lesson ideas and inspiring documentaries.

www.schoolpsychology.net – research learning disabilities, ADHD, functional behavioural assessment, autism, adolescence, parenting, psychological assessment, special education, mental health, and more.

Index